From the breakout star
of *The Game Changers*

Charity Morgan, plant-based chef to athletes and celebrities, lays out a plan for anyone who wants to eat less meat—whether they are looking to go completely vegan or just be a little bit more meat-free. Pulling inspiration from her Puerto Rican and Creole heritage as well as from the American South, where she lives with her family, Charity's recipes are full of big, bold flavor. Think Smoky Jambalaya; hearty Jerk-Spiced Lentils with Coconut Rice & Mango Salsa; Jalapeño-Bae'con Corn Cakes with Chili-Lime Maple Syrup; and a molten, decadent Salted Caramel Apple Crisp.

In her highly anticipated first cookbook she offers more than 100 recipes for living a meat-free life without giving up your favorite comfort foods. She guides readers on how to use oyster mushrooms to stand in for chicken and how to spice walnuts to taste like chorizo! Charity proves that vegan food can be fun, filling, healthy, and above all else unbelievably delicious.

unbelievably vegan

UNBELIEVABLY VEGAN
PROTEIN BURGER, PAGE 217

unbelievably vegan

100+ Life-Changing, Plant-Based Recipes

CHARITY MORGAN

CLARKSON POTTER/PUBLISHERS
New York

This book is dedicated to my "BFFs,"
my beautiful, supportive family:
my husband, Derrick, and our amazing
little humans, King-Elias and Love Lee.
I love you guys so much. Thank you for
being incredible.

CONTENTS

KICKOFF BREAKFASTS & BRUNCHES

SOUP'OR BOWL

CROWD-PLEASERS

PLAYMAKING MAINS

FOREWORD

In 2011, I was diagnosed with an autoimmune disease that forced me to stop playing tennis. I was experiencing chronic fatigue, swollen joints, and other issues that are not so unusual for people who are affected by these types of diseases. What I learned from this experience is that, unfortunately, many medical professionals are not sure how to treat or diagnose these types of autoimmune issues. I was completely committed to finding a way to take back control of my life and did a great deal of reading during this time. I learned that a plant-based diet could address many of the issues that I was experiencing.

I ultimately adopted a plant-based vegan diet, which was quite frankly overwhelming.

When making my own transition, I was lucky enough to get support from a variety of professionals. I struggled through many of the common questions: Am I getting enough protein? Am I getting the proper nutrients? Why am I still so hungry?

I had the privilege of meeting Charity, who is extremely impressive. Charity celebrates growth and creativity, which also means that she doesn't seem to shy away from making mistakes. I also enjoy the fact that she's candid about her own journey of how she got to where she is today. Like so many of us, her change did not happen overnight nor was it linear. I also love that Charity is taking a practical approach to a plant-based diet, which she has branded Pleganism. It's impressive that her approach is so constructive. She provides support and encouragement as she guides you through this exploration.

I hope that people's stereotypes about what plant-based eating is are flipped upside-down when they open Charity's book. That they see that they can have everything they love, but better for them and better for the planet. That they can transform everyday favorites like nachos and pound cake (yes, really!) into delicious plant-based meals without sacrifice. Charity has done the work and showed us a world full of opportunities. Now, with *Unbelievably Vegan* in our hands, we can dive in feeling supported and excited.

VENUS WILLIAMS,
World Champion Athlete,
Philanthropist, and Entrepreneur
August 2021

INTRODUCTION

Most people know me from *The Game Changers,* the documentary in which I transformed everyday comforting favorites into delicious plant-based meals. I was cooking for NFL players in the film, but in real life I cook for all kinds of clients from athletes to musicians and just regular people looking to change the way they eat.

Let me tell you, though, it was a *journey* to get here. I went plant-based—or "Plegan" as I call it (more about that on page 22)—in 2017. Shortly after, I made a grocery run and looked like a total madwoman—I loaded my cart with every vegetable you could imagine—you'd have burst out laughing if you'd seen it! When I got home that afternoon, my toddler daughter signed to me, "Eat, eat!" (one of her few toddler sign language words). I looked at my garden haul and I swear, I had a full nervous breakdown. I had bought tons of food . . . but what were we going to *eat*? What was my plan? I didn't have anything that she'd want, and I had no idea what to quickly toss together. I was so overwhelmed that I put my head down on my kitchen counter and prayed for encouragement.

Then, it came to me, in a *divine* voice:

"Make everything you love— just change the ingredients!"

Call it God, call it the universe, call it a stroke of genius—it was exactly what I needed to hear.

Suddenly I found myself halfway through my jambalaya recipe, but this time, there was no diced chicken, andouille sausage, or shrimp. Instead, I added smoked tofu and spicy blackened veggies for kick and flavor. That's when I found my mojo. I learned that I didn't have to reinvent the wheel. I could still rely on my favorite flavors, like traditional Puerto Rican and Creole spices and jerk seasoning, and make the foods I loved, now with plant-based ingredients swapped into the same dishes. I realized that I'd put up mental barriers about what could and couldn't go in certain recipes, what was traditional, what was authentic, and what the "rules" of the kitchen were.

Focusing on plants opened a whole world of opportunity. It made me become a better chef—I became more creative, with limitless ideas and even *more* conscious of ingredients and flavor.

And you know what? Everybody loved what I was cooking because I was still building layers of flavor like I learned in culinary school (don't worry, I will teach you how). Transitioning from meat to plant-based cooking for me was a mental shift. Rather than being limited by not eating certain things, being plant-based brought forward new and exciting ways to be creative, and taught me how to take my favorite dishes and make them brand-new. But make no mistake, eating plants doesn't mean eating rabbit food! One flip through these pages proves that.

This book is a collection of my favorite recipes, my family's favorites, and my clients' favorite recipes, too. I've come up with quite the arsenal—and they're all *unbelievably* flavorful. I use all kinds of amazing spices, surprising hits of acid, and lots of heat to make sure you don't feel as if you're missing out. Just try my Fried Chik'n with Spicy Maple Syrup (page 206) or a platter of Buffalo Cheezy Sweet Potato Fries (page 179) and tell me you're not satisfied!

If you want to jump into a fully plant-based way of eating, go right ahead. If you want to ease into it, that's fine by me, too—maybe you do meatless Mondays, meatless weekdays, or start with just one plant-based meal a day. It's all good. Maybe you just want some ideas of how to spice up your day-to-day and eat less meat—I'm here for it. Start slow: try a few recipes at first, learn some new techniques, and work them into your weekly meals. Maybe start with Papas & Walnut Chorizo Breakfast Tacos (page 103) for breakfast one day. Try a next-level Garbage Salad with Creamy Lemon-Peppercorn Dressing (page 144) for lunch. Make your family a Gochujang Jackfruit Noodle Bowl (page 215) with a side of Sesame Avocado Kale No-Egg Rolls (page 161) for dinner. Eventually, when you're comfortable, do what I did—try out one of your family favorites and just switch up the meat, fish, and dairy for plant-based alternatives. It really is that easy.

This book was curated with love. I love what I do, I love people, I love our earth, and I love sharing. I look at recipes as a guide, not something written in stone, and mine are no different. I hope this book will gently nudge you out of your normal routine, help break down barriers in the kitchen, and encourage you to explore your culinary creativity. Learn to be flexible, adventurous, and make everything just the way you like. If you don't like black beans, that's cool; use pinto or red beans instead. Not a fan of kale? Use spinach or arugula. The world has hundreds of thousands of grains, beans, vegetables, and edible plants to explore. Have a field day!

No matter how you decide to use this book, I'm here to support you, inspire you, and *empower* you. Because, as I'm hoping you'll learn, I haven't lost meat—I've gained life.

MY STORY

I grew up one of six children on a farm outside of Sacramento, California, to Creole and Puerto Rican parents. In both cultures, meat and seafood are vital. My dad is from Pacoima, California, born to Creole parents from Mermentau, Louisiana, who made jambalaya and gumbo full of sausage, shrimp, and crab. My mom grew up in Chicago, with parents from Maunabo and Humacao, Puerto Rico, who put pork and beef in just about everything—from Puerto Rican tamales called pasteles to fried pastelillos (hand pies). As a family, food was the center of everything, and my parents encouraged our love of it. While my dad couldn't cook to save his life, food was the way to his heart, and my mother cooked with that in mind. She is truly a great cook.

Looking back at my childhood, I find my culinary style makes a lot of sense. Growing up on a farm taught me to love vegetables and respect my ingredients. And my mom could work her magic on *anything*. One of my favorite foods was her fried zucchini (and homemade ranch dressing)— fresh from her garden. She always thought that the best way to truly connect with people was through food, so on weekends she'd be in the kitchen learning to make lumpia or curries from her Filipino or Indian friends. Fresh veggies paired with the new-to-me, amazing flavors opened my eyes early to a whole world of what food could be.

When I was fourteen, my friend Aura Trujillo introduced me to all the meatless "specials" at Taco Bell. There was no separate vegetarian menu back then; it was more of a certain way of ordering that vegetarians just knew. I had no idea you could mix beans, rice, cheese, salsa, and guacamole into so many different combinations to make a satisfying meal. I realized that I loved my meals without the texture and taste of meat, and I started cutting it out. I'd occasionally eat seafood, but from the age of fourteen on, I was mostly vegetarian.

Believe it or not, my parents didn't mind. My mom and I busied ourselves figuring out how to get the best flavor from Creole- and Puerto Rican–inspired meat-free meals. For the next ten years, I didn't miss meat at all.

After high school, I moved to Los Angeles to start modeling and used the money I saved to travel and explore the world. On my first trip to Europe, I kept hearing the word *culinary*. This word was new to me and represented not only a career, but also a whole world of flavors and techniques. When I returned home, I was so obsessed with my discoveries, I signed up for a two-year program at the California School of Culinary Arts in Pasadena (a Cordon Bleu program).

At culinary school, my mostly vegetarian ways became a point of contention. My classmates and instructors felt this restriction would hold me back, and I didn't want anything to block my path to success. At first it was just a bite here or there, maybe a seasoning check on a steak or a sip of broth to make sure it was ready. Eventually I was eating meat regularly again.

After graduating, I worked various apprentice jobs, shadowing and prepping in many kitchens in Southern California. After a few months at each restaurant, though, I became bored and frustrated. What I loved about food was coming up with recipes, and here I was making the same food over and over (and over) again.

I decided to create a personal chef business and took off on my own. I realized a lot of people in SoCal wanted homemade meals, but they didn't know how to cook or didn't have the time. That's where I came in. I specialized in meals to meet specific needs (like low-carb or family-friendly) and knew how to handle all dietary restrictions. Sometimes I just taught basic cooking lessons. I did it all.

In 2010, I met a gorgeous linebacker for the Tennessee Titans named Derrick Morgan. We fell in love, moved to Nashville, got married, and started a family. I made *so* many changes so fast. NFL life was unlike anything I had ever experienced. Our lives revolved around Derrick's incredibly intense football schedule and making sure he stayed in peak performance shape. Motherhood became my full-time job after we welcomed our son, King-Elias, and eventually our daughter, Love Lee, to the world.

What I didn't know at the time was that all these changes would become a whole new life, not just personally but professionally.

GOING PLANT-BASED

Each year in the off-season, Derrick took it upon himself to improve his body and skills (in the mind of an athlete, there's always room for improvement). After the 2016 season, his particular focus was nutrition and overall health. He met with Ashleigh Ignelzi, a nutritionist and plant-based-eating advocate who recommended he cut out meat and dairy to lower inflammation in his body. Inflammation, aches, and pains come with the territory because football, whether at the college level or in the NFL, is a *100-percent-guaranteed-injury sport*. Think about that for a second. For this reason, players are always looking for ways to bring down inflammation, which means a higher level of playing, fewer injuries, faster recoveries, and getting back out onto the field quickly.

At first, Derrick was unsure about this no-meat thing, but he didn't rule it out. He started researching on his own, and the more he read, the more it made sense. He learned about other professional athletes from nearly every sport who were plant-based. So out went eggs, fish, dairy, and meat, and in came leafy greens, tofu, and whole grains. Initially I didn't join him—I continued eating seafood, eggs, and tons of dairy (everything was better with extra cheese in my opinion).

A few weeks after he went plant-based, Derrick felt his energy soar. He was sleeping so much better, and his old aches started to fade away. At the same time, my own body started breaking down. My energy was low, and I was dizzy and had horrible digestion issues for weeks at a time. I saw traditional and naturopath doctors, but none of them found anything wrong. So I decided to become more serious about what I was eating. I took my health into my own hands and became (mostly) plant-based, too. In the beginning, I held out on a few things—like eggs, for their versatility, and cheese—but I eventually phased them out. All the while, I focused on creating flavorful plant-based dishes for Derrick and me.

PLANT-BASED KIDS

I needed the facts before I eliminated animal products from my kids' plates. As a mother, my job is to protect and nourish their little bodies and minds, which were still developing (and fast). I started doing my own research and enrolled in an online plant-based nutrition class with Dr. T. Colin Campbell, who laid out the evidence and debunked the myths. Like many other mothers, I had subscribed to the idea that milk "does a body good." How wrong I was.

I can just hear a parent saying, "But my kid doesn't like vegetables!" I often find that we parents would rather give in than deal with the drama of convincing our child to eat something new and nutritious. It takes time. Children's palates will develop to appreciate what they are exposed to over and over again.

Here's a thought: What's the first thing to touch a newborn's tongue? Formula or breast milk, and both are sweet. Then we move to puréed fruit and veggies, and most babies like the sweet ones, such as sweet potato and apple. Parents, these new foods are full of flavors that are *foreign* to our babies! As adults, we love all kinds of tastes beyond sweet, and bitter, acidic foods like beer, wine, coffee, hot sauce, and even onions become favorites. But these are all flavors we have *grown* to love. If you drink coffee, beer, or wine, think back to your first sip—not pleasant, right? But after repeated exposure, now you crave the taste.

For the first few years of our children's lives, the rule was "just one bite," no matter how many times I served that ingredient or dish. It was my job to develop their palates to appreciate bitter kale and sulfuric broccoli. (And since I'd been sneaking them into their baby purées with the sweet veggies they loved, it wasn't that difficult.)

When I was convinced our kids would be fine without animal products (and got the approval from our doctor), I slowly started to include our children in our plant-based meal planning. There was no way I was going to become a short-order cook and make one meal for us and another for them. I don't believe in kid meals—I believe in family meals. I started transitioning them away from dairy and meat with their favorite dishes (like mac and cheese and tacos), then it was up to me to come up with plant-based recipes that the whole family would love. Thankfully, this book is full of them.

FEEDING A TEAM

My family and I were off to a good start, but I knew Derrick's new way of eating would suffer when he went to the Titans' facility. We discovered that what many see as performance food—red meat and energy drinks—is not what aids in recovery or provides quality energy. Try eating a 12-ounce piece of Wagyu beef and a loaded baked potato washed down with Gatorade, then go crash up against 300-pound men and let me know if that equates to energetic food. (For some, that answer may be yes, because they haven't experienced true energy and clarity or have never pushed their bodies to this level of endurance.) Our livelihood was on the line, so I had decisions to make—fast.

I started sending Derrick to practice each day with my specially prepared meals. Then a funny thing happened. His teammates, who just a few weeks before had teased him about his "plants," watched him eat these delicious homemade meals and started saying, "Wait! That doesn't look like salad! That looks so good," or "What is that? Can you ask your wife if she can send me a meal, too?"

Within two weeks, I was cooking for four more players, then it soon became six, and a month later I was cooking for twelve. Holy smokes, I had an overnight business, and I was becoming the Tennessee Titans' unofficial vegan chef!

When a new player was thinking about signing up with me for plant-based meals, I'd give him my favorite pep talk: I'd ask him about his favorite car. This being the NFL, I got a lot of very exotic responses: Ferrari, Lamborghini, and the like. And I'd respond, "Don't you think your body is more valuable than a Ferrari?" Their minds were blown! None of them considered that they are working with something even more precious and complex than a six-figure sports car. Next we'd move on to fuel. You can put regular fuel into a Honda Civic, and it will run fine, but would you put that same fuel into a Lambo? You have to put high-octane gas into a performance sports car, and you *have* to put the highest quality fuel into any human body—especially one of a professional athlete. Your body is only as good as the fuel you put in.

When the players realized that eating plant-based foods didn't mean they'd collapse on the field, that their stats wouldn't go down, and that they *would* be back after injury sooner, more and more said, "Sign me up!" They were convinced that getting enough protein from plants wasn't just easy and absolutely delicious, but it was the fuel for optimal performance and health. That's when I realized there was something special and different about what I was doing.

And as you might remember, the Titans even went to the playoffs in 2017—for the first time since 2008. Maybe there is a correlation between eating right and performance, but overall I can only say it was just our time to shine.

The number of players eating my cooking continued to grow. By the 2018 training camp, I was providing 100 percent plant-based meals to more than nineteen players! In addition, I started to take on private clients and welcomed them into this inclusive space I call Plegan.

Plegan (**plant-based** + **vegan**) is a term I coined.

It refers to people with animal-free diets who avoid meat, fish, dairy, and eggs, but who may still use animal by-products, such as leather (I am not condoning leather, I am meeting people where they are). It's an *inclusive* space for people who have a non-animal-based diet.

WHY PLEGAN?

When I made the switch to plants and gained some attention for my work with athletes, I entered into a world of scrutiny. "Why don't you talk more about animal welfare?" "Are you teaching NFL players about our environment?" "These athletes are wearing leather shoes!" "You should be using only whole foods." "You shouldn't use these meat substitutes!" "Why aren't you oil-free?" I found myself always trying to explain my decisions and felt the frustration from my clients, too. They wanted to try something new but didn't want to tell people they were vegan or plant-based because with that statement comes judgment (which is why many people go vegan quietly). They wanted to eat vegan and play football *and* not be attacked because that football on the field is made of leather.

I hate boxes, borders, and rules. I looked at all these "categories" available to me and realized I don't want to be a part of any of them. But I knew I needed something for me and my clients: a space to grow—to make mistakes and to get up from those mistakes. So, being the rebel that I am, I created my own category.

I called it *Plegan*. It's a term for people growing in their awareness and consciousness, making an effort to discover the healthiest and most sustainable way of eating. I wanted to create an inclusive, welcoming space where we can intentionally grow and educate ourselves without judgment as we eliminate animal products from our plate and life.

In my experience, plenty of people will judge you for not doing "enough," but the hard truth is that we live in a society where it's nearly impossible to be 100 percent vegan. Animal products end up nearly everywhere. For every easy-to-identify animal-based product like leather, there's a laundry list of products (pun intended) that may contain animal ingredients and are much harder to avoid: fabric softeners, perfumes, car and bike tires, tattoo ink, LCD screens, even some countries' *currencies*. Same with food. It's easy to ask for "no bacon" but did you know beer, wine, gummy candies, and even soy cheese—yes, you read that right—may use animal products? I don't blame anyone for feeling overwhelmed or for not being a "perfect vegan."

In the meantime, it's nice to know you can keep the animal products off your plate and continue to grow in a loving, inclusive environment where you can make your own conscious decisions about your impact on animals, the environment, and yourself.

THE GAME CHANGERS

Our influence on the team was how we earned a spot in the 2018 documentary *The Game Changers*. Both Derrick and I appear in the film and were executive producers. If you haven't seen it—watch it tonight! The film is about the benefits of plant-based eating for athletes. (Talk about timing with our growing numbers on the Titans!) It covers multiple success stories of elite athletes on plant-based diets, interviews doctors and scientists about the benefits of plants (and the harm of animal products) for athletes, and argues that the benefits of a plant-based diet extend to everyone.

It went on to be the most popular documentary ever sold on iTunes, and millions more saw it when it launched on Netflix. And I can't tell you how many viewers reached out to me asking, "Charity, where can I buy your cookbook?" Well, now you know how that went!

TRANSITIONING: HOW TO GO PLEGAN

Changing your lifestyle is a marathon, not a sprint. Think about it: the way we eat is a habit built over a lifetime, and it reflects not just our own habits, but our parents' and grandparents' habits, too.

I am going to put myself out there and tell you that I actually first tried to go plant-based in 2015. I failed miserably. The biggest difference my second time around was preparation. I researched. I studied. I planned. It might seem like a lot of work, and for some people, it is, but I'm here to help you.

Begin here: to be successful, you need to understand your why, understand your how, and make a game plan.

UNDERSTAND YOUR WHY

The first time around I failed to educate myself on the benefits of a plant-based eating and the *why*—meaning, why did I want to do this?

Understanding why it was important to eliminate meat and animal products was very empowering for me. I was doing it because I wanted to feel like the best version of myself: not dealing with digestive issues, waking up with a burst of energy, and not having to rely on caffeine to get me through a day. Derrick's research showed that a plant-based diet provides all of the nutrients your body needs for training and competition, can reduce inflammation, and gives you a ton of energy. I wanted that, too!

Everyone's reason for trying out plant-based eating is unique. Take the time to do the research and really figure out *your* why. Is it because you want to lower your cholesterol? Are you doing it for environmental reasons? To do your part in ending factory farming? Do you have a chronic illness? Understanding your *why* will get you emotionally and mentally ready to make the giant leap.

Once I had my *why*, I shifted my thinking from "I can't" have bacon to "I choose" not to have bacon, and that decision was empowering. *You* are in control. And control is *everything*.

UNDERSTAND YOUR HOW

Back in 2015 I thought I could just jump into this new lifestyle without a game plan and wing it by transitioning to a diet of fruits, vegetables, and grains. Within seven days, I was hangry and back to my regular way of eating. Winging it rarely works. Understanding *how* to do it does, and that's what I'm going to show you with the recipes in this book, as well as giving my advice on how to make a game plan and all the tips and tricks that worked for me and my clients.

Nothing good comes easy. But me being me, I also started to overthink it. What was I going to eat for breakfast? What can I order at a restaurant? What will I do when I travel? What will I feed my children for dinner? I had all these roadblocks—and they were all put there by me.

All that I really needed to do was come up with a plan. I needed to take into account all the mental, emotional, and physical considerations, then start small and eventually graduate—all while shopping smart and doing just a little bit of planning if I wanted to eat out (ain't nothing wrong with going online and looking at a restaurant's menu before you go there). Then, I just needed to take a deep breath and go one day at a time. That's what I suggest you do, too.

MAKE A GAME PLAN

In every sport there is no game without a game plan. A game is only a few hours; a game plan is an approach that extends far beyond—and before—the game.

Making a major life change on a whim doesn't usually yield permanent results. After you tackle the mental and emotional commitment to a plant-based diet, it's time to make a plan and stick to it. Preparation and research will ready you for action and make the change much easier.

Mental, Emotional, and Physical Considerations

The first step in making a game plan you can stick to is taking into account all the variables that might come up.

Changing a lifetime of eating habits can be anxiety-provoking. The anxiety of change can cause major stress, and when we are stressed, we are less likely to resist temptation and more likely to throw in the towel. Partnering up with someone—a life partner, family member, or roommate—when starting a big change can make your journey more enjoyable and be an invaluable source of moral and mental support as you shift your way of eating and thinking about food.

Also, consider your timing. Unless you need to make this change immediately for health reasons, or you have unbreakable willpower, I don't recommend starting this journey around any holidays where food plays center stage and everyone's got opinions. Choose dates that are meaningful when it comes to change, like New Year's Day, Earth Day, or your birthday.

The pressure from others can easily throw you off track. When your family and friends hear that you've decided to go plant-based, all of a sudden they all become nutritionists and doctors!

Not only will you be feeling a lot of emotions, you're going to feel different physically almost immediately. You are definitely going to feel hungrier if you're eating only fruits and vegetables. Grains, beans, legumes, and nuts provide fiber, and our bodies also need to work harder to process the complex carbohydrates in them, making us feel fuller for longer.

I'm not going to lie: some may experience not-so-pleasant changes, too. You may have more gas, bloating, some constipation, or other digestive issues, especially if you're not used to eating so much fiber. This is completely normal. Going plant-based can be a big adjustment for the body, especially if fresh vegetables and fiber-rich foods haven't been part of your daily lifestyle. Starting your transition with cooked veggies rather than raw, drinking lots (and lots) of water, and taking a vegan probiotic daily will help lessen any unpleasantness. If your diet was filled with lots of processed foods and products with sugar (or hidden sugar), you may also experience headaches, fatigue, acne, insomnia, and irritability. This is your body's way of detoxing itself. Just know it's temporary. These physical symptoms will pass, and the long-term results will be worth it.

Some of the positive results I experienced included more radiant and clearer skin; shinier hair; healthier nails; more energy, stamina, and endurance; less inflammation in my body; and a clearer mind and more focus. I used to need cups and cups of coffee and espresso to feel alert; now I get my buzz naturally through what I eat (though I still do love the taste of an occasional oat milk latte).

By understanding what's going to happen in your mind and body as you make the transition, you'll be better prepared to stick to your game plan.

Small Steps to Big Change

Once you've made the decision to change your diet and know what to expect, begin with easy steps that you can put into action immediately. When you've got that step down, add another! Keep going and celebrate your wins.

Here are some of the small steps that have worked for my clients:

- **Pick one food to eliminate.** Give it a realistic goal. For example. "I am removing beef from my plate." Then, after a month, add another: "I am removing eggs from my plate." Keep going. These seemingly small accomplishments add up.
- **Change the proportion** of plant- and animal-based foods on your plate. It's easier to eliminate the foods if they're not the star of the meal.
- **Start with something simple,** like meatless Monday. It's not hard to eat plant-based one day a week, but, if a whole day feels like too much, pick a meal once or twice a week to make plant-based, then graduate to one meal *every day*, then two. . . .
- **If you're stuck on what to make,** use the Pro-Bowl chart on page 152— this is where I tell my clients to start because it makes putting together a plant-based meal super easy. Cooking up some grains and loading them with fresh and roasted vegetables, beans, and a fun sauce has always been my "I have no idea what to make today" default. It still is.
- **Toss out the store-bought snacks** full of overly processed and animal-based ingredients. Whip up some homemade options to keep around instead, like my queso (page 167). It's great as a dip for chips or crispy veggie sticks, and it's rich and satisfying.
- **Meal kits** (meals that come totally prepared or meals that you need to prepare yourself) are a great way to get familiar with vegan options without the sometimes-overwhelming task of meal planning and shopping. You can find out what you like and what you don't like and get lots of inspiration for creating meals on your own.

Soon enough, eating a 100 percent plant-based diet will feel natural and easy.

Shop Smart

Remember my story about my disaster of a shopping trip? Don't be like me!

Plan your meals and make a list before you go to the grocery store—and stick to it (that's the hard part!). If you *really* hate meal planning or want to be able to freestyle for a few meals a week, make sure you add ingredients from every column in the Pro-Bowl chart on page 152 to your list and get the ingredients for a dressing or two.

While you're making a list, add minimally processed snacks. I was never a big snacker outside of guacamole and chips. However, Derrick can snack his way through a whole day and still eat a large dinner and dessert. So I load up my cart with things like nuts, dried fruit, fresh fruit, chickpeas for hummus, fresh vegetables, fresh salsa, healthier chips and crackers, and lots and lots of peanut butter. Keeping fun snacks on hand helps get you through cravings and prevents hanger.

When you are first deciding to eliminate animal products, it can be confusing to figure out which foods are free of hidden animal ingredients, like gelatin and whey (see Ingredients to Watch Out For, page 32). Obviously, if we lived in a perfect world, everything we put into our body would be whole and fresh and without a long list of additives that could win you a spelling bee. But we don't, so I *always* **READ LABELS.**

READ LABELS.

READ LABELS.

This is the only way to make sure they're free of animal by-products, and also to be sure there aren't tons of sodium, sugar, or other not-good-for-you sneaky additions.

MY GAME PLAN

My *why* for going vegan is: _____

My *how* for going vegan is: _____

I am going to start by: _____

Next I am going to: _____

Eventually I will work up to: _____

The foods I will miss the most are: _____

Plegan recipes I can use to replace my favorites include: _____

INGREDIENTS TO WATCH OUT FOR

This is a list of ingredients that come from animals. If any of them appear in an ingredient list, the product is *not* plant-based or vegan (there are a few ingredients that can be either animal- or plant-based; they're noted). While this may seem like a long list, there are plenty of alternatives that are made without any of the ingredients below. Once you know what to look out for, it becomes easy to spot non-vegan foods.

Albumen/albumin: From eggs

Aspic: Made from clarified meat, fish, or vegetable stocks; sometimes also contains gelatin

Casein: Milk protein

Collagen: From the skin, bones, and connective tissues of animals such as cows, chickens, pigs, and fish

Elastin: Found in the neck ligaments and aorta of cow; similar to collagen

Gelatin: Obtained by boiling skin, tendons, ligaments, and/or bones, usually from cows or pigs

*Glycerin: Also known as glycol or glycerol, this thickener can be made with plant-based or animal-based oils, so you'll need to look for other indications on the label that your product is plant-based

Keratin: From the skin, bones, and connective tissues of animals such as cows, chickens, pigs, and fish

Isinglass: A substance obtained from the dried swim bladders of fish that is used mainly for the clarification (fining) of wine and beer

Lactose: Milk sugar

Lard/Tallow: Animal fat

Pepsin: From the stomachs of pigs, a clotting agent used in vitamins

Red Dye #40 or Red 40/ Carmine/Cochineal: Made from the dried and crushed bodies of female insects known as cochineal to give a red tint to food; you might also see it listed on a label as cochineal extract, crimson lake, carmine lake, or natural red 4

Royal Jelly: Secretion of the throat gland of the honeybee

Shellac: Obtained from the bodies of the female *Kerria lacca* insect and most commonly used to coat candy

*Stearic Acid: Like glycerin, this fat used in processed foods and cosmetics (and car and bike tires) can be animal-derived or plant-based, so you may need to do more research to find out where your specific product's comes from

*Vitamin D3: Often from fish liver oil or sheep's wool (there are vegan options of vitamin D3)

Whey: Milk by-product

Restaurant Tactics

Don't think for one second that restaurants are off-limits to you! Do your homework and get familiar with vegan-friendly and plant-based restaurants in your area. There are also apps like Happy Cow and Vanilla Bean to help with that. (They're great resources for vacations or road trips when you are less familiar with restaurants in the area.)

If you want to keep going to your favorite spots, and they have options that seem like they could work for you, don't be afraid to ask about the ingredients in a dish (never assume they're totally plant-based, even if no animal products are listed in the description). The easiest approach is to ask if the soup is made with meat or seafood broth, or if the dish is cooked with butter or cheese.

If the restaurant you're going to doesn't offer plant-based options, call ahead of time and ask if the chef can create something for you. Giving the chef a heads-up can be the difference between a creative vegan meal that blows you away and a bowl of pasta with marinara sauce.

BE KIND TO YOURSELF

Weaning yourself off of animal proteins, cheese, and eggs can be hard. You may find yourself longing for a burger or a wedge of oozing, smelly, stinky ripe cheese so much that it begins to consume your every thought. If you fall off the wagon, you can always get back on. It will become easier and easier, and eventually you won't have these cravings at all. And when you do and you eat that pulled pork sandwich or extra-cheesy grilled cheese, you will likely realize that your body doesn't want it anymore.

Above all, please remember this: Allow yourself forgiveness. Always count your wins and not your losses.

THE PLEGAN KITCHEN

My plant-based cooking philosophy is about two things: preparing super flavorful food that tastes incredible and making sure no one ever feels like they're missing out on anything. Along with a fully-stocked pantry, here's a list of my favorite and most-used ingredients. They help my food taste so good that people forget there's no meat or dairy in it.

I also included some essentials you might not be using regularly in the kitchen—yet. They're everything from ingredients I use to make Plegan versions of my favorite dishes to pantry staples that have amped up health benefits.

BUILDING BLOCKS

Agar-Agar

A vegetable thickener made from red algae that is used to replace gelatin. It's fairly easy to find now, thanks to the prevalence of plant-based cooking. Eden Foods, a brand sold in many grocery stores, makes a flaked version, and it can also be found online as a fine powder. It's key for making plant-based cheeses with nice, thick textures like my Cream Cheeze (page 56). Stored in your pantry, it lasts about a year.

All-Purpose Gluten-Free Flour Blend and Gluten-Free 1-to-1 Baking Flour

Since I'm all about inclusivity, I try to make sure our friends on gluten-free diets can eat as much of my food as possible. That's why I prefer to use a gluten-free flour blend whenever I can. Bonus: These blends often include rice flour, which fries up nice and crispy! You can, of course, sub in regular all-purpose flour for all my recipes that call for gluten-free flour.

Avocado Oil (and Other Oils)

Avocado oil is my preferred everyday oil for sautéing because it has a very high smoke point (375°F to 400°F) as well as a neutral flavor. It is heart-healthy, due to being high in oleic acid (an unsaturated fat), contains vitamin E, and also helps the body absorb fat-soluble antioxidants like carotenoids. Grapeseed oil is a good alternative. For frying, I use rice bran oil because of its high smoke point (490°F) and naturally mild flavor, and it's a great non-GMO source of monosaturated fat and beneficial compounds such as oryzanol and tocotrienols. Safflower is my choice for baking because of its good heat tolerance, light texture (it won't weigh down your baked goods), and neutral flavor and aroma. I always opt for an expeller-pressed oil, because the process uses a mechanical force to expel the oil rather than solvents and chemicals.

Brazil Nuts

This nut—actually a seed—has a rich and buttery texture and is perfect for making dairy substitutes, like Brazil Nut Sour Cream (page 57). It's also loaded with selenium, which is great for your immune system, skin, and hair.

Cashews

I love cashews so much that they get their own special section (see box). I always try to have a bulk stash of raw cashews at home. They are high in fat, so store them in your freezer to keep them at their freshest.

Coconut (Palm) Sugar (and Other Sugars)

Coconut sugar is subtly sweet and has a nice caramel flavor and a low glycemic index (good for blood sugar level management). The brand Sugar In The Raw is a good substitute. For baking, I use organic sugars because conventional sugar isn't vegan.

CASHEWS: The Superhero of the Nut World

My favorite nuts, cashews, are a gift from God. Each one is a nutritional powerhouse rich in beneficial plant compounds and contains almost the same amount of protein as an equivalent quantity of cooked meat (5 grams for 1 ounce of cashews versus 7 grams for 1 ounce of red meat). Shall I go on? Okay, I will.

This rich, buttery, sweet, and creamy nut, which is actually a seed, can be used to make delicious plant-based milk, heavy cream (page 55), ice cream, and cheeses (try the queso on page 167). I use them to create creamy dishes that no one will believe are dairy-free, like Lobzter Bisque (page 132) and Sweet Potato Cheezecake (page 278). When using them in a savory recipe, don't be shy with salt. Adding a little extra salt will help balance the cashew's natural sweetness. I also suggest always having a little extra liquid reserved to thin out the dish, if needed; cashews tend to thicken when heated.

SOAKING CASHEWS (And Other Nuts)

Soaking cashews is a must for nutritional and textural reasons. Cashews contain phytic acid that makes them hard to digest, but soaking eliminates the enzyme and allows for an extra-smooth consistency after blending.

Put the cashews in a bowl and cover with filtered water by 2 inches (the cashews will swell during soaking), then cover the bowl and leave at room temperature for at least 3 hours to guarantee a smooth, creamy, digestible dish. I like to add a generous pinch of salt at the beginning to help break down the enzymes that may be present. Cashews can be soaked for up to about 12 hours, but note that over-soaking can lead to sliminess and an altered taste. If you forgot to soak your cashews, don't stress it! Simply cover them with boiling filtered water, add a pinch of salt, and set aside for 30 minutes, then drain, rinse, and proceed with the recipe. Bonus: The same technique works for all other nuts.

Hemp Hearts

One of only a few plant foods that is a complete source of protein, hemp hearts (shelled hemp seeds) are the main ingredient in my Hemp Parm (page 58). They're also great for blending in smoothies or sprinkling on salads for added nutrition.

Pink Himalayan Salt

Using enough salt can take a recipe from good to great. My go-to salt contains 84 minerals and trace elements including calcium, magnesium, potassium, copper, and iron. If you're concerned about sodium, know that eating processed foods (canned sauces, soups, frozen prepared foods) is generally where the problem lies. Of course, if your doctor recommends using less salt, then heed their advice. Pink Himalayan salt comes in coarse and fine grinds or crystals. I like fine grinds because they dissolve faster.

SPROUTING SUPERFOODS

To be sprouted, legumes (including soybeans), seeds, grains, and even some nuts are left in a damp environment long enough to grow a sprout—the beginning of a plant. It's a process that dates back thousands of years. Sprouting provides a number of added health benefits, including improved digestion and increased nutrient absorption. Any time I can choose a sprouted ingredient over another, I will.

Tofu

Many people complain that tofu is bland, but that's when I have to remind them that tofu is a blank slate ready to show off whatever flavors you put into it. Allow yourself to be creative not just with the flavor but with the technique, too—tofu can be marinated, fried, baked, roasted, blackened, creamed, fermented, crumbled . . . its uses are endless.

Hot tip: Keep a few blocks of firm or extra-firm tofu in the freezer. Once you thaw and press out all of the water, the tofu will be able to soak up your desired marinade like a dream, plus it will have a spongy, meaty texture I like.

Just make sure you are buying only organic tofu, preferably sprouted. Organic tofu is free from GMOs, and sprouted tofu (see box, below) is more easily digested.

PLANT-BASED SWAPS
Applesauce

The *best* egg-replacer for baking. I love unsweetened applesauce in my sweet and savory baking (use it in my Skillet Cornbread on page 241) because it adds moisture, binds beautifully, and helps make baked goods a lovely golden color, thanks to the natural sugars in apples.

Banana Blossoms

Also known as banana hearts, these flowers create a wonderfully flaky, meaty texture that mimics fish and tastes more like a mild artichoke than banana. They're available canned and packed in brine in many Asian markets or online. They're a must-have for my Beer-Battered Fysh & Chips with Tartar Sauce (page 195).

Chickpea Flour

Great for making batters and soft, light "omelets" (see page 106) and scrambled eggz (see page 108). It's high in protein and naturally gluten-free.

Coconut Milk and Cream

These two are the richest nondairy milks out there, and either one can be used as the key ingredient in my whipped cream substitute, Vanilla Coco Whip (page 244). Coconut milk has savory uses, too, like in my Pumpkin Red Curry Rice Bowl (page 135). I don't use either as an all-purpose milk because of their distinct coconut flavor.

Flax Eggs or Other Egg Replacers

Mixing ground flaxseeds with water is the easiest egg-replacer option, but there are plenty of others to explore. If you go the flax egg route, you can buy whole flaxseeds and grind them yourself in a coffee grinder or high-speed blender or buy them pre-ground. Either way, store flaxseeds in the freezer as their abundant healthy fats go bad quickly.

For each flax egg needed, combine 1 tablespoon ground flaxseed with 3 tablespoons warm water. Mix until well combined and let stand for 5 minutes to thicken.

Jackfruit

This unripe fruit has a texture like shredded meat, which makes a great replacement for pulled pork, shredded beef, and even crab in dishes like Hot Krabby Dip (page 164). You're most likely to find jackfruit canned in brine or frozen at Asian grocery stores, though some big supermarket chains now stock it, too. Look for packaging labeled "young," "unripe," or "green" jackfruit—not ripe.

Kala Namak

A pungent black Himalayan salt that gets its smell due to a high mineral content of . . . you guessed it: sulfur. This salt adds an awesome flavor that will give your plant-based dishes like Hollandaze Sauce (page 98), Tofu Scramble (page 108), and protein-packed Chickpea Omelets (page 106) an "eggy" aroma and taste. This delicious, mineral-packed salt can be found at co-ops and some markets, and many online sources carry it.

Mock Meats/Faux Meats

Many criticize the plant-based burgers, sausages, ground "meat," veggie "chicken," and so on as being highly processed, containing soy, or even being unhealthy (due to increased amounts of sodium or fat). But I think meat replacements are a good choice for people who can't seem to part ways with animal meat and crave the flavor and texture but want to go plant-based. There are some great brands out there that focus on clean, non-GMO ingredients. Read your labels and give some a go if you feel it will help you stay on your meat-free journey. It's all about balance!

Soy Curls

These are *awesome*. Soy curls are made from the whole soybean and are non-GMO and chemical-free. They're a great alternative to meat because of their chew. Just like tofu, they're a blank canvas—only as good as the love you put into them. I love to marinate them as long as possible since they soak up flavor *beautifully*. One of my all-time favorite fillings for anything is leftover saucy soy curls from the Buffalo Chik'n Tacos on page 168. Think perfect meaty texture and spicy flavor penetrating every bite. If you haven't seen them at a health food store near you, order online. To rehydrate soy curls, cover with hot water for 8 to 10 minutes (up to 15 minutes if using the whole package), then gently squeeze out any excess water.

TPP (Texturized Pea Protein)

This is a gluten- and soy-free ingredient that's also a high-quality plant protein and a good source of iron. It's great for making your own plant-based meats like Unbelievably Vegan Protein Burger (page 217). Since it's created from peas (i.e., yellow split peas), it can be much gentler on the stomach than TVP if you have soy sensitivities. TPP is a specialty item that is just making its way to stores but can be easily found online.

TVP (Texturized Vegetable Protein)

This is similar to TPP but it contains soy.

PLANT-BASED DAIRY

One of the easiest plant-for-animal swaps you can make!

Butter

There are many great plant-based butter options available made from cashews, oats, and coconut, and with none of the funky stuff that's in margarine. These butters bake perfectly and add a nice buttery touch to dishes. Going out on a limb for the first time? Try Miyoko's Creamery European-Style Cultured Vegan Butter (salted or unsalted).

Cheese

I hear everyone screaming at me—BUT WHAT PLANT-BASED CHEESE IS THE BEST? This is where I say try them all! Get a different one every time you go grocery shopping. Yup, I never stop picking up new ones to try as long as they contain honest, plant-based ingredients. What I like is not what others may like. We all have different taste buds. There was once a time when you had only one or two brands to choose from. Now grocery stores have full sections dedicated to plant-based cheese. Have fun with them!

Cream Cheese

Luckily for you, there are phenomenal options out there to try. Or go on an adventure and make my simple homemade Cream Cheeze (page 56).

Milks

Soy milk is essential for making my Mayonnaise (page 53). Oat and cashew milks are rich and perfect for baking. Rice and almond milks are nice and mild. Coconut milk I use for specific purposes (see page 36). For cooking, look for unsweetened, unflavored varieties (meaning no vanilla!). A sweetened milk is fine for baking, but no need to keep both on hand. Find the types you like best and keep one or two in your fridge at all times.

FLAVOR ENHANCERS

Bouillon Cubes

I use mushroom bouillon cubes to get a rich, layered flavor in my French Onion Soup (page 131). With its deep color and natural umami, it's a great option for replacing beef stock in any of your favorite recipes. When I don't have Chik'n Broth (page 50) in the house, I will use a vegan bouillon in a pinch, such as Better Than Bouillon No Chicken or Vegetable paste.

Classic Latin Seasonings

Since I'm all about continuing to make the foods I loved growing up—that take me right back to mom's kitchen—I always keep a supply of these fundamental ingredients. Adobo seasoning is a traditional all-purpose spice mix that can be used for flavor layering or simply sprinkled on sliced avocado and tomato. There are many varieties; original or with cumin are my favorites. Sazón is used as a seasoning for just about anything from tacos, "meats," soups, stews, rice, and beans. It adds tons of flavor and aroma from its savory blend of garlic, coriander, cumin, oregano, pepper, and achiote. I always seek out brands that don't contain MSG. The achiote in sazón is ground from the annatto seed, which is another ingredient I always stock. It's used whole in many traditional Latin dishes such as Arroz con Gandules (page 237) for the seed's nutty, earthy flavor and colorful bright reddish-orange hue.

Dried Mushrooms

Dried shiitakes are key to getting the right depth of flavor for Fyshy Sauce (page 65). Dried lobster mushrooms have that spot-on slightly sweet taste and meaty texture that *make my*

Hot Sauce

I LOVE HOT SAUCE!

It's not just a plant-based cooking essential, it's an every-kind-of-cooking essential. If you want your food to pop, I strongly encourage you to get out there and try different kinds (there are plenty of mild ones, too) and incorporate them into dishes as a spice and hit of acid, not just as a condiment. I love adding hot sauce into sauces, marinades, and a couple splashes into my braising liquids. My go-tos are cayenne pepper sauces like Frank's RedHot Sauce for Buffalo dishes, Tabasco for creamy ones like Hollandaze Sauce (page 98), and Louisiana-style for dishes like jambalaya (page 212), but I also love sriracha as a condiment and for making sauces. I like chile pastes like sambal oelek and harissa for cooking. There are so many good ones out there, I could write a whole book on hot sauces, but I digress. You get the point of how amazing hot sauces can boost flavor!

Lobzter Bisque (page 132) and Lobzter Penne alla Vodka (page 198). I order mine—and lots of them—online.

Hickory-Smoked Salt

This is the secret ingredient in my Smoke Signal (page 87), which I use any time I want a big, bacon-y hit of flavor. Finishing a dish with smoked salt adds a nice hint of smoky flavor.

Kelp Powder or Nori Dust

This is a must-have for adding a seafood-like taste to dishes and for making my Vegan Anchovy Paste (page 140). Kelp powder is a ready-made product found at health food stores or online. If you can't find it, make Nori Dust: pulverize five plain or roasted nori sheets in a blender or food processor into a fine powder. Store in an airtight container in a cool, dry place for up to 2 months.

Liquid Amino Acids

With their concentrated, deep, and hearty flavor, aminos can be used in place of traditional Worcestershire sauce. Coconut aminos add a salty, savory, slightly sweet taste; it is made from the fermented sap of the coconut palm and is similar in color and consistency to light soy sauce. It is also packed with seventeen amino acids, potassium, vitamin C, and vitamin B. Regular liquid aminos are made from soybeans and don't taste as sweet as the coconut aminos. It contains an impressive sixteen amino acids. Both types are great for building flavor, but if you are avoiding soy, choose coconut aminos.

Liquid Smoke

No matter how many plant-based bacons you taste, they're never quite right and what's missing is an intense smoke. I like hickory liquid smoke for Smoke Signal (page 87) and all

my bae'con needs. Just like the name implies, this is smoke in liquid form. Wood chips are burnt, the smoke is collected and condensed (as when water drops form on the lid of a boiling pot), then that liquid is filtered to remove any impurities. This stuff is cooking gold.

Marmite or Vegemite

These are both thick, dark, yeast-based spreads that are the by-product of the beer brewing process and are used in vegan cooking to add a rich, salty, meaty, umami flavor—they're key to my Chili con Chili (page 136). Vegemite is thicker and stronger in flavor and is available in a gluten-free version, while Marmite has gluten and is a little milder and more syrupy. For my recipes, they're interchangeable.

Nutritional Yeast

I think most people are familiar with this ingredient as a cheese replacement—and a great popcorn topping—but it's also useful in getting rich, umami, not-at-all-cheesy flavors in recipes like my Chik'n Broth (page 50) and Garlic Ramen Noodles (page 238). It is similar to the yeast that is used to make bread and beer, but is loaded with minerals, protein, and B vitamins.

Pure Vanilla Powder and Vanilla Paste

When you're not baking with eggs and dairy, you need to find ways to make your sweets pop. I use vanilla powder and vanilla paste in many of my recipes to add a rich, concentrated vanilla flavor to desserts instead of alcohol-based extract, because the extract evaporates and loses its flavor. But if you can't find powder or paste, don't worry, I'll tell you how much extract to use, too.

Vegan Worcestershire Sauce

So much flavor packed into one little bottle! Regular Worcestershire sauce has anchovies, but there are plenty of vegan versions out there with the same tangy, complex flavor and ingredients you can feel good about, such as apple cider vinegar, tamarind paste, and garlic. I use it liberally in my cooking.

FLAVOR LAYERING

Having a well-stocked pantry *and* refrigerator/freezer is like having money in the bank. It makes preparing food at home easy and will cut down on last-minute takeout or trips to the grocery store.

A full pantry to me means having everything you need to turn your fresh produce into meals every week: staples like rice, pasta, grains, dried and canned beans; seasonings like vinegar, oil, lots of spices, dried chiles; and canned goods like tomatoes, tomato paste, and (more) chiles. Baking essentials like flours and leaveners mean you're that much closer to dessert or a side like cornbread. Plus, ingredients like cacao powder, dried fruit, and sugars make their way into my savory cooking, so I always have them around.

Along with the ingredients in the previous section, I always have the following on hand to help layer everything I make with *loads* of flavor.

Capers

Carrots

Celery

Citrus: limes, lemons, oranges, tangerines, grapefruit

Cooking alcohol: dry white and red wine, port wine, sherry, dark ale, whiskey

Herbs, fresh: Culantro (for making sofrito; see page 74), cilantro, basil, Thai basil, flat-leaf parsley, rosemary, mint, thyme, oregano, dill

Garlic

Ginger

Harissa

Ketchup

Kimchi (without shrimp paste or fish sauce; to make your own, see page 80)

Lemongrass

Mushrooms, fresh: shiitake, oyster, cremini, or any variety

Mustard: yellow prepared, Dijon, Creole, dry

Nondairy yogurt

Nut butters: hazelnut, cashew, almond, peanut

Olives: green, black, kalamata, Manzanilla

Onions: red, white, yellow

Peppers and chiles: sweet, mild, and hot such as jalapeños, bell peppers, ají dulce, and Thai chiles

Pickled things: dill pickles, sweet and dill relish, jalapeños, pepperoncini

Sauerkraut

Scallions

Shallots

Tahini

Vegan mayonnaise (or make your own; see page 53)

CHOOSE ORGANIC CONDIMENTS

I have a few favorite condiment recipes in this book that I prefer to make myself rather than buy. These include mayo (page 53), barbecue sauce (page 60), and ranch dressing (page 66). That said, I also live in the real world and don't always have time to make *everything* from scratch. When I'm adding condiments like ketchup or mustard to my cart I buy only organic. That way I can avoid harmful dyes, artificial flavors, and unnecessary chemicals. Always make sure the condiments you buy do not contain high fructose corn syrup.

ESSENTIAL KITCHEN EQUIPMENT AND TOOLS

People *always* ask me about cooking equipment! Maybe it's because, while shopping for kitchen equipment, many people buy tons of unnecessary items (myself included) that don't help them cook any more easily at home. Don't clutter your kitchen—get only the items you need and will actually use. This is a list of the tools you might not have at home that are necessary for great cooking and when using this book. (I assume you already have a sauté pan and pot you like, and basic tools such as tongs, wooden spoons, a spatula or two, and a strainer.)

Balloon Whisk

An absolute necessity for creamy grits, vinaigrettes, a smooth roux, and getting things whipped up evenly.

Chef's Knife

Please don't waste your money and buy a huge cutlery block filled with ten less-than-stellar knives, seven of which you will never use. You can achieve a lot of things—nearly everything—in the kitchen with one *great* chef's knife. I use it for slicing, dicing, and chopping fruits and vegetables, mincing herbs, and cutting through the tough rinds of melons and winter squashes. If you want to add to your collection, everything else can be handled by a good serrated knife (also called bread knife) and a small paring knife.

Cutting Boards

I like using wooden cutting boards, preferably made with a sustainable wood such as bamboo. Since I don't handle raw meat, it's easy to keep a wooden board clean without worrying about cross contamination. However, if you still cook meat or fish, always keep a separate board that can be easily sanitized, such as a recycled plastic one.

Dutch Oven

I use mine for *everything*. The heavy bottom gets a great sear on foods, and you can sauté and braise in one like nothing else. If you get one that's big enough, you can make stock, a good pot of beans, or a one-pot meal like jambalaya (page 212) in it.

High-Speed Blender

Hands-down my favorite piece of equipment. It's powerful and versatile and doesn't take up much space. I use it for smoothies, like you probably do, too. But I also use it to make the freshest nut butters, creamy salad dressings, and plant-based dairy substitutes. You can use a less powerful blender, but your end result will never be as smooth and creamy as one you make with a pro-level blender.

Immersion or Stick Blender

A convenient tool for creaming sauces and making purées. I use my immersion blender when I want to add creaminess to a pot of beans or soup while leaving a good amount of texture and chunkiness, like for my Cream of Broccoli Chedda' Soup (page 128). Plus, they're easy to clean and store.

Microplane

It's all about quick and easy, right? Many of my recipes call for citrus zest or grated garlic (see more on pages 43 and 47). This is best achieved by using a Microplane zester. It's also fantastic for grating fresh ginger and turmeric and whole spices, such as cinnamon and nutmeg.

Multicooker or Pressure Cooker

To make beans and grains without the hours of a traditional soak-and-simmer process, I use a multicooker or pressure cooker. (I use mine just about every day.) It's also great for cooking hard vegetables such as beets, artichokes, and potatoes, and for stews and one-pot meals that come together super fast.

Parchment Paper

This is where frustration-free baking starts! Parchment paper is an excellent choice for making sure items do not stick to the pan when roasting and baking and makes cleanup a breeze.

Pastry Blender

Excellent for cutting butter into flour for the most perfect Butta Biscuits (page 94) or Flaky Pie Dough (page 253). If you love rich, flaky baked goods (and who doesn't), this is a worthwhile addition to your kitchen.

Rubber Spatula

I call this my squeegee. A rubber spatula is great not only for scraping the sides of bowls and pans but also for removing sauces from a blender. You often can find me "squeegee-ing" out the sauce to get every last drop.

Sheet Pans

Necessary not only for making perfect cookies but for achieving beautifully roasted vegetables, tofu, Shiitake Bae'con (page 88), and all your baking needs. Have *at least* two half-sheet pans (they're cheap!) so you can roast and bake more efficiently.

A FEW TECHNIQUES

Here are a few key techniques to rely on for developing great flavor.

Blackened Vegetables

I serve these flavorful vegetables with nearly anything, but I especially love them with jambalaya (page 212). Heat 1 tablespoon plant-based butter and 1 tablespoon neutral oil in a cast-iron skillet over medium-high heat. When the butter is browned, toss in a combination of vegetables, such as cauliflower, broccoli, and my favorite, okra. Season with Creole-Cajun Seasoning (page 85) and cook until the veggies have softened and have crispy, browned/blackish edges, 5 to 7 minutes.

Caramelizing Onions (and More)

Nothing frustrates me more than ordering caramelized onions at a restaurant and just getting sautéed onions. *There is a difference.* Caramelized onions should be well . . . caramel colored! This is achieved by allowing the sugars to release and brown, making a sweet and beautiful product. (It works for more than just onions, too—try this method using garlic cloves, mushrooms, peppers, and even apples.)

I caramelize mine in about half the typical time. Here's how: Start with a large, hot sauté pan. Add a touch of oil, then your sliced or chopped ingredient, such as onions. Make sure the heat is on medium to high. Sprinkle with salt to pull out the moisture. Stir often—you do not want to burn them. Adding 2 to 3 tablespoons of liquid once they start to brown helps to deglaze the pan (see opposite page) and retain moisture, and creates steam to cook them faster. I love adding a little coconut sugar to my pan with the liquid—yup, to help them out and get them even sticky-sweeter. Once the onions are a deep golden amber, you can add red or white wine or some whiskey for extra color and flavor. Cook until the alcohol is mostly evaporated. This whole process should take 10 to 15 minutes. This is the method I use for whiskey-caramelized onions that top the Southern Poutine on page 178.

Cooking Grains

I'm always picking out different kinds of grains when shopping. I love to get creative with less common varieties in my cooking, and I use any and all grains as a base for Pro-Bowls (page 152). I throw them in my multicooker and cook according to the grain's liquid-to-grain ratio. There's a whole world of grains out there, and not enough space in this book to tell you how to cook each one. Check the package for the correct liquid-to-grain ratio for each grain.

Deglazing Pans

After sautéing vegetables, there is often deep brown flavor magic stuck to the bottom of your pan (referred to as the fond). You want to use it in whatever you're making. Once your ingredients have browned, remove them from the pan and add about ¼ cup of liquid (veg stock, wine, or other alcohol) and scrape the bottom of the pan to get off all those bits of flavor. Reduce the liquid by half and proceed with your recipe.

Grating Garlic

I will often ask for grated garlic in a recipe. By grating, I mean using a Microplane to grate it directly into a sauce or dip. This way, you get all of the garlic's essential oils and flavors. If you don't have a Microplane, use a garlic press or the smallest size holes on your grater (just take care not to skin your knuckles or fingers). Either way, make sure you give the Microplane or grater one good hit against your pot or bowl to release all the garlic and allicin collected. Allicin, one of the sulfur compounds of garlic, possesses antioxidants and is an antibacterial agent.

Reading Recipes

Get in the habit of reading recipes all the way through before starting—even if you don't plan on fully following them. There are lots of tips in my recipes, and by reading the whole thing first, you can make note of them and even prevent missteps once you start cooking. It will give you insight into the meal you're preparing and might even teach you a thing or two!

Roasting Peppers

Many of my recipes call for roasted, peeled, and seeded bell peppers or poblano chiles. Here's how I fire-roast them at home for *much* better flavor than you can get from a jar: Place the pepper over an open flame on your stovetop or on a foil-lined sheet pan under the broiler. Use tongs to turn the pepper until charred all over. Put the pepper in a bowl and cover. Let stand for 5 minutes. Run the pepper under cool running water (don't worry, you're not losing any flavor), rubbing to remove the charred skin. Discard the skin, seeds, and stem. Place the pepper on a paper towel to absorb any excess water.

CAULIFLOWER MARBELLA, PAGE 190

Roasting Vegetables (and More)

Let's set the record straight: roasting is not the same as baking! Roasting gives you a tender veg with a crisp, deeply browned, and caramelized exterior. This can only happen with *high heat*. Quick and high is what roasting is all about, so oven temperatures should be anywhere from 400°F to 425°F. Make sure to toss whatever you're roasting in oil, then season with salt and pepper. Add tougher herbs like rosemary and thyme, too. Save other spices for the last 5 minutes or sprinkle over the veg before serving; otherwise they'll burn and become bitter. Do not crowd the pan either—vegetables need space so heat can circulate around each piece to allow it to crisp (rather than steam). Make sure to shake the pan or flip larger vegetables so they roast evenly. Roasting should take 15 to 20 minutes. I love to roast chickpeas, too—they get so crisp! Just keep your eye on smaller items; they can dry out pretty fast, so finish closer to a 15-minute mark.

Sautéing Anything

Add ingredients to a *hot pan* unless otherwise stated. When you do, you will hear your ingredients erupt into applause.

That applause is called a sizzle (and if you don't hear it, your pan wasn't hot enough). It gets your vegetables caramelizing right away so the natural sugars can create super-complex flavors and aromas.

"Your ingredients should applaud you as they hit the pan."

Seasoning Everything

Season throughout the entire cooking process so that the final dish is as flavorful as possible. Also get into the habit of tasting as you go, so that you know if more seasoning is needed before you bring the dish to the table. It's not enough to simply sprinkle a little salt and pepper on your food at the end of cooking; if you add salt only at the end, it provides a more concentrated, surface coating that immediately hits your tongue. Your food will just taste salty, but not flavorful from the inside out.

"I see vegetables, tofu, and legumes as a canvas ready to soak up bold flavors."

Soaking Beans

All grains, dried beans, legumes, and nuts can be soaked in advance, which helps to eliminate hard-to-digest enzymes and fibers. Soaking beans helps minimize gas and bloating caused by a carbohydrate called oligosaccharide and makes them gentler on the stomach. It also helps shorten the cooking time needed to get a tender bean. Make sure to drain and rinse beans after soaking and before cooking, because all those oligosaccharides will now be in the water. I recommend soaking for at least 8 hours, or overnight. If you forgot to soak, don't worry: You can also put the beans in a pot with plenty of water and bring it to a boil. Cook for just a few minutes, then turn off the heat, cover, and soak for an hour. Drain, rinse, and proceed.

Toasting Bread Crumbs

I use panko bread crumbs often (not the other kind of sawdust in a box), but a simple ingredient like *fresh* bread crumbs can pull dishes like Mac & Cheezy (page 192) and Lobzter Penne alla Vodka (page 198) together beautifully. Toasted bread crumbs give them texture by adding crunch and visual appeal with hues of golden brown. The greatest part is that they can be made from the butts, scraps, and less desirable parts of the loaf. Whenever I have these kinds of pieces, I toss them in a plastic bag in my freezer. Once the bag gets full, I'm off to make fresh bread crumbs.

Preheat the oven to 300°F. Cut the bread into pieces small enough to pass through the chute of a food processor. Place the grating disk attachment on your food processor (I like the disk with larger size holes so I can get a variety of sizes). Process until all the pieces are fine and pick out any larger or flat pieces that refuse to cooperate. Spread the crumbs on a sheet pan and bake for 20 to 25 minutes, shaking and or stirring every 5 minutes, until golden. Cool and store in an airtight container in the refrigerator for up to 1 month. Note: These can be flavored with melted butter, herbs, and garlic.

Toasting Nuts and Seeds

Whether you're a seasoned vet or a first-time nut toaster, you may end up with burnt nuts; they do not discriminate. Here's my no-fail tip for never burning nuts again: Preheat the oven to 325°F and set the oven rack in the middle position. Place the nuts on a sheet pan in an even layer and leave the oven door slightly ajar. It will annoy you so much that the oven door is open that you will not forget about the nuts. Set the timer for 5 minutes, then turn off the oven. Allow the carryover heat of the oven to finish the job. You're welcome.

Zesting Citrus

When grating citrus zest to add to recipes, I like to use a Microplane grater to zest the fruit directly over what I'm making. This way I capture all of those essential oils that are released once I start scraping the peel. If you zest onto a cutting board and then put the scrapings into your food, you'll lose some of those potent essential oils—you want them in your food, not on your cutting board! Use organic citrus (free from pesticides) and make sure to thoroughly wash them before grating. Only zest the outer, colorful skin, not the bitter white pith under the skin.

"Food needs love. The more love you put into it, the better the results."

SHIITAKE BAE'CON, PAGE 88

FUNDAMENTALS

CHIK'N BROTH

2 large yellow onions, quartered

8 celery stalks (including leaves), coarsely chopped

6 carrots, scrubbed and coarsely chopped

10 garlic cloves, smashed

1 bunch flat-leaf or curly parsley

6 sprigs fresh thyme

4 bay leaves

2-inch piece fresh turmeric root, scrubbed, or
1 teaspoon ground

3 tablespoons nutritional yeast

2 tablespoons fine pink Himalayan salt, or to taste

2 teaspoons whole black peppercorns

¼ teaspoon ground cayenne pepper

16 cups water

¼ cup fresh or freeze-dried minced chives (optional)

MAKES 10 CUPS

TIP:
This broth is amazing during cold and flu season; for extra immune-boosting magic, add a 2-inch piece of peeled ginger and an extra pinch of cayenne to the finished broth and simmer for 10 minutes. Sip warm.

The first week of culinary school is knife skills 101. The next few weeks? All about stock. That's because in French cuisine, chicken stock is the backbone of great soups, sauces, and braising liquids. I use my chik'n broth the same way. And because it is the base of everything from Sopa Azteca (page 127) to Savory Brown Gravy (page 91), I make it myself so I can control the quality and quantity of the ingredients that go into it and the final flavor—and this broth is *just* as good as the stuff I made back when I was in school. The nutritional yeast lends a rich, umami flavor, and turmeric gives it that lovely, golden color associated with homemade chicken broth.

In a very large stockpot or Dutch oven, combine the onions, celery, carrots, garlic, parsley, thyme, bay leaves, turmeric, nutritional yeast, salt, peppercorns, cayenne, and water. Bring to a boil over medium-high heat. Reduce the heat to low and simmer, uncovered, for 45 to 60 minutes for a deep, concentrated vegetable flavor.

Let the broth cool slightly, then strain it through a fine-mesh strainer into a large bowl. Discard the solids.

Stir in the chives (if using). Use immediately or cool completely and store. You can divide among freezer-safe containers, like deli containers, reusable plastic bags, or ice cube trays, and freeze for up to 6 months or refrigerate in an airtight container for up to 1 week.

CASHEW HEAVY CREAM,
PAGE 55

MAYONNAISE, PAGE 53

BRAZIL NUT SOUR CREAM,
PAGE 57

CREAM CHEEZ
PAGE 56

MAYONNAISE

½ cup unsweetened, unflavored soy milk, at room temperature, or aquafaba (see below)

2 teaspoons nutritional yeast

1 teaspoon fine pink Himalayan salt, or to taste

½ teaspoon dry mustard

1 cup neutral oil, such as avocado or grapeseed

2 teaspoons fresh lemon juice

2 teaspoons apple cider vinegar

MAKES 1½ CUPS

TIP:

If the mayonnaise breaks and looks curdled, don't panic—even I've had my share of broken mayo. Transfer it to a bowl and place it in the freezer for 20 to 30 minutes. Put about half of the broken mayonnaise in the blender, then, with blender running, slowly add 1 cup of fresh oil, a little at a time, alternating with the remainder of the broken mayonnaise, until the mayo thickens (it will be the same consistency, you'll just have more—not a bad thing!).

AQUAFABA

This is the liquid from cooked or canned chickpeas and can be blended, frothed, and used as a thickener. Basically, wherever you'd use egg whites, you can use aquafaba. You can't technically buy it, but having a few cans of chickpeas or dried chickpeas ready to throw in your multicooker is a quick and easy way to get the best of both worlds. Aquafaba keeps in the refrigerator for up to 1 week and the freezer for up to 6 months.

I love empowering people with options! Having lots of delicious, convenient vegan swaps for your favorite foods will prepare you for the most successful plant-based journey—and one that sticks. This soy milk mayo is thick, creamy, made in minutes, and so much better than the store-bought stuff.

Soy milk emulsifies better than other dairy-free milks and gives you the thickest, creamiest consistency. If you're avoiding soy, substitute ½ cup of the liquid from cooked or canned chickpeas (called *aquafaba*).

In a high-speed blender (or beaker if using an immersion blender), combine the soy milk, nutritional yeast, salt, and dry mustard (add the oil now if using immersion blender and blend until thick). Cover and blend on medium-high speed until smooth. Turn the blender off and remove the small-ingredient stopper from the center of the blender top.

Turn the blender to medium speed. Very slowly drizzle in the oil through the top to emulsify the mayonnaise. Once you've added all the oil and the mayo is thick, add the lemon juice and vinegar and blend for a few seconds, just until incorporated. (I add the acid at the end to allow the mixture to fully emulsify first.)

Use immediately or store in an airtight container in the refrigerator for up to 8 days.

BÉCHAMEL

1 bay leaf

½ small yellow onion

2 whole cloves

¼ cup plant-based butter

¼ cup all-purpose flour or all-purpose gluten-free flour blend

2½ cups unsweetened, unflavored plant-based milk

1 teaspoon fine pink Himalayan salt, or to taste

½ teaspoon ground white pepper

¼ teaspoon freshly grated nutmeg (optional)

MAKES 2 CUPS

Béchamel is the foundation of creamy dishes like my Truffle Cream'd Corn (page 225). Essentially a gravy—butter, flour, and milk create a creamy sauce. It's a great alternative to cashew-based sauces like the one I use to make my Mac & Cheezy on page 192, if you have an allergy or don't have time to soak cashews.

Place the bay leaf on the flat side of the onion half. Secure the bay leaf in place with the cloves and set aside.

In a medium saucepan, melt the butter over medium heat. Add the flour and whisk to make a paste (called a roux). Cook, whisking constantly, for 1 to 2 minutes to cook the flour, being careful not to let it turn golden (turn the heat down if you need to); otherwise you'll have a brown sauce rather than a white one.

Continue whisking vigorously and begin to slowly pour in the milk. Whisk until smooth, then add the prepared onion half. Bring the liquid to a simmer and cook until slightly thickened, 4 to 5 minutes. Turn off the heat. Season with the salt, white pepper, and nutmeg (if using). Remove and discard the onion. Use immediately or cool and store in an airtight container in the refrigerator for up to 5 days.

CASHEW *HEAVY* CREAM

1 cup raw cashews, soaked and drained (see page 35)

1 cup unsweetened, unflavored plant-based milk

½ teaspoon fine pink Himalayan salt, or to taste

MAKES 2 CUPS

Along with Smoke Signal on page 87, this is one of the recipes that I rely on the most. Cashews blended with a nondairy milk *truly* act like heavy cream, and it has the perfect consistency for creating velvety sauces and soups like Lobzter Bisque (page 132) and Salted Caramel Sauce (page 245). Using cashews and plant milk creates the richest cream—much more luscious and milder in flavor than using solely plant-based milk or just cashews and water in a recipe.

In a high-speed blender, combine the cashews, milk, and salt. Cover and blend for 2 to 3 minutes, until very smooth.

Use immediately or store in an airtight container in the refrigerator for up to 1 week or freeze for up to 6 months.

CREAM *CHEEZE*

2 cups raw cashews, soaked and drained (see page 35)

½ cup unsweetened, unflavored plant-based milk

⅓ cup plain plant-based yogurt

2 tablespoons fresh lemon juice

2 teaspoons fine pink Himalayan salt, or to taste

½ cup water

3 tablespoons agar-agar (see page 35)

MAKES 3 CUPS

Yet another reason to love cashews: Their high fat content makes them perfect for a homemade vegan cream cheese. They just need a little boost from yogurt and lemon juice for the right tang, and agar-agar for that extra-thick consistency. Slather Cream Cheeze on bagels (obviously), use it for the golden and bubbly crostini that top my French Onion Soup (page 131), or turn it into a Sweet Potato Cheezecake (page 278).

In a high-speed blender, combine the cashews, milk, yogurt, lemon juice, and salt. Cover and blend until very smooth.

In a small saucepan, combine the water and agar-agar. Bring to a simmer over medium-low heat, whisking constantly, until thickened, about 1 minute.

Immediately pour the thickened agar-agar mixture into the blender with the cashew mixture (otherwise it will get too hard to incorporate). Cover and blend for 30 seconds, or until everything is well incorporated. Transfer the mixture to a glass dish.

Cover and chill in the refrigerator until completely cold and solid, 1 to 2 hours. Once chilled, use immediately or store in an airtight container in the refrigerator for up to 1 week.

GET CREATIVE!
Make flavored Cream Cheeze. Just add these ingredients when you incorporate the agar-agar:

- 1 tablespoon white miso paste and 1 recipe (2 tablespoons) Smoke Signal (page 87) for a smoked cream cheeze
- 5 to 10 whole roasted garlic cloves
- A few tablespoons chopped fresh chives and/or scallions (green parts only)
- 1 to 2 chopped chipotle chiles in adobo sauce and chopped roasted and seeded red bell pepper (see page 43) for a smoky-spicy chipotle option
- A few tablespoons fruit preserves, such as strawberry jam, for a sweet and tangy spread

BRAZIL NUT
SOUR CREAM

2 cups raw Brazil nuts, soaked and drained (see page 35)

1 cup unsweetened, unflavored plant-based milk

3 tablespoons distilled white vinegar or apple cider vinegar

2 tablespoons nutritional yeast

1 tablespoon fresh lemon juice

1 teaspoon fine pink Himalayan salt, or to taste

MAKES ABOUT 3 CUPS

GET CREATIVE!
Add a few teaspoons of onion powder, chopped fresh chives, dehydrated onion flakes, a minced garlic clove or two, and a dash of liquid aminos for a tasty onion dip. Serve with potato chips.

This is one of the condiments that never lasts long in my home. Zesty and silky smooth, my kids love it with just about anything. Brazil nuts—actually seeds—are rich, buttery, and loaded with selenium, an essential mineral and antioxidant that maintains the basic functioning of the body's immune system and is *great* for your skin and hair. So, if you need an excuse to eat more sour cream, here you go. Dollop it on top of Nacho Average Nachos (page 167), Chili con Chili (page 136), or a fluffy baked potato.

Rub the soaked Brazil nuts between two clean kitchen towels to remove as much of the skins as you can, but don't drive yourself crazy—Brazil nut skins are tough to remove, and the speckles in the sour cream add a nice natural touch. Discard the skins.

In a high-speed blender, combine the nuts, milk, vinegar, nutritional yeast, lemon juice, and salt. Cover and blend for about 2 minutes, or until super smooth and velvety.

Store in an airtight container in the refrigerator until the sour cream firms up and is chilled throughout, 1 to 2 hours. Once chilled, you can use it immediately or store in the refrigerator for up to 1 week.

HEMP *PARM*

½ cup hemp hearts

½ cup raw Brazil nuts, raw cashews, or blanched almonds

3 tablespoons nutritional yeast

1½ teaspoons extra-virgin olive oil

½ teaspoon onion powder

½ teaspoon garlic powder

½ teaspoon fine pink Himalayan salt, or to taste

MAKES 1½ CUPS

If I can use something in my cooking that has more nutritional value than the standard choice, I'm going for it. Hemp hearts (shelled hemp seeds) are the perfect example: they're fiber-rich, full of essential fatty acids, and one of relatively few plant-based foods that are complete sources of protein. I turn them into a Parmesan substitute by blitzing them in a blender with a few flavor components, and it's so good *and* so good for you that you can basically use this superfood on everything: pasta for the kids, Lobzter Penne alla Vodka (page 198), or sprinkled over Lemon Parm-y Kale Salad (page 139).

In a food processor or blender, combine the hemp hearts, nuts, nutritional yeast, olive oil, onion powder, garlic powder, and salt. Pulse until the mixture has the consistency of grated Parmesan.

Use immediately or store in an airtight container in the refrigerator for up to 2 weeks.

GET CREATIVE!
Swap out the pink Himalayan salt for truffle salt to make truffle Parm.

CHIPOTLE *BBQ* SAUCE

2 cups ketchup, preferably organic (see page 40)

½ cup (packed) dark or light brown sugar (either is fine)

1 to 2 minced chipotle chiles in adobo sauce (depending on how spicy you want it)

2 tablespoons organic yellow mustard

1 tablespoon molasses

2 teaspoons hickory-flavored liquid smoke (see page 38)

2 teaspoons ground cumin

½ teaspoon ground black pepper

MAKES ABOUT 2½ CUPS

My husband is a sauce guy—he needs to put some on everything. Once we were plant-based, I started reading the labels on the barbecue sauces we were buying at the store and was not happy with what I saw. Questionable ingredients like high-fructose corn syrup, tons of white sugar, artificial flavors and colors, and even animal by-products were in many of them. *My* recipe is tangy, sweet, spicy, all-natural, and it uses mostly pantry ingredients so you can throw together a batch easily. Use it as a dipping sauce for fries or slather on Unbelievably Vegan Protein Burgers (page 217) like Derrick does. It also makes a fantastic marinade for anything you want to grill.

In a medium saucepan, combine the ketchup, brown sugar, chiles, mustard, molasses, liquid smoke, cumin, and pepper and whisk to combine. Bring to a simmer over medium-high heat. Reduce the heat and simmer for 10 minutes, whisking occasionally.

Remove from the heat and allow to cool completely. Use immediately or store in an airtight container in the refrigerator for up to 2 weeks.

ROJO *SAUCE*

2 dried guajillo chiles, stemmed and seeded

2 dried ancho chiles, stemmed and seeded

4 ripe beefsteak or 5 ripe Roma tomatoes (or other plum tomato), stemmed and halved lengthwise

½ yellow, white, or red onion

3 garlic cloves

½ cup Chik'n Broth (page 50) or any vegetable broth

2 teaspoons dried oregano

2 teaspoons fine pink Himalayan salt, or to taste

1 teaspoon sweet or smoked paprika

1 teaspoon ground cumin or cumin seeds (optional)

½ teaspoon ground black pepper

Juice of 1 lime

MAKES 3 CUPS

This smoky, spicy, bright enchilada sauce is so much better than anything available at the store. You can make it entirely in a blender, and it easily doubles for storing in the freezer. How else can I turn out these delicious meals like the enchilada casserole Pay Azteca (page 205) or Chilaquiles with Tofu Scramble (page 113) during the week?

Set an oven rack in the middle position of the oven and heat the broiler on high.

While the oven heats, put the guajillo and ancho chiles in a heatproof bowl. Cover with boiling water and let soak for 10 to 15 minutes, or until soft and rehydrated; drain and reserve the soaking water.

Line a large sheet pan with foil. Arrange the tomatoes, onion, and garlic on the pan. Broil until charred, about 25 minutes, turning everything over halfway through.

In a high-speed blender (or large beaker if using an immersion blender), combine the chiles, tomatoes, onion, garlic, broth, oregano, salt, paprika, cumin (if using), pepper, and lime juice. Cover and blend for 1 to 2 minutes on high until smooth. I like the consistency of rojo sauce as is, but if you prefer yours on the thinner side, add the chile-soaking water, a few tablespoons at a time, until your desired consistency is reached.

Use immediately or cool and store in an airtight container in the refrigerator for up to 2 weeks.

GET CREATIVE!

Spread a thin layer of Rojo Sauce on the inside of tortillas when making quesadillas with plant-based cheese. It's also great mixed with a few tablespoons of mayonnaise and a pinch of smoked paprika to make a creamy taco sauce.

CREAMY *BUFFALO* SAUCE

1 cup hot sauce
(the classic choice is
Frank's RedHot Sauce;
see Note)

½ cup tahini

3 garlic cloves

½ cup water

MAKES 1⅔ CUPS

This kickin' sauce is so addictive, you'll start planning your meals around it. Tahini adds a luscious mouthfeel and richness to the sauce and makes it ridiculously creamy. As a bonus, tahini is more stable than plant-based butter, which has a tendency to break in an acidic sauce. This is so good tossed with baked chickpeas and roasted vegetables (see page 44), as a dip for crudités platters, and for taking plain vegetables or tofu to the next level. You'll thank me later.

In a high-speed blender (or beaker if using an immersion blender), combine the hot sauce, tahini, garlic, and water. Cover and blend until very smooth. Use immediately or store in an airtight container in the refrigerator for up to 2 weeks.

GET CREATIVE!
When making Lemon-Pepper Wingz (page 171), toss half of the cooked and battered wingz with the lemon-pepper sauce and the other half with this sauce for a poppin' party platter.

NOTE:
If you want less heat in your Buffalo sauce, use just ½ cup of hot sauce.

QUICK *STIR-FRY* SAUCE

½ cup coconut aminos
(see page 38)

3 tablespoons soy sauce,
tamari (if you're gluten-
free), or Fyshy Sauce
(page 65)

1 tablespoon coconut sugar
or maple syrup

2 teaspoons chile paste or
hot sauce (I like sambal
oelek or sriracha)

2 teaspoons toasted
sesame oil

1 teaspoon Chinese
five-spice powder

1½-inch piece ginger,
peeled and grated

2 garlic cloves, minced

¼ cup minced scallions
(green and white parts)

MAKES ABOUT ¾ CUP

Let's face it—we all have those days when cooking is not a priority, but we still need something quick, healthy, and filling. Or maybe it's the end of the week and your produce bin is looking a little less than perfect. Stir-fries are the answer for those nights. Serve over steamed rice, ramen, or your favorite grain.

In a medium bowl, whisk together the aminos, soy sauce, coconut sugar, chile paste, sesame oil, five-spice powder, ginger, and garlic. Mix well to combine. Add the scallions and stir.

To use immediately, add to a pan of stir-fried vegetables over high heat, allowing the sauce to heat through and the sugar to caramelize for 1 to 2 minutes. Or refrigerate in an airtight container for up to 1 week.

GET CREATIVE!
Pour Quick Stir-Fry Sauce over vegetables after roasting (see page 44), then bake on high heat for 5 minutes to allow the sugars to caramelize.

FYSHY *SAUCE*

3 dried shiitake mushrooms

1 (9- by 10-inch) sheet of kombu, broken into a few pieces

2 tablespoons coconut sugar

2 tablespoons soy sauce or tamari (if you're gluten-free)

1 tablespoon fine pink Himalayan salt, or more to taste

1 tablespoon Nori Dust (page 38) or kelp powder

2 teaspoons coconut aminos (see page 38)

Juice of 1 lime

3 cups water

MAKES 2½ CUPS

Asian fish sauce (there are Thai, Vietnamese, and lots of other varieties—it's often labeled nam pla, nuoc mam, or nam pa) brings a totally unique, rich, salty, and truly incredible flavor to any dish that it touches. The real stuff contains small fish (like anchovies) fermented with salt in barrels for anywhere from a few months to several years. So what are you supposed to do if you don't eat fish but you want to add that special salty-tangy-pungent flavor to a dish? Make Fyshy Sauce! It gets its rich flavor from coconut aminos and shiitake mushrooms, and that hit of deep savoriness from sea vegetables: kombu and kelp. A batch of this in your fridge means no compromising on favorite dishes like Vegetable Pho (page 183) and other take-out favorites you can now make at home.

In a small saucepan, combine the mushrooms, kombu, coconut sugar, soy sauce, salt, Nori Dust, coconut aminos, lime juice, and water. Bring to a simmer over medium heat. Simmer for 20 minutes, stirring occasionally.

Remove from the heat and allow to cool completely. Strain through a fine-mesh strainer and discard the solids.

Use immediately or store in an airtight container in the refrigerator for up to 3 months.

RANCH *DRESSINGS*

Classic Herby *Ranch*

2 cups Mayonnaise (page 53) or any plant-based mayonnaise

2 garlic cloves

3 tablespoons nutritional yeast

1 tablespoon onion powder

1 tablespoon fresh lemon juice

2 teaspoons distilled white vinegar, red wine vinegar, or apple cider vinegar

2 teaspoons fine pink Himalayan salt, or to taste

1 teaspoon garlic powder

½ teaspoon ground black pepper

¾ cup chopped fresh herbs, such as dill, chives, thyme, cilantro, basil, flat-leaf parsley, oregano, and/or rosemary, or ¼ cup dried

Unsweetened, unflavored plant-based milk (optional)

MAKES 2¼ CUPS

When I was growing up, my mom made ranch dressing from scratch, and we loved it so much, I swear we practically drank it. Into it we dunked raw vegetables, fried zucchini, French fries, and even pizza! Keeping with tradition, I make mine from scratch, too, now with plant-based ingredients and herbs from my garden (especially when it's overflowing in the spring and summertime). Watching my children enjoy something that was such a huge part of my childhood makes me so happy. Talk about full circle!

Between the six of us (Derrick counts as three people!), it always disappears quickly, so I make big batches (I double this recipe), but if you want to make less, the recipe also halves easily. The best ranch dressing uses fresh herbs, but there's nothing wrong with dried herbs if that's what you have.

Spoon the mayonnaise into a medium bowl. Using a Microplane, grate the garlic into the bowl (make sure to give the Microplane a good whack to release all of the garlic). Add the nutritional yeast, onion powder, lemon juice, vinegar, salt, garlic powder, and pepper and whisk until smooth. Stir in the herbs. (If you like your dressing a little thinner, add a few tablespoons of plant-based milk.)

Use immediately or cover and chill before serving to allow the flavors to meld. Store in an airtight container in the refrigerator for up to 1 week.

Avocado-Lime *Ranch*

1 large ripe avocado, halved and pitted

1 cup Mayonnaise (page 53) or any plant-based mayonnaise

2 garlic cloves

2 tablespoons nutritional yeast

2 teaspoons onion powder

1 teaspoon fine pink Himalayan salt, or to taste

½ teaspoon ground cumin

¼ teaspoon ground black pepper

Zest and juice of 1 lime

3 tablespoons finely chopped fresh cilantro leaves

MAKES 2 CUPS

Ranch dressing is amazing, but ranch dressing with avocado and lime is next level. I was preparing a taco lunch that was missing a little something, and I didn't want to just slap salsa on it (I love salsa but it just wasn't the right move here). I saw some ranch in my fridge, started vibing, and ended up with a sauce that's *even better* than the original. Now I use this richer, zestier version to make simple green salads incredible and as a dip for almost everything. Tossed with shredded cabbage, it makes a picnic-worthy coleslaw that's also used to top off Buffalo Chik'n Tacos (page 168).

Scoop out the avocado, add the flesh to a medium bowl, and smash with a fork. Add the mayonnaise. Using a Microplane, grate the garlic into the bowl (make sure to give the Microplane a good whack to release all of the garlic) and whisk until smooth. Add the nutritional yeast, onion powder, salt, cumin, pepper, and lime zest and juice; whisk again. Add the cilantro and whisk until smooth.

Use immediately or cover and chill before serving to allow the flavors to meld. Store in an airtight container in the refrigerator for up to 1 week.

HARISSA-TAHINI
DRESSING

2 garlic cloves

½ cup tahini

2 tablespoons harissa

Juice of 1 lemon or lime

2 teaspoons agave or pure maple syrup

1 teaspoon fine pink Himalayan salt, or to taste

½ teaspoon ground black pepper

½ teaspoon ground cumin

¾ cup water

MAKES A GENEROUS 1 CUP

This dressing is similar to the rich, spice-forward Creamy Buffalo Sauce (page 63), but with notes of roasted red peppers from harissa, a vibrant red chile paste originating from Tunisia. Haven't tried harissa yet? Made from dried chiles, roasted red peppers, olive oil, and warm spices like coriander, it's a cornerstone condiment used across many North African countries. Combined with smooth tahini, it sure can perk up any dish—I love it drizzled over roasted vegetables or simply cooked lentils.

Using a Microplane, grate the garlic into a medium bowl (make sure to give the Microplane a good whack to release all of the garlic). Add the tahini, harissa, lemon juice, agave, salt, pepper, and cumin and whisk until smooth.

Whisk the water into the mixture a little at a time until it transforms into a creamy sauce. (You may not use all of the water—I like thick, creamy, pourable sauce.)

Use immediately or store in an airtight container in the refrigerator for up to 5 days. If the sauce thickens during storage, stir in water a teaspoon or two at a time to reach the desired consistency.

CITRUS-MISO *DRESSING*

4 tangerines or 2 oranges (any variety)

¼ cup raw cashews, soaked and drained (see page 35), or ½ cup Mayonnaise (page 53) or any plant-based mayonnaise

3 tablespoons white miso paste

3 tablespoons soy sauce or tamari (if you're gluten-free)

3 tablespoons agave or pure maple syrup

2 tablespoons rice vinegar

1 teaspoon chile paste or hot sauce (I like sambal oelek or sriracha)

1 teaspoon toasted sesame oil

1- to 1½-inch piece ginger, peeled

1 garlic clove

Juice of 1 lemon

MAKES 1½ CUPS

This one goes out to our homie (Derrick's teammate) Brian Orakpo. I came up with this dressing when I had a fruit basket full of tangerines that my kids just couldn't eat fast enough, so I used them to make a spinach salad dressed with this sweet-umami dressing. When I started putting it in the guys' lunch, Brian would save any of his extra dressing in the team fridge with a "do not touch" disclaimer—he loved it that much. So here you go, Brian, now you can make as much as you want, and pour it over everything! It's excellent as a marinade for tofu, sautéed with mushrooms, brushed on cauliflower steaks after grilling, and as a dip for plant-based chik'n. Use it to dress my cold soba noodle salad on page 148.

Using a Microplane, zest 2 of the tangerines or 1 orange. Juice all of them.

Combine the cashews in a high-speed blender with the tangerine zest and juice, miso paste, soy sauce, agave, vinegar, chile paste, sesame oil, ginger, garlic, and lemon juice. Blend on high until very smooth. Use immediately or store in an airtight container in the refrigerator for up to 2 weeks.

ROASTED RED PEPPER, *CHIPOTLE* & LIME DRESSING

1 red bell pepper, roasted, peeled, and seeded (see page 43)

½ cup apple cider vinegar

½ cup neutral oil, such as avocado or grapeseed

2 teaspoons ground cumin

1 teaspoon fine pink Himalayan salt, or to taste

½ teaspoon chili powder

½ teaspoon smoked paprika

5 to 7 pitted Medjool dates (depending on how sweet you want it)

2 chipotle chiles in adobo sauce

Juice of 1 lime

1 garlic clove

½ cup water

¼ cup fresh cilantro leaves, left whole

MAKES 2¾ CUPS

I used to purchase "gourmet" store-bought salad dressings, looking for something interesting and convenient to spruce up a dish. Unfortunately, I was always disappointed. Not only by the unnecessary ingredients in the dressing (like loads of sugar, high-fructose corn syrup, and additives to keep it shelf-stable) and high amounts of sodium, but also the taste—or rather lack of. So I started developing my own dressings. This one makes an insane taco salad (page 147) and adds a smoky-sweet boost to just about anything else. I start by fire-roasting red peppers on the stovetop (so easy, you'll never buy the jarred ones again!) and add chipotles in adobo sauce for the main flavor profile, plus Medjool dates for natural sweetness and body as well as fiber.

In a high-speed blender (or beaker if using an immersion blender), combine the roasted pepper, vinegar, oil, cumin, salt, chili powder, smoked paprika, dates, chipotle chiles, lime juice, garlic, and water. Cover and blend on high until very smooth. Add the cilantro and blend for another 5 to 10 seconds, until the leaves are chopped. Use immediately or store in an airtight container in the refrigerator for up to 2 weeks.

THE MARINADE

¼ cup vegan Worcestershire sauce

¼ cup liquid aminos (see page 38)

¼ cup avocado oil or extra-virgin olive oil

1 garlic clove, minced or grated

2 teaspoons smoked paprika

½ teaspoon ground black pepper

½ teaspoon fine pink Himalayan salt, or to taste

MAKES ABOUT ¾ CUP

Food needs love. The more love you put into it, the better the results. To me, a marinade is like the first step of dating—it's intense and sets the stage for the rest of the relationship. I use this umami bomb of a marinade to smother tofu, soy curls, chickpeas, beans, mushrooms, cauliflower, tomatoes, or just about anything with affection. I see vegetables, tofu, and legumes as a canvas ready to soak up bold flavors, and this marinade has them all.

In a medium bowl, whisk together the Worcestershire sauce, liquid aminos, oil, garlic, paprika, pepper, and salt. Use immediately to marinate ingredients for at least 2 hours (though overnight is superb if you want to make a flavor impact) or store in an airtight container in the refrigerator for up to 1 week.

"People always say to me, 'I hate tofu' and 'Tofu is bland.' Stop blaming tofu for your lack of creativity!"

PUERTO RICAN *SOFRITO*

2 Spanish or yellow onions, quartered

12 sweet ají dulce peppers, stemmed, halved, and seeded (see Note)

2 green bell peppers, stemmed, quartered, and seeded

1 red bell pepper, stemmed, quartered, and seeded

15 to 18 garlic cloves, smashed (from about 2 heads)

1 bunch cilantro, about 2 inches from stem ends trimmed off

1 bunch culantro (recao), about 2 inches from stem ends trimmed off, or another bunch cilantro

2 teaspoons fine pink Himalayan salt, or to taste

½ teaspoon whole black peppercorns

MAKES 4 CUPS

TIP:

If using a blender to purée the sofrito and the blade gets stuck, turn it off and use a long-handled spoon to rearrange the vegetables and clear the bottom of the jar. Once the onion is puréed, it creates liquid, which is why I don't add water or oil to my sofrito.

NOTE:

If you can't find sweet and mild miniature ají dulce peppers, use an additional 1 green and 1 red bell pepper.

Garlicky and pungent with onion and a healthy dose of culantro (cilantro's cousin), sofrito is the building block of Latin cooking. While the base is always made from a mixture of onions, peppers, garlic, and herbs, each Latin American country has its own version, sometimes adding vegetables like tomatoes, leeks, scallions, or carrots, and olive oil, wine, or vinegar. My Puerto Rican mother and her family add oregano, cumin, and capers, while I keep mine pretty basic (sometimes, I'll add tomato if I have a few extra that I need to use). It's traditional to freeze sofrito in ice cubes trays, popping out one to three cubes per recipe (about 2 to 6 tablespoons total). Add it to your pan as the first step for a well-seasoned dish or pop it into a simmering pot of stew or beans. I always have this flavor-boosting staple ready to go when making Arroz con Gandules (page 237) and Pastelillos with Saffron Aïoli (page 173).

Put the onions in a high-speed blender or food processor first (see Tip), then add the peppers, garlic, cilantro, culantro, salt, and black pepper. Blend until the purée has a pesto-like consistency. Transfer to an airtight jar. Use immediately, store in the refrigerator for up to 2 weeks, or divide among ice cube trays for 2-tablespoon-size servings; once frozen, pop out the cubes and keep frozen for up to 6 months in a freezer-safe container.

PICKLE *IT!*

KIMCHI, PAGE 80

Pickled and fermented vegetables are great for boosting flavors by adding salty, vinegary, and spicy notes—plus they add great textures, too. Fermented vegetables are also beneficial for your gut health, and unless you have been living under a rock, then you know how important gut health is to maintaining general health and well-being. Here are my favorites to make at home. If you're feeling intimidated with fermenting, start with simple Pickled Red Onions (see opposite page), then work your way up to Kimchi. Use my recipes as a starting point and get creative by adding different herbs and spices (or switching up the veg) to create your own versions.

TIP:
I like to recycle large 32-ounce glass jars and use them for pickling. All the recipes except for Kimchi fit into one *perfectly.*

PICKLED RED ONIONS, OPPOSITE PAGE

Pickled Red Onions

2 cups distilled white vinegar

⅔ cup organic sugar or (packed) dark brown sugar

1 tablespoon fine pink Himalayan salt, or to taste

1 tablespoon pickling spice (optional)

2 red onions, halved and cut into ¼-inch-thick slices (about 3 cups total)

2 garlic cloves, smashed

MAKES ONE 32-OUNCE JAR

These are good alongside just about any savory dish and can be made in under 10 minutes. They add zest to avocado toast, salads, tacos—even chili. When I've finished a batch, I like to save the liquid and add more fresh red onions, then place in the refrigerator overnight to "pickle." Talk about stretching your pennies!

In a medium saucepan, combine the vinegar, sugar, salt, and pickling spice (if using). Bring to a simmer and cook, stirring occasionally, until the sugar is completely dissolved. Remove from the heat and allow to cool slightly for 5 minutes.

Pack the onions and garlic in a large glass jar (see Tip, opposite page). Pour the warm pickling brine over the onions. Let sit, uncovered, until liquid comes to room temperature. Tightly secure the lid on the jar and refrigerate. The onions are ready to eat in 1 hour, however, the longer they sit, the better they get. Store in the fridge for up to 2 weeks.

GET CREATIVE!
Use the same brine to pickle thinly sliced carrots, beets, or a combination of vegetables. Don't like (or don't have any) pickling spice? Simply omit it for a basic brine.

Escabeche

1 tablespoon neutral oil, such as avocado or grapeseed

1 large yellow onion, sliced ¼ to ¾ inch thick

5 garlic cloves, crushed

2 large carrots, sliced ¼ to ¾ inch thick

4 large jalapeños, sliced ¼ to ¾ inch thick

1 cup 1-inch cauliflower florets (optional)

5 or 6 small radishes, sliced ¼ to ¾ inch thick (optional)

1 cup distilled white vinegar

½ cup water

1 tablespoon organic sugar

1 tablespoon fine pink Himalayan salt, or to taste

½ teaspoon dried oregano

½ teaspoon dried thyme

MAKES ONE 32-OUNCE JAR

These pickled vegetables and peppers are traditionally used as a condiment in Mexico. I fell in love eating them in the mom-and-pop Mexican restaurants of my home state, California. Soon I was seeking out restaurants with salsa bars just for the escabeche—I could eat a whole meal consisting of just these pickles, chips, and salsa (try it!). I also love them on nachos, a crunchy tostada, or a bowl of rice and beans to liven it up. Sweating (sautéing without browning) the vegetables to bring out their flavor before they soak up the tart and addictive brine is an essential step—so don't skip it!

Heat a large pot or Dutch oven over medium heat. Add the oil. Once the oil is hot and shimmering, add the onion and garlic. Sauté, stirring often, until fragrant, about 1 minute, then add the carrots, jalapeños, cauliflower (if using), and radishes (if using). Sauté for another minute, but don't let the vegetables brown at all.

Add the vinegar, water, sugar, salt, oregano, and thyme. Bring to a simmer and cook, stirring occasionally, until the sugar is completely dissolved. Remove from the heat and allow to cool slightly for 5 minutes.

Using a slotted spoon, transfer the vegetables to a large glass jar with a lid (see Tip on page 76). Strain the brine through a fine-mesh strainer into the jar, making sure to keep the jalapeño seeds out of it (unless you want your escabeche super spicy!). Allow the vegetables and brine to cool to room temperature.

Cover tightly with the lid and chill in the refrigerator for at least 1 hour before serving. The vegetables can be stored in the refrigerator for up to 2 weeks and will become more delicious the longer they sit.

Vietnamese Pickled Vegetables

1 small daikon radish, peeled and sliced into matchsticks

1 tablespoon plus 1 teaspoon fine pink Himalayan salt, or to taste

2 carrots, sliced into matchsticks

1 large English cucumber, sliced into matchsticks

2 serranos, stemmed, seeded, and cut into rings (optional)

1 cup rice vinegar

½ cup warm water

¼ cup organic sugar

MAKES ONE 32-OUNCE JAR

TIP:
Add extra flavor to your pickles with a 1-inch piece of ginger, peeled and sliced into coins, or half a red onion, cut into thin slices.

GET YOURSELF A MANDOLINE OR JULIENNE PEELER

Not many people want to slice vegetables into juliennes or matchsticks by hand. I personally find it therapeutic, but for a shortcut, buy either of these nifty handheld tools. They don't cost much and will get all your knife cuts done in a fraction of the time.

When I lived in Southern California, I would plan my weekends around excursions with my dear friend Suzie Vuong. We'd go to various markets and restaurants and try countless versions of our favorite Vietnamese dishes. I fell in love with these spicy, briny, crunchy vegetables that accompanied so many of my favorites, like banh xeo (Vietnamese crepes). The rice vinegar in the brine is low in acid and won't overpower the produce like other vinegars. This recipe really can be as simple as daikon radish and carrots and will still be awesome on a tofu or mushroom banh mi, as a beautiful complement to a lettuce cup platter (try mine on page 158), or eaten straight out the jar, as I do. For less heat, leave out the serranos.

In a medium bowl, sprinkle the daikon radish with 1 tablespoon of the salt and let stand for 15 minutes. Rinse well with cool water, then squeeze out excess water. (This step also helps remove some of the strong daikon fragrance.)

In a large bowl, combine the daikon, carrots, cucumber, and serranos (if using). Toss gently to combine. Transfer the vegetables to a large glass jar with a lid (see Tip on page 76).

In a medium bowl, whisk together the vinegar, warm water, sugar, and remaining 1 teaspoon salt until the salt and sugar are dissolved.

Pour the brine over the vegetables. Cover tightly with the lid and chill in the refrigerator for at least 1 hour before using. Store in an airtight glass container in the refrigerator for up to 2 weeks.

Kimchi

3 pounds napa cabbage, trimmed, quartered, cored, and coarsely chopped into 2- to 3-inch pieces

1 cup plus 1 tablespoon coarse sea salt

2 tablespoons sweet glutinous rice flour

1 cup water

¼ cup Fyshy Sauce (page 65)

10 garlic cloves, crushed

1-inch piece fresh ginger, peeled and sliced

1 white or yellow onion, halved and thinly sliced

1 cup gochugaru (Korean hot pepper flakes)

6 scallions (green and white parts), sliced diagonally

1 large Korean radish or daikon radish (about 1 pound), julienned

2 large carrots, julienned

½ cup cut Asian chives (2- to 3-inch lengths) (optional)

2 tablespoons toasted white sesame seeds

MAKES TWO 1-QUART JARS

My former neighbor, Choe, would make me fresh batches of kimchi (and the best fried rice I have *ever* had to go with it). She'd always caution me, saying it's fresh, so it'd be "better in a few days." I never got to a few days—I would always eat it right away—and it still tasted amazing. Inspired by Choe and encouraged by my dear friend Alice Kim, I whipped up a version using Fyshy Sauce to add complexity and depth that usually comes from fish sauce. All you need is a quick trip to an international grocery store (or an even faster trip online) to get your gochugaru and sweet glutinous rice flour for the flavor paste. While you're there, pick up some Asian chives (also called garlic chives or buchu), which have an extra-garlicky flavor. The most well-known kimchi is made with napa cabbage, but once you get the technique down, you can literally turn just about any vegetable into kimchi. Other traditional versions use daikon radish, scallions, or cucumber. Make sure to use disposable gloves when mixing the kimchi—those hot pepper flakes seeping into your skin will not feel good.

In a very large bowl, gently sprinkle the cabbage with a little bit of water, allowing the leaves to get slightly wet but not saturated.

Layer a handful of the dampened cabbage in the bottom of another very large bowl. Sprinkle with some of the 1 cup of salt. Add another handful of cabbage and more salt, repeating with the remaining cabbage and salt until both are gone. Let stand for 2 hours at room temperature, stirring gently every 30 to 45 minutes to evenly distribute salt on all of the cabbage.

recipe continues >>

Meanwhile, make the rice flour paste. In a small saucepan, combine the rice flour and water. Bring to a simmer over medium-low heat. Cook, stirring constantly, until the mixture begins to thicken, about 3 minutes. Remove from heat and allow to slightly cool.

In a blender or food processor, combine the rice flour mixture, Fyshy Sauce, garlic, ginger, onion, and the remaining 1 tablespoon salt. Blend until the mixture is smooth. Transfer to a bowl. Add the gochugaru and stir until well combined. Set aside.

Very carefully pour off any liquid released by the cabbage. Fill the bowl with cool water, swirling the cabbage around to rinse it. Discard the water and repeat three or four times to remove all of the salt. Drain the cabbage in a colander, pressing gently to get rid of all excess water. Return the cabbage to the bowl.

Add the scallions, radish, carrots, chives (if using), and sesame seeds. Add half of the rice paste seasoning mixture. Wearing disposable kitchen gloves, mix well with your hands. Add the remaining rice paste mixture and mix well again until all the ingredients are evenly distributed.

Divide the cabbage mixture between two glass jars with tight-fitting lids, packing each well. Cover tightly with lids, leaving 1 inch of headspace at the top of each jar. (The kimchi will produce gases as it ferments, and you need to allow for some space for the gases to expand.)

Let the kimchi stand on the counter for 1 to 2 days to allow for fermentation, then refrigerate. The kimchi will continue to ferment in the fridge for 2 to 3 weeks and is good for up to 6 months. The longer it stays in the refrigerator, the deeper the flavors become, and then it will become sour. Once sour, use for noodles, stews, and rice dishes.

TIP:
Salting the cabbage is the first and one of the most important steps. *Do not* skip this. It helps to clean the cabbage, create an environment that harmful bacteria don't like, and encourage the growth of good bacteria. It also primes the cabbage to absorb seasonings and be compactible after the water in the leaves is released.

GET CREATIVE!
Using kimchi to make kimchi fried rice, adding some to ramen, or topping off a Pro-Bowl (page 152) or Gochujang Jackfruit Noodle Bowl (page 215) are all very tasty ways to add healthy, gut-beneficial microbes to your plant-based meals.

BBQ
SEASONING

3 tablespoons (packed) light or dark brown sugar or coconut sugar

2 tablespoons chili powder

1 tablespoon smoked paprika

1 tablespoon ground cumin

1 tablespoon garlic powder

1 tablespoon fine pink Himalayan salt, or to taste

MAKES ABOUT ½ CUP

When I want the flavor of barbecue but not the messiness of the grill or the sauce, this is my go-to seasoning. Try rubbing or sprinkling it on tofu, cauliflower steaks, or portobello mushrooms before roasting or grilling them for an intense bite of smoky, spicy, sweet backyard barbecue flavor. Add it to the Unbelievably Vegan Protein Burger mix (page 217) for a bold patty. Or go all out and toss with freshly fried French fries and make Southern Poutine with Whiskey Caramelized Onions (page 178).

In a small bowl, combine the sugar, chili powder, smoked paprika, cumin, garlic powder, and salt. Use immediately or store in an airtight container in a cool dry place for up to 6 months. Stir or shake before using.

CREOLE-CAJUN
SEASONING

6 tablespoons sweet paprika

2 tablespoons onion powder

2 tablespoons garlic powder

1 tablespoon dried thyme

1 tablespoon fine pink Himalayan salt, or to taste

2 teaspoons ground black pepper

2 teaspoons ground white pepper

1½ teaspoons dried oregano

1½ teaspoons ground cayenne pepper (use ¾ teaspoon if you don't like heat)

1 teaspoon smoked paprika (optional)

MAKES ABOUT ¾ CUP

TIP:
Save old condiment jars or other small glass jars for storing your homemade spice blends.

People often use the terms Cajun and Creole interchangeably, but there are differences between the two, especially when it comes to spices. Cajun seasoning focuses on the peppers in the blend and often contains cayenne, black, or white pepper (or all three) and usually has more of a kick. Creole seasoning has a stronger herbal presence and often includes thyme, marjoram, basil, oregano, parsley, and sometimes rosemary. My version takes a little bit from each to create one universal seasoning that I use in many dishes in this book, including my Grandma Duplechan's Creole Gumbo (page 209) and Fried Chik'n with Spicy Maple Syrup (page 206). It's also great for seasoning tempeh or tofu strips before blackening them in hot oil in a cast-iron skillet on the stovetop (see page 42).

In a small bowl, combine the sweet paprika, onion powder, garlic powder, thyme, salt, black pepper, white pepper, oregano, cayenne, and smoked paprika (if using). Use immediately or store in an airtight container in a cool dry place for up to 6 months. Stir or shake before using.

TACO *SEASONING*

3 tablespoons chili powder

2 tablespoons ground cumin

1 tablespoon fine pink Himalayan salt, or more to taste

1 tablespoon ancho chile powder

1 tablespoon sweet paprika

1 tablespoon smoked paprika

1 tablespoon onion powder

1 tablespoon garlic powder

2 teaspoons dried oregano

¼ teaspoon ground black pepper

MAKES ABOUT ¼ CUP

If I'm starting to sound like a broken record about making things myself, it's because I get so frustrated with the options available at the grocery store! Sure, those packets in the spice aisle are convenient, but they are also full of fillers and unnecessary ingredients of mysterious origin. Making your own taco spice blend at home allows you to control the flavor and skip the preservatives. It's also a great way to get one last use out of spices in your pantry that have been sitting there for only God knows how long. Give your food that extra loving touch it needs, all for about 5 minutes of work.

In a small bowl, combine the chili powder, cumin, salt, ancho chile powder, sweet paprika, smoked paprika, onion powder, garlic powder, dried oregano, and pepper. Use immediately or store in an airtight container in a cool dry place for up to 6 months. Stir or shake before using.

SMOKE SIGNAL

1 tablespoon vegan Worcestershire sauce or liquid aminos (see page 38)

1 tablespoon hickory liquid smoke

1 teaspoon hickory-smoked salt

½ teaspoon smoked paprika

⅛ teaspoon hot sauce (I like Tabasco)

MAKES 2 TABLESPOONS

This is a flavor bomb you will find *alllll* throughout this book. I use it when I'm trying to replicate the taste of bacon, ham, or other smoked meats. The key ingredient is liquid smoke (or, as I call it, cooking gold; read why I love it on page 38). This seasoning gives vegetables, pastas such as Bae'con Mac & Cheezy (page 194), and mushrooms like Shiitake Bae'con (page 88) a deep, smoky flavor. The amounts below make enough to flavor one or two recipes—if you want to make more, simply double or triple the amounts.

In a small bowl, combine the Worcestershire sauce, liquid smoke, hickory-smoked salt, paprika, and hot sauce. Stir well to combine and make sure the sugar and salt are dissolved. Use immediately or store in an airtight container in the refrigerator for up to 2 weeks.

SHIITAKE
BAE'CON

It was essential for me to capture all the amazing sweet, smoky, salty, fatty notes of good bacon for my clients (and my family), otherwise they were going to have a real hard time staying plant-based. Meaty shiitake mushrooms along with flavor bomb Smoke Signal nails all those flavors to give you exactly what you crave. If you're constantly disappointed by plant-based bacons, look no further—and you're welcome.

1 pound fresh shiitake mushrooms, stemmed

⅓ cup neutral oil, such as avocado or grapeseed

1 recipe (2 tablespoons) Smoke Signal (page 87)

2 teaspoons maple syrup or (packed) light or dark brown sugar

MAKES 2 CUPS

Preheat the oven to 375°F (if your oven has convention bake mode use it, because the fan helps crisp up the mushrooms nicely, but preheat to 350°F in that case). Line two large sheet pans with parchment paper.

Rinse the mushrooms under cool running water. Drain, pat dry with paper towels, and let air-dry completely. Once they are completely dry, cut the caps into ¼-inch-wide strips.

Put the mushroom strips in a medium bowl. In a small bowl, combine the oil, Smoke Signal, and maple syrup. (If using sugar, allow it to dissolve before mixing.) Drizzle over the mushrooms and toss well to coat. Let the mushrooms stand for 10 minutes, stirring halfway through.

Spread the mushroom strips evenly in a single layer on the prepared pans. Bake until golden brown, 25 to 30 minutes. Turn the oven off and let the mushrooms sit in the oven for an additional 20 minutes. (This allows the carryover heat to crisp up the mushrooms a bit without burning or overcooking them.)

Remove from the oven and cool completely on the sheet pans before using. Store in an airtight container in the refrigerator for up to 3 days.

GET CREATIVE!

Use this Shiitake Bae'con to add crunch and smoky flavor to anything you would have previously used pork bacon for—veggies, pasta, salads, even whipped into dips. My favorite is to use it in a hearty BLAT (bacon, lettuce, avocado, and tomato sandwich), or layer it in a grilled plant-based cheese sandwich.

SAVORY *BROWN* GRAVY

The quintessential sauce of the South, this gravy plays an important role at breakfast, ladled over biscuits (see the variation, below), and also is key at dinner smothering crispy fried chik'n. Can you imagine a holiday without a lustrous gravy on the table for pooling over a mound of creamy mashed potatoes?

⅓ cup plus 1 tablespoon plant-based butter

⅓ cup all-purpose flour or all-purpose gluten-free flour blend

½ yellow onion, diced

½ teaspoon fine pink Himalayan salt, or to taste

½ teaspoon ground black pepper, or to taste

2½ cups Chik'n Broth (page 50) or any vegetable broth, plus more if needed

1 bay leaf

1 teaspoon garlic powder

1 teaspoon poultry seasoning (optional)

2 teaspoons vegan Worcestershire sauce or liquid aminos (see page 38)

MAKES 2½ CUPS

In a medium saucepan, melt ⅓ cup of the butter over medium heat. Add the flour and whisk to make a paste (called a roux). When the butter and flour are well mixed, keep cooking and whisk occasionally to allow the mixture to get to a caramel color, 8 to 10 minutes. (You can increase the heat slightly to speed this process up, but you must stay at the stove, stirring constantly. This keeps the roux from scorching.)

When the roux is a nice brown shade, add the remaining 1 tablespoon butter and the onion, salt, and pepper and cook, whisking often, until the onion becomes slightly translucent, 3 to 4 minutes.

Slowly add the broth, whisking vigorously to prevent clumping. Add the bay leaf, garlic powder, and poultry seasoning (if using). Continue whisking vigorously until smooth. Bring to a simmer and cook, stirring frequently, until the gravy thickens, 8 to 10 minutes. Add the Worcestershire, taste, and adjust the seasoning, if necessary. If your gravy is too thick, don't panic! Just add broth or water, ¼ cup at a time, until the desired consistency is reached. Remove the bay leaf before serving.

Use immediately or cool and store in an airtight container in the refrigerator for up to 5 days.

GET CREATIVE!

Add fresh chopped herbs, such as rosemary, thyme, flat-leaf parsley, and/or oregano, to give your gravy a fresh top note. I'll also sometimes add sautéed or caramelized mushrooms for a mushroom gravy that is delicious over pasta or a plant-based burger.

CREAMY BREAKFAST GRAVY

Substitute 2½ cups any unsweetened, unflavored plant-based milk (except coconut milk) for the broth. Stir 2 cups (4 or 5 patties) cooked and crumbled Spicy Maple Breakfast Sausage (page 96), or any store-bought sausage, into the finished gravy. Serve over biscuits, breakfast potatoes, or creamy grits.

CHICKPEA OMELETS, PAGE 106

KICKOFF BREAKFASTS & BRUNCHES

BUTTA *BISCUITS*

My mother made fantastic, tall buttermilk biscuits with flaky layers and airy pockets. Just like Mom knows, the keys to making perfect biscuits are ice-cold butter and milk and not overworking the dough. That cold butter creates steam in a hot oven that bakes into flaky layers made to capture jam, gravy (see page 91), and good ole maple syrup. Yaasss! Use the dough to make the dumplings in Veggies & Dumplings (page 189).

2 cups self-rising flour (see below), plus extra for shaping

2 teaspoons baking powder

1 teaspoon organic sugar

¼ teaspoon fine pink Himalayan salt

8 ounces cold plant-based butter, cut into pieces, plus 1 tablespoon, melted

½ cup unsweetened, unflavored plant-based milk

MAKES 8 BISCUITS

GET CREATIVE!
Add herbs (fresh or dried), diced Shiitake Bae'con (page 88), and/or plant-based cheese shreds to the biscuit dough. For shortcakes (page 261) or scones, add a teaspoon of lemon or orange zest.

DIY SELF-RISING FLOUR
Don't have self-rising flour? Make your own: In a medium bowl, combine 2 cups all-purpose flour, 1 tablespoon baking powder, and ¼ teaspoon fine pink Himalayan salt. Whisk until well-combined. Makes 2 cups (enough for one batch of biscuits).

Preheat the oven to 425°F. Line a large sheet pan with parchment paper.

In a large bowl, whisk together the flour, baking powder, sugar, and salt. Add the butter to the flour mixture and use a pastry blender or clean hands (working fast and carefully, making sure the heat of your hands doesn't melt the butter) to cut the butter into the flour until mixture is the size of small peas. Do not overwork the butter, and make sure it remains cold—refrigerate the flour mixture for a few minutes if the butter is getting too warm.

Slowly add the milk, working the mixture with a pastry blender or a fork to combine. When the dough comes together into a semi-smooth ball (don't overwork the dough—you want it pliable and not to form much gluten), shape into a flattened disk. Cover the bowl and chill in the refrigerator for 10 to 15 minutes.

Lightly dust your work surface with flour. Roll the dough out to a 1½-inch thickness. Using a round 2½-inch biscuit cutter or an upside-down glass, cut out biscuits, dipping the cutter or glass in flour as necessary to prevent sticking. Place the cut biscuits on the prepared pan, leaving 1 inch between each to allow enough room for expansion. Reroll the scraps and repeat until all dough is used.

Brush the tops of the biscuits with the melted butter. Bake for 15 to 20 minutes, or until fluffy and golden. Serve immediately, or cool and store in an airtight container at room temperature for up to 2 days.

SPICY MAPLE *BREAKFAST* SAUSAGE

I had a tasty vegan breakfast sausage at a restaurant in Miami called Uninhibited Honey, owned by Carlos Dunlap, an NFL colleague of Derrick's. The sausage was meaty, spicy yet sweet, and though it was vegan, it did not taste vegan (you know what I mean). There are many good brands of plant-based sausages in the grocery store, but there's something special about whipping up a big batch of my own. Plus, mine are nut-, soy-, and gluten-free. Crumble cooked sausage into a breakfast gravy (see page 91), or serve on a toasted vegan English muffin or Butta Biscuit (page 94). Add a slice of plant-based cheese for a healthier version of that fast-food sausage-egg-and-cheese favorite. The additional 2 tablespoons of oil adds fat to replicate a traditional sausage, but you can skip it if you prefer a leaner sausage.

1 to 3 tablespoons neutral oil, such as avocado or grapeseed

1 small red or yellow onion, finely diced

2 garlic cloves, minced

2 cups textured pea protein (TPP) or textured vegetable protein (TVP) (see page 37)

1 cup quick or rolled oats

½ cup flax meal

2 tablespoons tapioca starch

1½ cups Chik'n Broth (page 50) or any vegetable broth

1 tablespoon molasses

1 tablespoon pure maple syrup

1 tablespoon liquid aminos (see page 38)

2 teaspoons fennel seeds

1½ teaspoons Vegemite or Marmite (see page 38)

1 teaspoon poultry seasoning

1 teaspoon smoked paprika

1 teaspoon fine pink Himalayan salt, or to taste

½ teaspoon ground black pepper

½ teaspoon crushed red pepper flakes

Nonstick cooking spray

MAKES 12 TO 15 PATTIES

Heat a medium skillet over medium-high heat. Add 1 tablespoon of the oil. When the oil shimmers and is hot, add the onion and sauté until translucent, 5 to 7 minutes. Add the garlic and sauté for 30 seconds, or just until fragrant. Remove from the heat and set aside.

In a medium bowl, combine the textured pea protein, oats, flax meal, and tapioca starch. Add the reserved onion mixture. Mix well and set aside.

In a large pot, combine the broth, molasses, maple syrup, liquid aminos, fennel seeds, Vegemite, poultry seasoning, smoked paprika, salt, black pepper, and red pepper flakes. Heat over medium until steaming. Pour the warm broth over the TPP mixture. Add the remaining 2 tablespoons of oil (if using) and mix well. Cover and let stand for 10 to 15 minutes to allow the liquid to be absorbed.

Form the mixture into twelve to fifteen patties, about 3 inches in diameter and ¼ inch thick.

NOTE:
An optional final sear will result in a crispier sausage. Heat a griddle or large pan over medium-high heat. When hot, add some oil to the pan and sear the baked patties in batches for 2 to 3 minutes on each side, or until browned and crisp, adding more oil as needed for additional patties.

Preheat the oven to 375°F. Line a sheet pan with parchment paper and lightly coat with nonstick cooking spray.

Arrange as many patties as you plan to serve on the prepared sheet pan. (Freeze any extra patties in an airtight container between layers of parchment paper to prevent them from sticking. Thaw at room temperature before cooking.) Spray the patties with nonstick cooking spray and bake for 30 minutes, flipping the patties halfway through the baking time.

SPINACH *& ROASTED* TOFU BENNY

FOR THE HOLLANDAZE SAUCE

7 ounces firm or extra-firm tofu

1 cup raw cashews, soaked and drained (see page 35)

2 tablespoons nutritional yeast

1 tablespoon fresh lemon juice

2 teaspoons kala namak (fine black salt) or fine pink Himalayan salt, or to taste

¼ teaspoon crushed red pepper flakes or pinch ground cayenne pepper

¼ teaspoon ground turmeric

¼ teaspoon dry mustard

1 teaspoon Tabasco sauce (optional)

¾ cup water, plus more if needed

SERVES 4

FOR THE ROASTED TOFU

1 cup liquid aminos (see page 38), soy sauce, or tamari (if you're gluten-free)

¼ cup water

1 recipe (2 tablespoons) Smoke Signal (page 87)

1 (16-ounce) extra-firm tofu, pressed (see page 101)

Nonstick cooking spray

FOR ASSEMBLING

1 tablespoon neutral oil, such as avocado or grapeseed

1 pound spinach, washed, stemmed, and spun dry in a salad spinner

Fine pink Himalayan salt and ground black pepper

4 vegan English muffins, split and toasted

Sweet or smoked paprika, for garnish

Back when I was eating eggs, if I was out for brunch and eggs Benedict was on the menu, I had to order it—it was my go-to! Now I'm serving up this version at home to get that creamy taste and toasty texture. The tofu doubles as the egg *and* a thick piece of Canadian bacon, thanks to a smoky, well-seasoned marinade and high-heat roasting to get those crispy edges. I pop it onto a toasted English muffin and top with sautéed spinach for freshness and color. The silkiest Hollandaze Sauce—made with a sulfuric black salt called kala namak (see page 36) for an egg-like flavor—brings it all together. No one will know it's vegan unless you tell them.

MAKE THE HOLLANDAZE SAUCE: Wrap the tofu block in a double layer of paper towels and press firmly a few times (it's okay if the block breaks—you're blending it) to release most of its water.

In a high-speed blender, combine the soaked cashews, tofu, nutritional yeast, lemon juice, salt, red pepper flakes, turmeric, dry mustard, Tabasco (if using), and water. Blend on high until very creamy and pourable, adding up to ¼ cup more water to achieve a pourable consistency, if necessary. Use immediately or store in an airtight container in the refrigerator for up to 1 week.

MAKE THE ROASTED TOFU: In a medium bowl, combine the liquid aminos, water, and the Smoke Signal. Make sure the sugar and salt in the Smoke Signal are dissolved.

recipe continues >>

Cut the tofu into eight even pieces. Put it in a shallow dish and pour the liquid amino mixture over it. Cover and marinate for at least 1 hour at room temperature, or up to overnight in the refrigerator, turning halfway through the marinating time.

Preheat the oven to 450°F. Grease a sheet pan with nonstick cooking spray.

Remove the tofu from the marinade and gently press out the excess marinade, reserving it in a dish. Put the tofu on the prepared sheet pan and roast until brown with crispy edges, about 15 minutes. Turn the tofu over, spoon a little of the reserved marinade on each piece, and continue baking until the second side is browned and crispy, 10 to 15 minutes more. Spoon a little more marinade on top and bake for a final 5 minutes, until the tofu edges are even more crispy. Remove the tofu from the oven. Discard any remaining marinade or save for another use.

In a very large skillet, heat the oil over medium-high heat. Once the oil is hot and shimmering, add the spinach and, using tongs, very quickly sear the leaves in the oil until wilted. Immediately remove from the heat. (This should take only 1 minute—if the spinach is left over the heat for too long, it will overcook into a watery mush.) Season to taste with salt and black pepper.

To assemble, place one piece of tofu on each English muffin half. Top with spinach, then drizzle generously with Hollandaze Sauce. Garnish with a sprinkle of paprika and serve immediately.

GET CREATIVE!

Top with thick slices of roasted tomato, grilled portobello mushroom, or sliced avocado in place of the spinach, or with it. Want to get fancy like my all-time-favorite brunch? Use Creole Krab Cakes (page 201) in place of the tofu. Add fresh chiles, citrus zest, and/or fresh herbs, such as tarragon, thyme, basil, flat-leaf parsley, or rosemary, to give the Hollandaze a little more dimension.

PRESSING TOFU

If I'm using tofu to make a scramble (page 108) or crumbling it into salads, I don't bother pressing it. A quick paper towel wrap, press, and release will always do. I really only press tofu when I'm marinating it so it can soak up as much flavor as possible, or if it was frozen to release much of its stored water. That said, I do marinate tofu a *lot*, and if you plan to as well, a tofu press is nice to have.

If you don't have a press, wrap the tofu in two layers of paper towels and place on a sheet pan. Set another sheet pan on top, then top with a cast-iron skillet or other heavy pan for more weight. Press for 30 minutes to release as much water from the tofu as possible before cooking.

PAPAS &
WALNUT CHORIZO
BREAKFAST TACOS

3 tablespoons neutral oil, such as avocado or grapeseed

3 potatoes (russet or Yukon gold), diced but left unpeeled

1 sweet potato, peeled and diced

½ yellow or Spanish onion, diced

1 small green or red bell pepper, stemmed, seeded, and diced

2 teaspoons Taco Seasoning (page 86) or any Mexican seasoning blend

1 teaspoon fine pink Himalayan salt, or to taste

Ground black pepper

1 cup Walnut Chorizo (page 105) or any store-bought Soyrizo, at room temperature

12 (6-inch) yellow or white corn tortillas, warmed

Optional toppings: Chopped fresh cilantro, Brazil Nut Sour Cream (page 57), plant-based cheese shreds, and/or guacamole or sliced avocado

MAKES 12 TACOS

Between visitors in town for football games and family visiting from California, Georgia, or Pennsylvania, our weekends are always filled with tons of guests. I often use these tacos to feed a crowd. Serve them with an array of fresh toppings on platters to create a fun self-serve brunch. They're a great way to introduce a flavorful yet filling plant-based meal to sceptics: "I hate tacos," says no one! Load up on spicy Walnut Chorizo or store-bought Soyrizo, warm up some fresh tortillas, and whatever you do, don't skip the sweet potato—it adds a nice balance without taking over.

Heat a large cast-iron skillet over medium-high heat. Add 1 tablespoon of the oil. When the oil is hot and shimmering, add the potatoes. Shake the pan or stir to distribute the potatoes in an even layer, then cover and cook, undisturbed, for 3 minutes. Uncover, stir, then cover and cook for another 3 to 4 minutes, or until most of the potatoes are browned. Add another 1 tablespoon of oil and stir in the sweet potato. Cover and cook for 5 minutes.

Add the remaining 1 tablespoon of oil to the pan, then stir in the onion and bell pepper. Cook for 2 to 3 minutes, uncovered, stirring only occasionally, to allow the potatoes and vegetables to get crispy-brown edges. Season with the Taco Seasoning, salt, and pepper. Turn off the heat and crumble the Walnut Chorizo into the pan. Stir to combine and heat through.

Spoon the hash into warm tortillas, garnish with the desired toppings, and serve.

GET CREATIVE!

For added flavor and protein, add Tofu Scramble (page 108), Scrambled Chickpea Eggz (page 106), or 1 cup cooked black beans to your taco spread for super-filling breakfast tacos. The filling works great for wraps, burritos, enchiladas, and quesadillas.

WALNUT *CHORIZO*

2 dried guajillo chiles

2 cups sun-dried tomatoes not packed in oil (see Tip)

2 teaspoons ancho chile powder or chili powder

2 teaspoons fine pink Himalayan salt, or to taste

1½ teaspoons ground cumin

1 teaspoon sweet paprika

1 teaspoon dried oregano

¼ teaspoon ground black pepper

⅛ teaspoon ground cinnamon

⅛ teaspoon ground cloves (omit if using chili powder)

½ white onion, coarsely chopped

2 garlic cloves, crushed

2 cups walnut halves, lightly toasted (see page 47)

1 tablespoon apple cider vinegar

MAKES 4 CUPS

With the pronounced flavor of garlic, fruity dried guajillo chiles, and six different spices, this recipe delivers the same robust flavor and smoky edge as the classic Mexican sausage, plus on-point meaty texture due to walnuts and, surprisingly, sun-dried tomatoes. Walnuts have more ALA (plant-based omega-3 fatty acid) than any other tree nuts and are an excellent source of magnesium and protein, plus they add fat, which helps carry the flavors of all those delicious spices. It's a flavorful, vegan, and *raw* (yes, you can get all this flavor without using a pan!) addition to any meal: try it on breakfast tacos (page 103) or nachos (page 167).

Combine the guajillo chiles and sun-dried tomatoes in a medium heatproof bowl. Pour enough boiling water over to cover the peppers and tomatoes and soak for 15 minutes to rehydrate. Drain well. Remove the stem and seeds from the peppers and discard. Set aside.

In a small bowl, combine the ancho chile powder, salt, cumin, paprika, oregano, black pepper, cinnamon, and cloves (if using); set aside.

In a food processor, combine the soaked peppers and sun-dried tomatoes, onion, and garlic; pulse until coarsely chopped. Add the spice mixture, walnuts, and vinegar. Pulse until well combined, scraping the bowl as needed. Use immediately or store in an airtight container in the refrigerator up to 3 days. Walnut Chorizo can be used cold or warm.

TIP:
I like using sun-dried tomatoes that have not been packed in oil in this recipe, because the oil-packed variety make the chorizo too greasy. If all you have are oil-packed sun-dried tomatoes, rinse them first with hot water, then drain on paper towels for at least 10 minutes before adding them to the food processor.

EGGZ

Chickpea Omelets

FOR THE EGGZ

1 cup chickpea flour

1 cup unsweetened, unflavored plant-based milk

1 tablespoon nutritional yeast

1 teaspoon kala namak salt (black salt) or fine pink Himalayan salt, or to taste

½ teaspoon onion powder

½ teaspoon garlic powder

½ teaspoon ground black pepper

¼ teaspoon ground turmeric

¼ cup water

Nonstick cooking spray

MAKES 4 OMELETS

FOR THE FILLING

(about 1 cup total per omelet)

COOKED ITEMS: **Sautéed mushrooms, diced and roasted potatoes, sautéed seitan or tofu, cooked Spicy Maple Breakfast Sausage (page 96), crumbled Shiitake Bae'con (page 88), Walnut Chorizo (page 105), or other plant-based meats**

FRESH ITEMS: **Plant-based cheese, diced fresh tomato or sun-dried tomato, chopped spinach, chopped kale, diced bell peppers, minced onion, sliced scallion (green and white parts)**

Protein- and fiber-rich chickpeas magically transform into a batter with a velvety texture and mild flavor that reminds me of eggs when combined with spices and nondairy milk. I add kala namak (see page 36), a sulfuric salt that gives the batter its "eggy-ness" and makes it an eggz-cellent substitute. Many online sources carry it, if you want to try it out in your cooking. If a mineral flavor isn't your thing, replace the kala namak with pink Himalayan salt.

MAKE THE EGGZ: **In a medium bowl, whisk together the chickpea flour, milk, nutritional yeast, salt, onion powder, garlic powder, pepper, turmeric, and water. Mix until smooth.**

Heat an 8-inch nonstick pan with flared sides over medium-high heat. Spray with nonstick cooking spray. Add enough of the chickpea mixture (about ⅓ cup) to the pan to cover the bottom completely and make a layer of batter about ¼ inch thick.

Reduce the heat to low. Cover the pan and cook until the batter is firm, about 2 minutes. Remove the lid and place about 1 cup of the desired filling—cooked and/or fresh—on one side of the omelet. Use a rubber spatula to fold the empty side over the filling, then remove the pan from the heat. Serve immediately or, if cheese is one of your fillings, cover the pan and let stand for 1 to 2 minutes, or until the cheese is melted.

Slide the omelet onto a plate and serve right away, or place it on a plate and loosely cover with foil to keep warm. Repeat with remaining batter and fillings, or store extra batter in an airtight container in the refrigerator for up to 5 days.

SCRAMBLED CHICKPEA EGGZ

For a scramble, cover the pan with a lid after pouring in the batter and allow the batter to firm up for about 2 minutes. Uncover and stir and scramble as you would regular eggs. Cover the pan again and let cook for 1 minute. Remove lid, stir, and scramble again. Remove the pan from the heat, cover, and let stand for 2 minutes to allow the eggz to set before serving. Any fillings can be added at the end.

GET CREATIVE!

For a sweet crepe, omit the turmeric, onion powder, garlic powder, black pepper, and salt. Add a pinch of cinnamon and a splash of vanilla. Proceed with the recipe, pouring only enough batter to create a very thin, even layer in the pan. Cover and cook on low heat until firm, 3 to 5 minutes. Fill with berries, fresh fruit, Vanilla Coco Whip (page 244), and/or chocolate sauce.

Tofu Scramble

1 (14-ounce) package extra-firm tofu, drained

1 tablespoon neutral oil, such as avocado or grapeseed

½ yellow onion, or 1 large shallot, finely chopped

2 tablespoons nutritional yeast

1 teaspoon kala namak (see page 36) or fine pink Himalayan salt, or to taste

1 teaspoon garlic powder

½ teaspoon chili powder

½ teaspoon ground cumin

¼ teaspoon ground turmeric

Ground black pepper

2 cups cooked thinly sliced mushrooms, baby spinach, diced bell peppers, diced tomatoes, and/or plant-based sausages

2 tablespoons snipped fresh herbs (optional)

Plant-based cheese shreds (optional)

SERVES 4

The two things I tell people to try cooking at home when they first embark on plant-based eating are Pro-Bowls (page 152) and scrambled tofu. A tofu scramble is a quick and easy way to start the day with high energy, plus it has all the protein of eggs but is lower in fat and cholesterol-free. No need to overly press the tofu: the water helps prevent it from drying out during cooking and gives the scramble a nice, light, and moist texture. I leave the seasonings pretty basic so you can be creative with flavors mix-ins. It's simple enough to add to all your breakfast faves like burritos, bowls, and sandwiches.

Wrap the tofu block in a double layer of paper towels and press firmly a few times (it's okay if the block breaks—we're scrambling it) to release most of its water.

Heat a large skillet over medium-high heat. Add the oil. Once the oil is hot and shimmering, add the onion and sauté until slightly translucent, 3 to 4 minutes. Crumble the tofu into the pan—large chunks can be broken up with a spatula. Add the nutritional yeast, kala namak, garlic powder, chili powder, cumin, turmeric, and black pepper to taste, mixing well to incorporate the spices into the tofu. Heat for 2 to 3 minutes to warm through. Stir in the vegetables and herbs (if using).

If you are using cheese, turn off the heat, add the cheese, and cover. Let stand for 2 minutes. (The residual heat will melt the cheese without drying out the tofu.) Serve immediately.

GET CREATIVE!

I love to use a batch of this scramble when making fried rice to replace the usual eggs. Alternatively, you can cool the scramble completely, then add plant-based mayonnaise, a tiny bit of prepared mustard, minced celery, chives, and a dash of Tabasco sauce for a delicious eggz salad that is perfect scooped over slices of toasted bread (or however you like your eggz salad sandwich).

CHEEZY GRITS BOWLS

with Kale, Chickpea Scramble & Grilled Avocado

2 ripe-but-firm avocados, halved, pitted, and peeled

Nonstick cooking spray

1 tablespoon neutral oil, such as avocado or grapeseed

2 garlic cloves, minced

8 cups chopped kale leaves (any variety; discard stems)

1 tablespoon liquid aminos (see page 38)

1 recipe Cheezy Sweet Potato Grits (page 227), warmed

2 cups Shiitake Bae'con (page 88), or 8 strips of any cooked plant-based bacon

1 recipe Scrambled Chickpea Eggz (page 106), warmed

1 cup cherry tomatoes, halved

SERVES 4

GET CREATIVE!

I love a flexible (and hearty) recipe: add your favorite plant-based sausages, roasted potatoes, and/or vegetables.

I love, love, *love* grits—especially cheesy grits (which mine are thanks to plenty of nutritional yeast and Cream Cheeze). I developed this hearty, creamy, savory meal-in-a-bowl when I started offering breakfast options for my athletes. How could I give them a filling breakfast that was loaded with nutrition and would hold up long enough for transporting? These grits with seasoned, juicy greens were the answer. Packed full of protein, fiber, and nutrient-dense kale, sweet potato, and avocado, it's the perfect way to fuel your body for a strenuous day ahead (whether your day consists of NFL-level training or running after a toddler).

Heat a grill pan or griddle over high heat. Lightly spray the avocado halves with nonstick cooking spray. Place on the grill and cook for 2 minutes, to get char marks. Remove and set aside.

Heat a large pot or Dutch oven over high heat. Add the oil. Once the oil is hot and shimmering, add the garlic and sauté just until fragrant, about 30 seconds. Add the kale, stir once, then cook undisturbed for 1 to 2 minutes to allow the kale to crisp around the edges. Stir and repeat. Do this a couple times until the kale wilts and some pieces are tender. (Keep the heat on high so any liquid the kale releases quickly evaporates—you want it to get crisp on the edges, not steam.) Add the aminos and mix well.

Divide the Cheezy Sweet Potato Grits among four bowls. Top with the kale, Shiitake Bae'con, and Chickpea Eggz. Garnish with a grilled avocado half and cherry tomatoes.

CHILAQUILES
with Tofu Scramble

15 (6-inch) yellow corn tortillas, or 1 (14-ounce) bag unsalted totopos (tortilla chips)

1½ cups Rojo Sauce (page 61), plus more as needed

1 cup water

1 recipe Tofu Scramble (page 108)

Optional toppings: Diced white onion, chopped fresh cilantro, sliced avocado, plant-based crumbled cheese or cheese shreds, and/or cooked pinto or black beans

SERVES 6

A traditional Mexican dish that's usually served at breakfast, chilaquiles are made with *totopos* (fried corn tortilla chips) cooked in a red (*rojo*) or green (*verde*) sauce and then topped with fried eggs, onions, crumbled Cotija cheese, and sometimes black beans. To make a plant-based version, I use my versatile smoky, chile-based Rojo Sauce, fresh-baked tortillas, and eggy Tofu Scramble. I prefer baking the tortillas in the oven for a lighter, healthier brunch or breakfast-for-dinner meal, but you can swap in store-bought unsalted tortilla chips for a quicker version.

IF USING TORTILLAS: Preheat the oven to 400°F. Cut the tortillas into triangles or 1-inch squares. Arrange them in a single layer on one or two large sheet pans and bake until crisp, 8 to 10 minutes, turning and shaking the pan(s) halfway through. Remove the pan(s) from the oven and allow the chips to cool completely.

In a large cast-iron skillet or Dutch oven, combine the Rojo Sauce with the water. Bring to a simmer over medium-high heat and cook until thickened, 6 to 8 minutes. Add the baked tortilla chips or totopos and use a rubber spatula to gently stir, making sure all of the chips are coated in sauce. (You can add more Rojo Sauce at this point if you want a saucier final dish.) Heat for 1 to 2 minutes, stirring occasionally to fold the chips into the sauce. Remove from the heat.

Quickly transfer the tortilla mixture to a large serving bowl. Top with the Tofu Scramble and whatever toppings you like. Serve immediately.

JALAPEÑO-*BAE'CON* CORN CAKES

with Chili-Lime Maple Syrup

FOR THE CHILI-LIME MAPLE SYRUP

1 cup pure maple syrup

½ teaspoon ground cumin

½ to 1 teaspoon chili powder (depending on how much spice you like)

Juice of ½ lime

MAKES 18 TO 20 (4-INCH) PANCAKES

GET CREATIVE!

Turn these into an appetizer by topping with a little Brazil Nut Sour Cream (page 57), sautéed fresh corn kernels, fresh diced tomatoes, chopped cilantro leaves, and bae'con pieces.

FOR THE CORN CAKES

1¼ cups medium- to fine-grind yellow cornmeal

1 cup brown rice flour

1 tablespoon organic sugar

2 teaspoons baking soda

1 teaspoon fine pink Himalayan salt

2 cups unsweetened, unflavored plant-based milk

2 flax eggs (see page 36)

2 tablespoons neutral oil, such as avocado or grapeseed

½ cup diced Shiitake Bae'con (page 88) or any cooked plant-based bacon

1 to 2 jalapeños (depending on how much heat you like), stemmed, seeded, and minced

¼ cup thinly sliced scallions (green parts only)

Nonstick cooking spray

OPTIONAL TOPPINGS

Diced tomato, diced avocado, sliced fresh jalapeño, fresh cilantro, and/or Brazil Nut Sour Cream (page 57)

Tell your gluten-free friends you got them covered, because these hearty pancakes happen to be just that—gluten-free! They have an abundance of mouthwatering flavor from smoky Shiitake Bae'con, fresh jalapeños, and cornmeal. Rice flour brings it all together and cooks up nice and golden. I love them drizzled with chili- and lime-spiked maple syrup for breakfast or brunch. Can you say bliss point!

MAKE THE CHILI-LIME SYRUP: In a small saucepan, combine the maple syrup, cumin, chili powder, and lime juice. Heat over low, stirring occasionally, until warmed through. Keep warm.

MAKE THE CORN CAKES: In a large bowl, combine the cornmeal, brown rice flour, sugar, baking soda, and salt. Whisk until well combined. Add the milk, flax eggs, and oil. Whisk again until the mixture is smooth. Stir in the Shiitake Bae'con, jalapeños, and scallions.

Heat a griddle or large pan over medium-high heat. Spray with nonstick cooking spray. Spoon about 2 heaping tablespoons of batter per pancake onto the hot griddle and cook until golden brown, 1 to 2 minutes per side. Repeat with the remaining batter, wiping off the griddle with a paper towel periodically and coating with nonstick spray as needed. Serve warm with warm Chili-Lime Maple Syrup and any additional toppings you like.

EGGLESS FRENCH TOAST

The secret to golden brown, slightly crispy French toast with a spongy interior—without relying on egg or dairy—is a smooth and creamy custard made with an extra-rich milk like oat or full-fat coconut, chickpea flour, banana, and a flax egg. Use a standard sliced loaf (fresh or stale), or elevate the plate with a thick-sliced baguette, sourdough, or raisin bread—though make sure to read the label because many store-bought breads contain eggs and dairy. Serve with warm maple syrup (the real stuff please), or go all out and top with dollops of plant-based whipped cream and fresh berries for an extra special treat.

1¼ cups unsweetened, unflavored plant-based milk

½ cup chickpea flour

1 ripe banana, peeled

1 tablespoon pure maple syrup

2 teaspoons vanilla powder or vanilla extract

2 teaspoons ground cinnamon

¼ teaspoon freshly grated nutmeg

1 flax egg (see page 36)

Neutral oil, such as avocado or grapeseed, for greasing the griddle

8 slices bread

Optional toppings: Fresh fruit, pure maple syrup, and/or Vanilla Coco Whip (page 244)

SERVES 4

In a small bowl, whisk together the milk and chickpea flour until combined.

In a large shallow bowl, smash the banana with a fork until it turns into a thick mash. Add the milk mixture, then stir in the maple syrup, vanilla, cinnamon, nutmeg, and flax egg, and whisk until well combined. Let stand for 2 to 3 minutes to allow the custard to thicken.

Preheat the oven to 200°F or the warming setting. Heat a griddle or large skillet over medium-high heat. Grease the griddle with oil. When hot, dip a slice of bread into the batter and allow it to soak for 20 to 30 seconds, turning to coat both sides. Let excess batter drip off into the bowl. Griddle until lightly browned on both sides, 4 to 5 minutes total. Transfer to the oven to keep warm. Repeat with the remaining bread slices and batter.

Serve warm with the toppings (if using).

FLUFFY *VANILLA* PANCAKES

(or Waffles)

1¼ cups self-rising flour (to make your own, see page 94)

2 tablespoons vanilla powder or vanilla protein powder

2 teaspoons organic sugar

½ teaspoon baking soda

½ teaspoon baking powder

¼ teaspoon fine pink Himalayan salt

1 to 1¼ cups unsweetened, unflavored plant-based milk

1 tablespoon apple cider vinegar

1 tablespoon neutral oil, such as avocado or grapeseed, plus more for the griddle

Pure maple syrup, for serving

MAKES ABOUT 8 PANCAKES

Airy egg-free pancakes and waffles are possible—all you need to do is add extra leavening to self-rising flour and a splash of vinegar . . . yes, vinegar! When vinegar is combined with baking soda, it creates a chemical reaction that makes the mixture fizz and produces baked goods that are light and fluffy. (This is similar to the reaction that happens when acidic buttermilk and baking soda are combined—and exactly what happens in those third-grade science experiments.) Then I steam the pancakes with a few drops of water in the pan for that last little bit of lift. I prefer to use vanilla powder to extract for a more concentrated vanilla flavor, and if it so happens to be vanilla protein powder, it's just a little added flex to your pancakes.

In a large bowl, sift together the flour, vanilla powder, sugar, baking soda, baking powder, and salt. Gently whisk to blend.

In a medium bowl, whisk together 1 cup of the milk, the vinegar, and oil. Make a well in the center of the dry ingredients. Add the wet ingredients all at once, whisking to blend. This batter is thicker than your traditional pancake batter to make the pancakes extra fluffy—if you want thinner pancakes, add the remaining ¼ cup milk.

Preheat the oven to 200°F or the warming setting. Heat a griddle or large skillet over medium heat and grease with oil. When the griddle is hot, use a ladle to add about ¼ cup of batter onto the griddle for each pancake (do not overcrowd; the pancakes need room to expand and rise). Splash about ½ teaspoon water around the pancakes, then cover with a lid large enough to cover all (or most) of the griddle. Cook the pancakes for about 1½ minutes per side, or until golden brown. Transfer to a plate or sheet pan and keep warm in the oven. Repeat with the remaining batter.

Serve warm with maple syrup.

NOTE:

For waffles, heat a waffle iron, lightly spray with nonstick cooking spray, and add the batter per your manufacturer's recommendations. Close the lid and cook until golden brown. Repeat until all the batter is used.

GET CREATIVE!

My kids love to add colored sprinkles to the batter for a funfetti vibe, but fresh blueberries, diced bananas, toasted nuts, peanut butter, and even bittersweet vegan chocolate chips are great additions, too. For chocolate pancakes, add 1 tablespoon of unsweetened cacao powder to the batter.

OVERNIGHT OATS TRIO

These no-cook overnight oats saved me from having to wake up at 4:00 a.m. each morning to make Derrick breakfast before he had to run off to practice. Instead of standing over a pot and cooking oatmeal for 30 minutes before dawn (for real), I mixed the raw oats with nondairy milk before going to bed. While I slept, the oats soaked in the fridge overnight until the liquid was absorbed and the oats were soft enough to eat. These three versions—green matcha, cacao and nut butter, and tropical fruit—are Derrick's favorites, but the sky's the limit when it comes to flavor combinations. Overnight oats can be served cold or warm and can be made up to 5 days in advance, so double, triple, or quadruple the recipe as needed.

SERVES 1

Cinnamon-Matcha Oatmeal

1 cup unsweetened, unflavored plant-based milk

1 tablespoon pure maple syrup or agave

2 teaspoons matcha powder

1 teaspoon vanilla powder or vanilla extract

½ to 1 teaspoon ground cinnamon

1 cup rolled oats

OPTIONAL TOPPINGS

Chopped nuts, hemp seeds, fresh berries, and/or sliced bananas

Cacao–Nut Butter Oatmeal

1 cup unsweetened, unflavored plant-based milk

1 tablespoon pure maple syrup or agave

2 teaspoons unsweetened cacao powder

2 tablespoons smooth or chunky peanut butter or almond butter

1 teaspoon vanilla powder or vanilla extract

1 cup rolled oats

OPTIONAL TOPPINGS

Chopped nuts, hemp seeds, fresh berries, banana slices, and/or cacao nibs

Tropical (Mango-Pineapple-Coconut) Oatmeal

1¼ cups cold full-fat or light coconut milk

1 tablespoon coconut sugar, or your favorite sweetener

1 teaspoon vanilla powder or vanilla extract

1 teaspoon orange zest (optional)

2 tablespoons diced fresh or frozen pineapple

2 tablespoons diced fresh or frozen mango

2 tablespoons toasted coconut flakes

1 cup rolled oats

OPTIONAL TOPPINGS

Chopped nuts, hemp seeds, diced pineapple, diced mango, and/or toasted coconut flakes

Pour the milk into a 1-pint glass or ceramic jar with a lid. Add the sweetener, flavorings, and any other additional ingredients, such as fruit. Place the lid on tightly and shake vigorously. Add the oats and shake again. Top with the desired toppings. Cover the jar tightly with the lid and refrigerate for at least 8 hours, or up to 5 days.

CHILI CON CHILI, PAGE 136

SOUP'OR BOWL

IMMUNE-
BOOSTING
SOUP

One of the most common culprits for a weakened immune system is poor nutrition. During the cold and flu season, you can find me sending quarts of this wholesome, gluten-free, oil-free, and nut-free soup to players whether they're feeling under the weather or just in need of an immunity boost. (I remember a time I sent a double portion to a player so he could eat it for a few days. Well, let's just say he didn't get that second container thanks to his lovely wife, who downed it all before he got a chance!) Make a double batch and freeze it in 32-ounce deli containers so you always have it when you're feeling a bit off your game.

1 cup peeled and diced butternut squash or pumpkin

1 red onion, diced

2 celery stalks, diced

2 carrots, diced

¼ cup water (optional)

2-inch piece ginger, peeled and minced

5 garlic cloves, minced

2 teaspoons fine pink Himalayan salt, or to taste

1 teaspoon crushed red pepper flakes

1 teaspoon ground turmeric

½ teaspoon ground black pepper

8 cups Chik'n Broth (page 50) or any vegetable broth

1 cup short- or long-grain brown rice

½ cup fresh lemon juice (about 3 lemons, reserve 1 juiced half)

6 cups chopped kale leaves (any variety, stems discarded; about 1 bunch) or spinach

SERVES 4 TO 6

Heat a large pot or Dutch oven over medium-high heat (do not add oil). When hot, add the squash, onion, celery, and carrots, and cook, stirring frequently, until the edges of the vegetables start to brown, 8 to 10 minutes. (If the vegetables start to stick to the pot, add ¼ cup of water and allow it to evaporate).

Add the ginger, garlic, salt, red pepper flakes, turmeric, and black pepper. Sauté for 30 seconds, or just until fragrant. Pour in the broth and bring to a simmer.

Add the rice and the reserved juiced lemon half and stir. Cover and cook on low until the rice is tender, about 30 minutes. Stir in the kale by the handfuls, allowing it to wilt before adding the next handful. Once all the kale is wilted, stir, cover, and continue to cook for an additional 10 to 15 minutes, or until the kale is tender.

Remove the lemon half and stir in the fresh lemon juice. Serve immediately or cool and store, covered, in the refrigerator for up to 5 days.

GET CREATIVE!

This is a foundation recipe, so feel free to add or subtract ingredients. I often throw in zucchini, broccoli, sweet potato, and any other vegetables I happen to have. You can also leave out the vegetables entirely for a broth to sip. The only nonnegotiables are the immune-boosting basics: the garlic, ginger, lemon, red pepper flakes, pink Himalayan salt, turmeric, and red onion—these are important to the nutritional aspects of the soup, as well as for the flavor.

SOPA AZTECA

(Vegetable Tortilla Soup)

There are almost as many versions of this rich, zesty, and slightly spicy soup as there are people in Mexico—some versions are thick like gravy and some are thin and brothy. My version is chunky with veggies and black beans and has a deeply flavored broth made from roasted and dried chiles thickened with tortillas that get cooked *into* the soup. Garnished with fried tortilla strips, avocado, fresh cilantro, and Brazil Nut Sour Cream, each bite is packed with flavor.

1 cup plus 2 tablespoons neutral oil, such as avocado or grapeseed

6 (6-inch) corn tortillas, halved and cut into short, ¼-inch strips

Fine pink Himalayan salt

2 dried ancho chiles

1 (15-ounce) can diced tomatoes

1 yellow onion, chopped

1 large carrot, diced

2 celery stalks, chopped

1 poblano chile, roasted, seeded, peeled (see page 43), and diced

3 garlic cloves, minced

1 teaspoon ground cumin

1 teaspoon dried oregano

½ teaspoon chili powder

5 cups Chik'n Broth (page 50) or any vegetable broth

1 cup cooked black beans (rinsed and drained, if canned)

1 teaspoon ground black pepper

Optional garnishes: Thinly sliced epazote or chopped fresh cilantro, diced avocado, plant-based cheese shreds, Brazil Nut Sour Cream (page 57), and/or lime wedges

SERVES 4 TO 6

GET CREATIVE!

To bulk up the soup even more, add roasted corn, chickpeas, diced and sautéed zucchini, butternut squash, or just about any other vegetables you like.

In a large, deep skillet, heat the 1 cup of the oil over medium-high heat until it reaches 350°F. Line a sheet pan with paper towels. Fry half of the tortilla strips until golden brown, 30 seconds to 1 minute. Drain on the lined sheet pan. Season lightly with salt; set aside. (Leave the remaining tortilla chips uncooked.)

In a small bowl, cover the ancho chiles with boiling water. Let soak for 5 minutes to rehydrate, then strain and discard the soaking water. Remove the stems and seeds and transfer the chiles to a high-speed blender. Add the tomatoes and blend for 1 to 2 minutes, or until smooth. Set aside.

Heat a large pot or Dutch oven over medium-high heat. Add the remaining 2 tablespoons of oil. When the oil shimmers and is hot, add the onion, carrot, celery, and poblano. Sauté until the onion is translucent, 5 to 7 minutes. Add the garlic, cumin, oregano, and chili powder and sauté for another 30 seconds, or until the spices are fragrant.

Add the broth and tomato-chile mixture and bring to a simmer. Add the uncooked tortilla strips and cook for 15 minutes to allow the tortillas to break down and thicken the soup. Add the black beans and season with salt and pepper.

Ladle the soup into bowls and top with the crispy tortilla strips and any other garnishes (if using).

CREAM OF BROCCOLI *CHEDDA'* SOUP

We all have those childhood favorites that only Mom could make with her special touch. This was mine: incredibly creamy, with just the right amount of broccoli bits, and so cheesy you could pull strings straight out of the bowl! Now when I make it for my kids, I get that smooth, velvety texture with homemade cashew cream and plant-based cheddar (that said, any other type of vegan cheese works just as well). Every spoonful of this soup is creamy, cheesy, and packed with broccoli flavor (just like mamacita's). I like to finish my bowl with a couple of heavy-handed splashes of Tabasco sauce and serve it with plenty of crusty bread for dipping.

¼ cup plant-based butter

¼ cup all-purpose flour or all-purpose gluten-free flour blend

1 small yellow onion, finely diced

3 garlic cloves, minced

6½ cups Chik'n Broth (page 50) or any vegetable broth

8 cups broccoli florets

2 large or 3 medium russet or Yukon gold potatoes, peeled and finely diced

2 cups unsweetened, unflavored plant-based milk

SERVES 6 TO 8

¼ cup nutritional yeast

2 teaspoons onion powder

2 teaspoons fine pink Himalayan salt, or to taste

1 teaspoon garlic powder

1 teaspoon ground black pepper

1 bay leaf

2 cups Cashew Heavy Cream (page 55)

1 large carrot, shredded (about 1 cup)

Plant-based cheddar cheese shreds, for garnish (optional)

Croutons or toasted baguette slices, for garnish (optional)

In a large pot or Dutch oven, melt the butter over medium heat. Add the flour and whisk to make a paste (called a roux). Add the onion and cook, stirring almost constantly, until slightly translucent, 3 to 4 minutes. Add the garlic and sauté for 30 seconds, or just until fragrant.

Pour in the broth and whisk until smooth. Add the broccoli, potatoes, milk, nutritional yeast, onion powder, salt, garlic powder, pepper, and bay leaf. Cover and simmer, stirring occasionally, until the potatoes and broccoli are tender, 15 to 20 minutes.

Uncover, remove the bay leaf, and, using an immersion blender, pulse two or three times for 10 to 20 seconds in spots where there are larger bits of vegetables. (If you don't have an immersion blender, remove 2 cups of the soup and carefully blend in a high-speed blender—leave the lid slightly cracked to allow steam to escape and protect your hand with a kitchen towel—until smooth. Return the soup to the pot.)

Stir in the Cashew Heavy Cream and the shredded carrot. Cook for an additional 5 minutes. Remove from the heat. Serve topped with cheddar shreds and croutons (if using).

GET CREATIVE!

For a broccoli-and-cheddar loaded potato, top a split baked potato with soup, Brazil Nut Sour Cream (page 57), Shiitake Bae'con (page 88), plant-based cheddar cheese shreds, and sliced scallions (green and white parts). So good!

MAKE YOUR OWN BREAD BOWL

Cream of Broccoli Chedda' Soup is fantastic in a home-made bread bowl. Buy 8- to 10-ounce sourdough boules, slice off the tops, then scoop out the bready insides (save it for bread crumbs—see page 46—or torn crouton pieces), leaving the crust "bowl" intact. Drizzle the inside of each bowl with 1 tablespoon of extra-virgin olive oil and bake at 400°F for 10 to 12 minutes, until the interior is dried out and firm. Remove from the oven and cool before using.

FRENCH ONION SOUP
with Cheezy Crostini

I fell in love with this soup—also known as soupe à l'oignon gratinée—in my early days of culinary school, so creating a plant-based version that is every bit as hearty and delicious as the original was important to me. This broth skips the beef or veal stock and gets its rich, deep flavor and color from red wine (instead of the customary white wine), sherry, mushroom bouillon for an intense umami boost, and glorious onions cooked slowly to a deep mahogany brown. Don't forget the gratinée: baguette slices slathered with Cream Cheeze and broiled until bubbly. Oh yasss!

2 tablespoons plant-based butter or neutral oil, such as avocado or grapeseed

4 yellow onions, thinly sliced (about 8 cups)

2 teaspoons fine pink Himalayan salt, or to taste

1 teaspoon ground black pepper

¼ teaspoon ground white pepper (optional)

1 cup dry red wine

4 cups water

2 mushroom bouillon cubes (see page 38)

1 bay leaf

2 sprigs fresh thyme

1 sprig fresh rosemary

¼ cup dry sherry

8 (½-inch-thick) slices baguette, toasted

1 cup Cream Cheeze (page 56), or 8 ounces any plant-based cream cheese

Minced fresh herbs, such as rosemary, flat-leaf parsley, or thyme, for garnish

SERVES 4

GET CREATIVE!
Stir chopped fresh chives, other herbs, and/or onion powder into your Cream Cheeze before spreading on the baguette for extra flavor.

In a large pot or Dutch oven, melt the butter over medium-low heat. Add the onions and cook, stirring occasionally, until the onions are softened and browned, 20 to 30 minutes. (If the onions are browning too quickly or start to get too brown, reduce the heat to low; do not rush this process by using heat that is too high.) Season with the salt, black pepper, and white pepper (if using).

Increase the heat to medium-high and add the wine. Cook and stir until slightly reduced, about 2 minutes. Add the water, bouillon cubes, bay leaf, thyme, and rosemary. Add the sherry and return the soup to a simmer. Cook for 2 minutes, then turn off the heat. Remove and discard the herb sprigs and bay leaf.

Set the oven rack one level down from the top position and heat the broiler to high. Place four oven-safe bowls or large ramekins on a sheet pan.

Ladle the soup into the bowls, leaving a little space at the top. Spread a thick layer of Cream Cheeze on the toasts. Place two pieces of toast, cheeze side up, on top of each bowl. Set the pan on the rack and, with the oven door ajar, broil until the cream cheeze is golden brown and bubbling, 2 to 3 minutes.

Cool for 5 minutes before serving, garnished with fresh herbs.

LOBZTER BISQUE

This soup is definitely in my top-five list of favorite recipes in this book. It's silky and velvety like a bisque should be, and the lobster mushrooms have a seafood-like essence, making them a perfect substitute for the real thing. I use dried mushrooms for a concentrated flavor, plus they are much easier to find (I get mine online). However, if you can score some fresh ones, call me! Lobster meat is sweet, so the addition of just a little sugar to the soup is essential, as are the sherry and saffron, which add a complex vibrancy.

1 ounce dried lobster mushrooms (about 1 cup)

6½ cups boiling water

½ teaspoon saffron threads

2 tablespoons plant-based butter or neutral oil, such as avocado or grapeseed

1 yellow or white onion, diced

2 large carrots, coarsely chopped

3 celery stalks with leaves, coarsely chopped

1 fennel bulb, trimmed, cored, and coarsely chopped (fronds reserved for garnish, if you like)

1 cup dry sherry

1 (6-ounce) can tomato paste

1 bay leaf

1 recipe Cashew Heavy Cream (page 55)

¼ cup nutritional yeast

2 teaspoons organic sugar

1 teaspoon fine pink Himalayan salt, or to taste

¼ teaspoon ground white pepper

Ground black pepper

Optional garnishes: Chopped fennel fronds, croutons, and/or plant-based heavy cream

SERVES 6 TO 8

In a medium pot, combine the mushrooms and boiling water. Cover and set aside for 30 minutes to rehydrate the mushrooms. Strain through a fine-mesh strainer over a large bowl, reserving the broth and mushrooms separately. Add the saffron to the warm liquid and set aside.

Heat a large pot or Dutch oven over medium-high heat. Melt the butter and then add the onion, carrots, celery, and fennel. Sauté for 8 to 10 minutes, until the vegetables are translucent and slightly browned.

Add the sherry and cook, stirring frequently, for 3 to 5 minutes, until most of the liquid has evaporated. Add the tomato paste and mix well. Add the mushroom-saffron liquid, bay leaf, and half of the mushrooms. Reduce the heat and simmer for 10 minutes, or until the veggies are tender. Turn off the heat and remove and discard the bay leaf.

Transfer half of the soup to a high-speed blender and carefully purée it, leaving the lid slightly cracked to allow steam to escape and protecting your hand with a kitchen towel. Repeat with the remaining soup, then return it to the pot over medium-low heat. Add the Cashew Heavy Cream, nutritional yeast, and sugar. Coarsely chop any large reserved mushrooms so they're bite-size; add to the pot. Season with salt and white and black pepper and heat, stirring frequently, until warmed through. Serve plain or topped with garnishes (if using).

PUMPKIN *RED CURRY* RICE BOWL

2 tablespoons neutral oil, such as avocado or grapeseed

4 cups peeled, seeded, and cubed pumpkin (about 1 small pumpkin)

2 red bell peppers, stemmed, seeded, and julienned

½ white onion, thinly sliced

3 tablespoons vegan red curry paste

2 (14-ounce) cans full-fat coconut milk

1 cup cut Chinese long beans or green beans (2-inch pieces)

2 dried Thai red chiles

3 Thai (Makrut) lime leaves

1 cup frozen green peas (no need to thaw)

½ cup whole Thai or Genovese basil leaves

1 tablespoon Fyshy Sauce (page 65), soy sauce, or tamari (if you're gluten-free)

1 to 2 tablespoons coconut sugar (depending on how sweet you like it)

Juice of 1 lime

1 teaspoon fine pink Himalayan salt, or to taste

Hot cooked jasmine rice, for serving

Optional garnishes: Fresh herbs such as Thai basil, mint, and/or cilantro leaves

SERVES 4 TO 6

GET CREATIVE!

Not quite pumpkin season yet? Swap out the pumpkin for any squash variety, such as butternut or kabocha, or for a root veg like sweet potato.

Growing up in California, I had friends from all over the globe—Jamaica, India, the Philippines, Thailand, Vietnam, Haiti, Indonesia, and Korea. I loved exploring new-to-me foods with them. At some point I realized one simple word brings all these cuisines to a delicious common ground: curry! All are different in their own unique way, and all are a great way to spice up your plant-based dishes with fiery, sweet, earthy, and savory flavors. This Thai-inspired pumpkin stew is creamy, rich, and comforting with a piquant kick from the chiles in the red curry paste. When shopping, be sure to check the label of the curry paste as many contain shrimp. A good vegan option is Thai Kitchen curry paste—but there are plenty more to try!

Heat a large pot or Dutch oven over medium-high heat. Add the oil. Once the oil is hot and shimmering, add the pumpkin and sauté, stirring frequently, until softened slightly, 5 to 6 minutes. Add the bell peppers and onion and sauté until the onion is slightly translucent, 3 to 4 minutes. Add the curry paste and sauté, stirring constantly, until aromatic and dark red in color, about 1 minute.

Add the coconut milk, beans, red chiles, and lime leaves. Bring to a simmer, stirring frequently. Reduce the heat to medium-low and gently cook until the vegetables are tender, about 20 minutes. Add the peas and cook until tender, about 5 minutes. Stir in the basil, Fyshy Sauce, sugar, lime juice, and salt. Serve over rice topped with fresh herbs (if using).

CHILI *CON* CHILI

I can assure you, when the Morgans are hosting a Super Bowl party, there's a large pot of Chili con Chili with an endless supply of zesty queso (page 167), avocado, and Pickled Red Onions (page 77) on the buffet line. I stir together a quick seasoning blend by adding spices like smoked paprika, ancho chile powder, and oregano to store-bought chili powder for more complexity. I also add a little cacao powder, which is rich in fiber, magnesium, iron, calcium, and antioxidants (I could go on), to create a complex, bitter flavor that melds well with the chiles and coconut sugar. Don't forget the Vegemite or Marmite for a rich, malty, umami flavor. This chili is hearty and flavorful enough to please even the most die-hard carnivores.

FOR THE SPICE BLEND

1 tablespoon coconut sugar

2 teaspoons sweet or smoked paprika

2 teaspoons chili powder

2 teaspoons fine pink Himalayan salt, or to taste

1 teaspoon unsweetened cacao powder

1 teaspoon ancho chile powder

1 teaspoon ground cumin

1 teaspoon dried oregano

1 teaspoon ground black pepper

SERVES 6

TIP:

For a meatier chili, add plant-based ground beef, Walnut Chorizo (page 105), or any Soyrizo.

GET CREATIVE!

Leftover chili is like gold in my house—add queso (page 167) to make chili-cheese fries, nachos, or a kid-approved chili mac. Or fill a Chickpea Omelet (page 106) with chili and plant-based cheese.

FOR THE CHILI

2 tablespoons neutral oil, such as avocado or grapeseed

1 yellow onion, diced

1 green bell pepper, stemmed, seeded, and diced

2 celery stalks, diced

3 garlic cloves, minced

1 (6-ounce) can tomato paste

4 cups Chik'n Broth (page 50) or any vegetable broth

3 cups cooked green or brown lentils (rinsed and drained, if canned)

3 cups cooked black beans or kidney beans (rinsed and drained, if canned)

1 tablespoon apple cider vinegar

2 teaspoons Vegemite or Marmite (see page 38) or liquid aminos (see page 38)

1 bay leaf

Optional toppings: Diced fresh tomatoes, Brazil Nut Sour Cream (page 57) or plant-based sour cream, chopped fresh cilantro, chopped fresh flat-leaf parsley, diced avocado, and/or sliced scallions (green and white parts)

MAKE THE SPICE BLEND: In a small bowl, combine the coconut sugar, paprika, chili powder, salt, cacao powder, ancho chile powder, cumin, oregano, and black pepper. Mix well to combine. Set aside.

MAKE THE CHILI: Heat a large pot or Dutch oven over medium-high heat. Add the oil. Once the oil is hot and shimmering, add the onion, bell pepper, and celery and sauté until the onion is translucent, 5 to 7 minutes. Add the garlic and sauté for 30 seconds, or just until fragrant.

Add the tomato paste and spice blend. Cook and stir for 1 to 2 minutes, until the tomato paste begins to darken slightly, then add the broth. Stir, scraping up browned bits from the bottom of the pan (this is called deglazing). Add the lentils, black beans, vinegar, Vegemite, and bay leaf. Bring to a simmer. Cover, reduce the heat to medium-low, and cook for 30 to 40 minutes, until the chili has thickened and the flavors have come together. Remove and discard the bay leaf.

Ladle into bowls and garnish with toppings (if using), or cool and store in the refrigerator for up to 1 week.

LEMON *PARM-Y* KALE SALAD

FOR THE DRESSING

½ cup extra-virgin olive oil

½ cup raw cashews, soaked and drained (see page 35)

¼ cup pure maple syrup

Zest of 2 lemons and juice of 4 lemons

3 garlic cloves, crushed

3 tablespoons nutritional yeast

2 teaspoons fine pink Himalayan salt, or to taste

1 teaspoon ground black pepper

¼ cup water

**SERVES 6
(PLUS EXTRA DRESSING)**

FOR THE SALAD

2 bunches kale (any variety), stems discarded, leaves thinly sliced crosswise

2 cups cooked quinoa

1 cup sliced or slivered almonds, toasted (see page 47)

1 cup dried cranberries or currants

½ cup hemp seeds

I've been making this kale salad forever, though now my dressing features cashews and nutritional yeast instead of the Parmigiano-Reggiano that I used to use. How do I know the new version tastes as good as the original? It has been my son's favorite salad since he was two years old—and when I changed the ingredients to be plant-based, he had no idea! To this day, he's always asking for more. This salad's got it all: a creamy, lemony dressing, bites of sweetness, tons of tang, and earthy quinoa that adds protein and fiber, making it a very filling meal. Bonus: This is a great make-ahead dish. Allow the flavors to marry with the fibrous kale for up to 2 hours in the refrigerator before serving.

MAKE THE DRESSING: **In a high-speed blender, combine the olive oil, cashews, maple syrup, lemon zest and juice, garlic, nutritional yeast, salt, pepper, and water and process until smooth and creamy. Use immediately or refrigerate for up to 5 days.**

MAKE THE SALAD: **Put the kale in a very large bowl. Add half of the dressing and toss to coat. Add the quinoa, almonds, cranberries, and hemp seeds. Toss to combine. Add more dressing, if desired, and toss again until everything is well coated. Serve immediately or cover and chill for up to 2 hours.**

TIP:

Have a nut allergy? Omit the almonds and substitute ½ cup extra-firm tofu for the cashews in the dressing. Instead of adding the olive oil with the other dressing ingredients, drizzle it in last while the blender is running and continue processing until the dressing is smooth and creamy.

GET CREATIVE!

When fresh berries are in season, replace the dried fruit with fresh raspberries, blueberries, or sliced strawberries for a beautiful and refreshing summer salad.

CAESAR SALAD
THREE WAYS

When I make a Caesar salad, I need my dressing to bite back! It's got to be garlicky and zesty and, most important, have that salty sea flavor. Here's a great example of how combining plants can mimic traditional animal-based ingredients: briny capers and fishy powdered seaweed coupled together bring you a *vegan anchovy paste*. Because I love Caesar salads so much, I couldn't stop myself at just one kind—so here are three unbelievably vegan versions.

VEGAN ANCHOVY PASTE

On a cutting board, finely mince 2 teaspoons drained capers. Sprinkle 1 teaspoon kelp powder or Nori Dust (see page 38) over the capers, then drizzle 1 tablespoon of caper brine over the kelp powder. Using the side of your knife, slide it back and forth to make a paste. Use immediately in Caesar dressing, pastas, homemade croutons, or roasted veggies for an anchovy-ish flavor. Makes about 1 tablespoon.

The Classic Caesar

FOR THE DRESSING

3 garlic cloves

1 recipe (1 tablespoon) Vegan Anchovy Paste (see above)

2 cups Mayonnaise (page 53) or any plant-based mayonnaise

3 tablespoons nutritional yeast

2 tablespoons fresh lemon juice

1 tablespoon red wine vinegar

2 teaspoons Dijon mustard

2 teaspoons vegan Worcestershire sauce

2 teaspoons Tabasco sauce

1 teaspoon fine pink Himalayan salt, or to taste

½ teaspoon ground black pepper

FOR THE SALAD

1 head romaine lettuce, coarsely chopped

1 bunch kale (any variety), stems discarded, leaves thinly sliced crosswise

Optional toppings: Hemp seeds, Shiitake Bae'con (page 88) or any plant-based bacon, croutons, roasted chickpeas (page 44), fried capers, fresh cherry or grape tomatoes halves, and/or oil-packed sun-dried tomatoes

SERVES 6 TO 8
(PLUS EXTRA DRESSING)

MAKE THE DRESSING: Use a Microplane to grate the garlic into a medium bowl (make sure to give the Microplane a good whack to release all of the garlic), then add the Vegan Anchovy Paste, mayonnaise, nutritional yeast, lemon juice, vinegar, mustard, Worcestershire sauce, Tabasco sauce, salt, and pepper. Whisk until completely combined. Use immediately or refrigerate in an airtight container for up to 1 week.

MAKE THE SALAD: In a large bowl, combine the romaine lettuce and kale. Add about a quarter of the dressing and toss the greens to make sure all are well coated. Add more dressing a little at a time, mixing as you go, until it's as dressed as you like—you won't use all the dressing. Divide the greens among bowls and serve with the toppings of your choice.

Fiesta Caesar Salad
with Crunchy Tortilla Strips

FOR THE DRESSING

3 garlic cloves

1 recipe (1 tablespoon) Vegan Anchovy Paste (see opposite page)

2 cups Mayonnaise (page 53) or any plant-based mayonnaise

¼ cup chopped fresh cilantro

1 to 2 chipotle chiles in adobo sauce (depending on how spicy you want it), minced, plus 2 teaspoons adobo sauce (see Tip)

3 tablespoons nutritional yeast

Juice of 1 large lime

1 tablespoon red wine vinegar, distilled white vinegar, or apple cider vinegar

2 teaspoons Dijon mustard

1 teaspoon fine pink Himalayan salt, or to taste

½ teaspoon ground cumin

½ teaspoon ground black pepper

**SERVES 6 TO 8
(PLUS EXTRA DRESSING)**

FOR THE SALAD

10 (6-inch) yellow corn tortillas, cut into ¼ by ¾-inch pieces

1 head romaine lettuce, coarsely chopped

1 bunch kale (any variety), stems discarded, leaves thinly sliced crosswise

1 cup cooked black beans (rinsed and drained, if canned)

1 cup corn kernels, fresh, frozen and thawed, or canned and drained

1 cup toasted pepitas (pumpkin seeds) (see page 47)

MAKE THE DRESSING: Use a Microplane to grate the garlic into a medium bowl (make sure to give the Microplane a good whack to release all of the garlic). Add the Vegan Anchovy Paste, mayonnaise, cilantro, chipotle chiles, adobo sauce, nutritional yeast, lime juice, vinegar, mustard, salt, cumin, and black pepper. Whisk until completely combined. Use immediately or refrigerate in an airtight container for up to 1 week.

MAKE THE SALAD: Prepare the tortilla strips first. Preheat the oven to 350°F. Line a large sheet pan with parchment paper. Arrange the tortilla strips in a single layer on the prepared pan. Bake for 10 to 12 minutes, until just firm. Let cool completely (the tortilla strips will crisp up as they cool).

In a large bowl, combine the romaine and kale. Add about a quarter of the dressing and toss the greens to make sure all are well coated. Add more dressing a little at a time, mixing as you go, until it's as dressed as you like—you won't use all the dressing.

Divide the dressed greens among bowls. Top with black beans, corn, toasted pepitas, and tortilla strips and serve.

TIP:
Use only 1 chipotle if you are sensitive to heat. If you are a heat-loving person like me, add 1 or 2 extra.

Kick'n Cajun Caesar Salad

with Crispy Black-Eyed Peas & Cornbread Croutons

FOR THE DRESSING

2 garlic cloves, peeled

1 recipe (1 tablespoon) Vegan Anchovy Paste (page 140)

2 cups Mayonnaise (page 53) or any plant-based mayonnaise

3 tablespoons nutritional yeast

2 tablespoons fresh lemon juice

2 teaspoons Tabasco sauce

2 teaspoons Creole mustard

2 teaspoons vegan Worcestershire sauce

1 teaspoon Creole-Cajun Seasoning (page 85)

1 teaspoon fine pink Himalayan salt, or to taste

¼ teaspoon ground black pepper

SERVES 6 TO 8 (PLUS EXTRA DRESSING)

FOR THE SALAD

Day-old Skillet Cornbread (page 241), cut into 1-inch cubes with a serrated knife

1 (15.5-ounce) can black-eyed peas, rinsed and drained

1 head romaine lettuce, coarsely chopped

1 bunch kale (any variety), stems discarded, leaves thinly sliced crosswise

MAKE THE DRESSING: Use a Microplane to grate the garlic into a medium bowl (make sure to give the Microplane a good whack to release all of the garlic). Add the Vegan Anchovy Paste, mayonnaise, nutritional yeast, lemon juice, Tabasco sauce, mustard, Worcestershire sauce, Creole-Cajun seasoning, salt, and pepper. Whisk until completely combined. Use immediately or refrigerate in an airtight container for up to 1 week.

MAKE THE SALAD: Preheat the oven to 375°F. Line two large sheet pans with parchment paper.

Arrange the cornbread cubes on one of the prepared pans and bake until dried out, about 20 minutes. Turn the cubes over and return them to oven. Spread the black-eyed peas in a single layer on the other prepared pan. Bake until the peas are crispy and the cornbread is browned and firm, 20 minutes more, shaking the pan to rotate the peas about halfway through. Cool the cornbread croutons and black-eyed peas completely.

Combine the romaine lettuce and kale in a large bowl. Add about a quarter of the dressing and toss the greens to make sure all are well coated. Add more dressing a little at a time, mixing as you go, until it's as dressed as you like—you won't use all the dressing.

Divide the dressed greens among bowls. Top with cornbread croutons and crispy black-eyed peas and serve.

TIP:

Day-old cornbread is easier to cut than fresh, which can be too crumbly before it's dried out a bit. The good news is that the cornbread croutons do not have to be perfect as long as they hold up while toasting.

GARBAGE SALAD

with Creamy Lemon-Peppercorn Dressing

FOR THE DRESSING

2 cups Classic Herby Ranch Dressing (page 66)

2 tablespoons fresh lemon juice

1 teaspoon fresh minced or ½ teaspoon dried tarragon (optional)

½ teaspoon Dijon mustard

½ teaspoon ground black pepper

**SERVES 8
(PLUS EXTRA DRESSING)**

FOR THE SALAD

2 heads romaine lettuce, thinly sliced

2 cups baby spinach, coarsely chopped

1 to 2 cups fried onion straws, croutons, and/or ½ cup toasted nuts (I use all three!)

1 cucumber, thinly sliced

1½ cups cooked chickpeas or other legumes (rinsed and drained, if canned)

1 (14-ounce) can hearts of palm or artichoke hearts, drained and sliced

2 carrots, shredded

½ cup sliced pepperoncini peppers or any olive variety

1 small to medium raw red or golden beet, peeled and shredded

1 cup Shiitake Bae'con (page 88) or any cooked plant-based bacon

1 cup plant-based cheese crumbles or crumbled raw or Roasted Tofu (page 98)

1 cup cherry or grape tomatoes, halved

1 Granny Smith apple, peeled, cored, and diced

¼ cup thinly sliced fresh basil

Contrary to popular belief, plant-based eating doesn't mean only salads. There are loads of creative ways in this book to eat vegetables and grains *without* tossing them into a bowl. But this isn't one of them—this is the best salad in the world. Why? Because you can throw anything in it! Don't have apples? Add pears or grapes. Don't like spinach? Use kale or arugula. Don't eat gluten? Replace croutons with crunchy nuts. You get the idea. Top it off with the creamy lemon-peppercorn remix of my Classic Herby Ranch that's everything you want a salad dressing to be.

MAKE THE DRESSING: In a medium bowl, combine the ranch dressing, lemon juice, tarragon (if using), mustard, and pepper. Whisk until smooth. Use immediately or refrigerate in an airtight container for up to 1 week.

MAKE THE SALAD: In a very large bowl, combine the romaine, spinach, onion straws, cucumber, chickpeas, hearts of palm, carrots, pepperoncini, beet, Shiitake Bae'con, cheese crumbles, tomatoes, apple, and basil. Toss until all ingredients are evenly distributed.

Add half of the dressing. Toss again to evenly coat all ingredients. Add more dressing, a little bit at a time, if desired. Divide among bowls, piling the salad high for a beautiful presentation, and serve.

TACO SALAD

in Baked Tortilla Bowls

Taco Tuesday in an edible bowl! Warm ingredients like my bomb Walnut Chorizo and tender beans with crisp lettuce and fresh toppings make this salad the kind of all-in-one meal that's fun to eat for the whole family. I offer two easy methods for baking the tortilla bowl—the muffin tin method is great for making multiple standard-size bowls, and the metal bowl method is great for a *mucho grande* taco salad bowl made with larger tortillas. If you are in the mood to show off, try this drizzled with spicy queso.

4 (8- or 11-inch) flour tortillas, warmed

Nonstick cooking spray

1 head romaine or green leaf lettuce, shredded

4 cups cooked black beans or pinto beans (rinsed and drained, if canned), warmed

2 cups Walnut Chorizo (page 105) or any store-bought Soyrizo, warmed

Optional toppings: Diced tomato, diced avocado or a scoop of guacamole, Brazil Nut Sour Cream (page 57), sliced black olives, warmed corn kernels, sliced fresh or pickled jalapeños, and/or sliced scallions (green and white parts)

Roasted Red Pepper, Chipotle & Lime Dressing (page 72), queso (page 167), Fiesta Caesar dressing (page 141), or Avocado-Lime Ranch Dressing (page 67)

SERVES 4

Preheat the oven to 350°F.

For the tortilla bowls, if using 8-inch tortillas, lightly coat both sides of each tortilla with cooking spray. Turn a 12-cup muffin tin upside down. Working with one tortilla at a time, set a tortilla over 4 cups and tuck the ends in to form a bowl; repeat with the remaining tortillas. Bake until the tortillas are firm and starting to brown, 8 to 10 minutes. Remove the tin from the oven and set aside to cool completely before inverting. Or, if you're using larger wrap-size (10- to 11-inch) tortillas, spray the inside of a medium ovenproof metal bowl (two if you have them and they'll fit in your oven at the same time) with cooking spray. Press a warm tortilla inside of the bowl (it's okay if you get some overlapping or scalloped edges). Bake until the tortilla is firm and starting to brown, 8 to 10 minutes. Remove the bowl from the oven and set aside to cool completely before inverting. Repeat with the remaining tortillas.

To build the salads, divide the lettuce among the tortilla bowls. Add the beans on top of the lettuce, then the Walnut Chorizo, followed by your favorite toppings. Drizzle the dressing over the salads and serve.

COLD SOBA *NOODLES*
with Citrus-Miso Dressing

8 ounces soba noodles

1 tablespoon neutral oil, such as avocado or grapeseed, or toasted sesame oil

1 red bell pepper, stemmed, seeded, and julienned

2 cups broccoli florets

2 carrots, shredded

2 cucumbers, seeded and julienned

3 scallions (green and white parts), thinly sliced

2 cups thinly sliced bok choy leaves or spinach

½ bunch fresh cilantro, coarsely chopped

10 ounces raw firm tofu, drained and cubed, or Roasted Tofu (page 98), cubed (optional)

1 recipe Citrus-Miso Dressing (page 71)

SERVES 6

I originally created my Citrus-Miso Dressing for a different salad, and it was a *huge* hit with my clients. They loved it so much that they asked if I could make more meals that show off its tangy-creamy-citrusy flavor. I created this soba noodle salad that's excellent at room temperature or chilled, which makes it a great option for make-ahead lunches and weekend picnics. Plus, it gets tastier when it sits in the refrigerator for a few hours or even up to 2 days.

Cook the noodles according to the package directions. Drain, rinse with cool water to stop them from cooking more, and drain again. Transfer to a large bowl and toss with the oil.

Add the bell pepper, broccoli, carrots, cucumbers, scallions, bok choy, cilantro, and tofu (if using). Toss to combine. Add half of the Citrus-Miso Dressing and toss to coat. If desired, add more dressing, a little at a time, until the noodles are dressed to your liking. Serve at room temperature or chilled (the soba can be refrigerated for up to 2 days).

TOONA
POKE BOWL
with Spicy Aïoli

When fish was an option for us, sushi dates were a go-to for Derrick and me, and spicy tuna rolls and tuna crispy rice used to be our thing. The key phrase was "used to," until one night I was struck by inspiration: while making *concasse* tomatoes (a fun cheffy term that means removing the skins and seeds), it dawned on me that these deep red plum tomatoes have a meaty texture that's perfect for a sashimi-like fish swap. After marinating for at least 2 hours (or even better, overnight) in poke seasonings like Nori Dust (for that fishy taste), soy sauce, ginger, sesame oil, and chile paste . . . it kinda throws you off for a second until you realize that it's actually tomato. Try it and you'll see it's pretty awesome.

FOR THE TOONA

8 ripe-but-firm Roma tomatoes (or other plum tomato)

½ cup soy sauce or tamari (if you're gluten-free)

2 scallions (green and white parts), thinly sliced

2 tablespoons minced shallot or sweet onion

1 tablespoon toasted sesame oil

2 teaspoons chile paste or hot sauce (I like sambal oelek or sriracha)

2 teaspoons toasted black or white sesame seeds, plus more for garnish

1 teaspoon Nori Dust (page 38) or kelp powder

½ teaspoon grated or minced fresh ginger

SERVES 4

FOR THE SPICY AÏOLI

½ cup Mayonnaise (page 53) or any plant-based mayonnaise

2 to 3 teaspoons chile paste or hot sauce (depending on how spicy you want it; I like sambal oelek or sriracha)

½ teaspoon toasted sesame oil

½ teaspoon fine pink Himalayan salt, or to taste

FOR SERVING

4 cups cooked short-grain brown rice or sushi rice

1 small cucumber, sliced

2 carrots, shredded

2 ripe avocados, halved, pitted, and sliced

4 radishes, sliced

½ cup Pickled Red Onions (page 77) or sliced red onions

½ cup thinly sliced pickled beets (page 77) or raw beets

½ cup shelled edamame, cooked and cooled

½ cup sliced scallions (green and white parts) or chopped fresh cilantro, for garnish

GET CREATIVE!
Add the toona to a sushi roll or serve a scoop on top of avocado toast to take it to the next level.

MAKE THE TOONA: Fill a large bowl with ice and water and set aside. Bring a large pot of water to a boil. Slice an X on the bottom of each of the tomatoes. Gently drop the tomatoes into the water and submerge them for no longer than 30 seconds. Use a slotted spoon to remove the tomatoes and immediately place them in the ice bath.

When the tomatoes are completely cooled, peel the skins off and discard. Starting where you made the X, quarter the tomatoes lengthwise and remove the seeds and cores. Dice or coarsely chop the tomatoes and place them in a strainer set in a large bowl for 12 to 15 minutes to allow excess juices to drain.

In a medium bowl, make the marinade by combining the soy sauce, scallions, shallot, sesame oil, chile paste, sesame seeds, Nori Dust, and ginger. Stir well to combine. (Taste and add more chile paste, if you like heat.) Add the strained tomatoes to the marinade and stir gently to coat. Cover and marinate in the refrigerator for 2 hours, or up to overnight.

MAKE THE SPICY AÏOLI: In a small bowl, combine the mayonnaise, chile paste, sesame oil, and salt. Stir well to combine. Cover and refrigerate until you are ready to serve, or up to 1 week.

TO SERVE: Divide the rice among four bowls. Use a slotted spoon to add a scoop of toona on top. Add cucumber, carrots, avocados, radishes, pickled onions, pickled beets, edamame, and scallions. Drizzle with the aïoli, garnish with additional sesame seeds, and serve.

PRO-BOWL

Cooked Grain Base
(CHOOSE 1; SEE PAGE 42)

Amaranth

Barley

Buckwheat

Bulgur

Couscous

Cracked wheat

Einkorn

Farro

Freekeh

Kamut

Quinoa

Rice: brown, black, white, wild, or mixed

Teff

Whole spelt

Whole-wheat kernels or wheat berries

Salad greens
(for a low-carb option)

Proteins
(I LIKE TO ADD 2)

Beans and legumes: black beans, chickpeas, edamame, fava beans, kidney beans, lentils, mung beans, pinto beans

Seasoned jackfruit from Gochujang Jackfruit Noodle Bowl (page 215)

Marinated (see page 73 for my go-to marinade) and roasted or grilled tofu or tempeh

Plant-based meats

Unbelievably Vegan Protein Burger patty (page 217) or any cooked plant-based burgers

Shiitake Bae'con (page 88) or any cooked plant-based bacon

Walnut Chorizo (page 105) or any cooked Soyrizo

Roasted, Sautéed, Grilled, or Steamed Vegetables
(CHOOSE UP TO 3)

Asparagus

Beets

Bell peppers

Bok choy

Broccoli

Brussels sprouts

Carrots

Cauliflower

Corn

Eggplant

Green beans or wax beans

Greens: collards, dandelion, kale, mustard, Swiss chard

Mushrooms

Okra

Potatoes

Pumpkin or squash (winter or summer)

Sweet potatoes

Tomatoes

Toppings (CHOOSE 2)

Avocado

Brazil Nut Sour Cream (page 57)

Kimchi (page 80)

Pickled Vegetables (pages 77, 78, and 79)

Plant-based cheese

Salsa, homemade or store-bought

Sea vegetables: arame, dulse, hijiki, kelp, kombu, spirulina, or dry-roasted or rehydrated wakame

Sriracha or other hot sauce

Pro-Bowls are a great place to start when you are beginning your plant-based journey (see "Small Steps to Big Change" on page 30). Building a bowl is easy when you have the right components on hand: a grain or greens for a base; a protein or two; cooked and raw veggies; healthy fats from avocado, toasted nuts, and legumes; and sauces for drizzling. Put it all together and you have a nutritious meal that you can eat for breakfast (yes, breakfast doesn't have to be eggs, pancakes, or oatmeal), lunch, or dinner. If you're cooking big batches, make up the bowls in advance and switch up the dressings for a quick remix of your meal prep.

Dressings & Sauces
(CHOOSE 1)

Chimichurri, homemade or store-bought

Chipotle BBQ Sauce (page 60)

Citrus-Miso Dressing (page 71)

Classic, Fiesta, or Cajun Caesar dressing (pages 140, 141, and 143)

Classic Herby Ranch Dressing or Avocado-Lime Ranch Dressing (pages 66 and 67)

Creamy Buffalo Sauce (page 63)

Harissa-Tahini Dressing (page 68)

Hollandaze Sauce (page 98)

Liquid aminos (see page 38)

Pesto, homemade or store-bought

Roasted Red Pepper, Chipotle & Lime Dressing (page 72)

Tahini thinned with lemon juice, liquid aminos, or water

Fresh Vegetables & Sprouts
(CHOOSE UP TO 3)

Baby spinach

Grated carrots

Celery

Sliced cucumbers

Microgreens: basil or cilantro

Mixed greens

Peas: English, snow, or sugar snap

Sliced radishes

Scallions

Snap peas

Sprouts: alfalfa, broccoli, kale, mung bean, sunflower, etc.

Tomatoes (sun-dried or raw)

Seeds & Nuts (Toasted or Untoasted)

Almonds

Cashews

Chia seeds

Flaxseeds

Hemp seeds

Peanuts

Pecans

Pepitas (pumpkin seeds)

Pine nuts

Pistachios

Sesame seeds

Sunflower seeds

Walnuts

CROWD-PLEASERS

SRIRACHA CAULIFLOWER WALNUT
LETTUCE CUPS, PAGE 158

CARIBBEAN CEVICHE

1½ cups soy curls
(see page 37)

2 cups canned or jarred
hearts of palm, drained and
sliced into ¼-inch pieces

¾ cup fresh lime juice
(from 7 or 8 limes)

½ small red onion, thinly
sliced

2 jalapeños or serranos,
stemmed, seeded, and
minced

2 tomatoes, seeded and
diced

SERVES 8

Juice of 1 orange

1 teaspoon fine pink
Himalayan salt, or to taste

½ teaspoon ground black
pepper

1 ripe mango, peeled and
diced (see Tip)

½ cup minced fresh cilantro

1 large ripe avocado,
halved, pitted, and diced

Plantain or tortilla chips,
for serving

My fresh, colorful ceviche is full of fun flavors: bold citrus, spicy jalapeño, and sweet mango. Hearts of palm add a calamari-like vibe (plus they have potassium and vitamin B_6) and protein-rich soy curls bring a Mahi-like texture. Finish it off with creamy avocado, bright cilantro, and tangy tomato to cut through the acid of the citrus juices and temper the heat of the jalapeños for a perfectly balanced bite.

In a small bowl, cover the soy curls with hot water and soak for 8 to 10 minutes, until rehydrated. Drain and gently squeeze out any excess water.

In a glass or other nonreactive bowl, combine the soy curls with the hearts of palm, lime juice, onion, jalapeños, tomatoes, orange juice, salt, and pepper. Mix well, then add the mango and cilantro, reserving the avocado until serving.

Cover and chill in the refrigerator for 30 to 45 minutes to allow the flavors to blend, carefully stirring halfway through.

Gently fold in the avocado. Serve with chips.

TIP:
To quickly dice a mango, cut down along both wide sides of the mango (leave the skin on) on either side of the pit, and as close to the pit as possible without hitting it. Place a mango half, round side down, on a cutting board. With a paring knife, score the flesh down to the peel in a crosshatch pattern. Press on the rounded side of the mango to turn the mango "inside out." Use your knife to slice the cubed flesh from the peel. Repeat with the other mango half.

SRIRACHA *CAULIFLOWER* WALNUT LETTUCE CUPS

2 heads cauliflower, cored and separated into florets

2 tablespoons neutral oil, such as avocado or grapeseed

1½ teaspoons fine pink Himalayan salt, or to taste

1 teaspoon ground black pepper

1 cup walnut halves, coarsely chopped

1½ cups Mayonnaise (page 53) or any plant-based mayonnaise

2 tablespoons sriracha

2 teaspoons white miso paste

2 teaspoons pure maple syrup

3 scallions (green and white parts), thinly sliced

2 garlic cloves, minced

1 tablespoon black sesame seeds

SERVES 8 TO 10

FOR SERVING

2 heads Bibb lettuce, leaves separated

3 large carrots, julienned

1 large cucumber, seeded and julienned

Leaves picked from ½ bunch fresh cilantro

Crunchy rice sticks or mung bean sprouts (optional)

Warm, roasted, crispy-edged cauliflower and meaty walnuts are tossed in a spicy-sweet, creamy aïoli, then tucked into cold, crunchy fresh lettuce leaves for a low-carb appetizer that will have your taste buds jumping! Arrange the lettuce cups on a platter with small bowls of toppings surrounding them so everyone can serve themselves, then kick back and wait for the compliments to roll in.

Preheat the oven to 400°F. Line a large sheet pan with parchment.

MAKE THE FILLING: In a large bowl, toss the cauliflower with the oil, 1 teaspoon of the salt, and ½ teaspoon of the pepper. Arrange in a single layer on the prepared sheet pan and roast for 25 to 30 minutes, until the edges are crisp and golden brown. Remove from the oven and allow to cool slightly.

Toast the walnuts in a medium skillet over medium heat for 2 minutes, shaking the pan every 30 seconds to prevent burning. Remove from the heat and allow to cool slightly in the pan.

Meanwhile, PREPARE THE SAUCE: In a large bowl, whisk the mayonnaise, sriracha, miso, maple syrup, two-thirds of the scallions, the garlic, and the remaining ½ teaspoon each of salt and pepper.

Add the cauliflower and walnuts to the bowl and very gently fold everything together, keeping the cauliflower intact. Transfer to a serving bowl. Sprinkle with sesame seeds and the remaining scallion.

TO SERVE: Build the cups by spooning the cauliflower mixture into one or two stacked lettuce leaves and topping with garnishes.

GET CREATIVE!

For a crispy version of this recipe, coat the cauliflower using the batter from Lemon-Pepper Wingz (page 171), but omit the lemon-pepper seasoning. Fry according to the wingz instructions. Or, make a beautiful bowl by serving the filling over steamed rice and topped with fresh vegetables, like carrots and cucumber, or Vietnamese Pickled Vegetables (page 79).

SESAME *AVOCADO* KALE NO-EGG ROLLS

6 ripe avocados, halved and pitted

1½-inch piece ginger, peeled

5 garlic cloves

⅓ cup coarsely chopped fresh cilantro

Juice of 1 lime

2 teaspoons fine pink Himalayan salt, or to taste

2 teaspoons toasted sesame oil

½ teaspoon Sichuan chile flakes or crushed red pepper flakes

1 bunch kale (any variety), stems discarded, leaves thinly sliced crosswise

24 egg-free eggroll or spring roll wrappers

Nonstick cooking spray for baking, or neutral oil for frying (I prefer rice bran oil)

Store-bought sweet chili sauce, for serving

MAKES 24 EGG ROLLS

I created these golden no-egg rolls when I had way too many ripe avocados. I wanted something more than just guacamole to offer friends who were coming over, and this was a delicious way to use up the avocados. Combined with garlic, ginger, sesame, red pepper flakes, and kale, every bite is packed with flavor. You can deep-fry the rolls or bake them in the oven—dealer's choice—both create satisfying and crispy rolls. They're delicious paired with a sweet chili sauce, or whip up a batch of Quick Stir-Fry Sauce (page 64) for dipping—sprinkle 2 teaspoons toasted sesame seeds over the sauce for extra crunch. Reminds me of those yummy avocado egg rolls that I used to order from that well-known restaurant chain that you will find in just about every shopping mall. Yeah! *That* one.

Scoop the avocados into a large bowl. Using a Microplane, grate the ginger and garlic into the bowl (make sure to give the Microplane a good whack to release all of the ginger and garlic). Add the cilantro, lime juice, salt, sesame oil, and chile flakes. Use a fork or a potato masher to mash the avocados, leaving some chunks for texture.

Add half of the kale to the bowl and stir to coat. Add the remaining kale and stir until all of the kale is coated in the avocado mixture. Cover the eggroll wrappers with a damp kitchen towel and fill a small bowl with water. If you plan to bake the rolls, line two large sheet pans with parchment paper and lightly coat each with nonstick cooking spray. If you're frying, skip this step.

recipe continues >>

Place a wrapper on your work surface with one corner pointed toward you. Add 2 tablespoons of the avocado mixture to the center. Pull the bottom pointed end completely over the filling. Fold the bottom corners (right and left) toward the center over the filling to create a cylinder. Moisten the remaining top corner with water. Roll the cylinder upward toward the moistened point, creating a large cigar-like roll. Place on the prepared sheet pan seam side down (or on an unlined sheet pan if frying). Repeat with remaining filling and wrappers.

TO BAKE THE ROLLS: Preheat the oven to 400°F.

Lightly coat the rolls with nonstick cooking spray (this helps to crisp up the wrappers). Bake until golden brown and crisp, 15 to 20 minutes. Remove from oven and allow to cool slightly.

TO FRY THE ROLLS: Fill a large, deep skillet or Dutch oven with 1½ inches of oil. Heat to 375°F. While the oil heats, line a sheet pan with paper towels. Fry the rolls a few at a time, making sure to not overcrowd the pan, until golden brown and crispy, about 1 minute per side. Drain on the paper towel-lined pan. Let the temperature of the oil return to 375°F before frying each batch.

Serve with the sweet chili sauce.

GET CREATIVE!
Don't have kale? Use shredded carrots, chopped mushrooms, and/or mung bean sprouts, or chopped cooked cabbage or collards for a hearty vegetable no-egg roll.

SPINACH-ARTICHOKE DIP

Creamy, wonderfully cheesy, and loaded with chopped spinach and artichoke hearts—I've always had a soft spot for spinach-artichoke dip so, of course, I had to create a vegan version. This dip is so similar to the dairy version, you might even change some of your friends' thinking about what dishes can be made without dairy. (Answer: All of them!)

3 tablespoons plant-based butter

½ yellow onion, finely diced

3 or 4 garlic cloves, minced

¼ cup all-purpose flour or all-purpose gluten-free flour blend

2¼ cups unsweetened, unflavored plant-based milk

¼ cup nutritional yeast

2 teaspoons fine pink Himalayan salt, or to taste

1 teaspoon ground black pepper

1 pound chopped frozen spinach, thawed

1 (14.5-ounce) jar marinated artichoke hearts, drained and coarsely chopped

1 tablespoon fresh lemon juice

1½ teaspoons vegan Worcestershire sauce

½ cup Brazil Nut Sour Cream (page 57), Mayonnaise (page 53), or any plant-based mayonnaise

1 cup plant-based cheese shreds

Tortilla chips, crackers, toast points, or fresh sliced baguette, for serving

SERVES 6 TO 8

GET CREATIVE!
Stuff leftovers into a tortilla to make spinach-artichoke quesadillas, or layer between lasagna noodles with marinara sauce to create a delicious spinach-artichoke lasagna.

Position an oven rack 6 to 8 inches from the top and preheat the oven to 375°F.

In a large saucepan, melt the butter over medium heat. When melted, add the onion and sauté until translucent, stirring occasionally, 5 to 7 minutes. Add the garlic and sauté for 30 seconds, or just until fragrant. Add the flour and whisk to make a paste (called a roux). Cook, stirring constantly, for 1 to 2 minutes. While whisking vigorously, slowly pour in the milk. Add the nutritional yeast and cook, whisking constantly, for 2 to 3 minutes, or until the sauce is thickened and bubbly. Remove from the heat and season with the salt and pepper.

Place the spinach in a clean kitchen towel and ring out the excess water over the sink, releasing and repeating until no more water comes out. Add the spinach to the sauce with the artichokes, lemon juice, and Worcestershire sauce and mix well. Fold in the Brazil Nut Sour Cream. Taste and adjust the seasoning, if necessary.

Transfer to a 1½-quart oven-safe baking dish. Sprinkle with the plant-based cheese. Bake for 25 minutes, or until bubbling.

Turn the oven to broil. Broil for 3 to 4 minutes, until the cheese begins to brown. Cool on a wire rack for about 10 minutes before serving with tortilla chips.

HOT *KRABBY* DIP

2 (14-ounce) cans young (green) jackfruit, drained

1 cup Cream Cheeze (page 56) or any plant-based cream cheese

½ cup Mayonnaise (page 53) or any plant-based mayonnaise

3 scallions (green and white parts), sliced

Zest and juice of ½ lemon

1 tablespoon nutritional yeast

1 tablespoon vegan Worcestershire sauce

2 teaspoons seafood seasoning (such as Old Bay)

2 teaspoons hot sauce (I like Tabasco or Frank's RedHot Sauce)

1 teaspoon garlic powder

Fine pink Himalayan salt and ground black pepper

½ cup panko bread crumbs

Crackers, crostini, or tortilla chips, for serving

SERVES 6 TO 8

This hot and bubbling crabby-ish dip is full of the flavors of the Chesapeake Bay. Young jackfruit, which is found canned in brine at most grocers and online, is mild in flavor and has a delicate, meaty texture, which makes it a perfect for absorbing the flavor of whatever you marinate or season it with. Even more impressive, when you pull apart the jackfruit, it takes on a texture similar to shredded crab meat. Oh, and it's a healthful source of vitamin C, potassium, and dietary fiber, too—so dip away!

Preheat the oven to 375°F.

Put the jackfruit into a bowl. Using two forks or your hands, shred the larger pieces until the jackfruit has the texture of shredded lump crabmeat; set aside.

In another bowl, combine the Cream Cheeze, Mayonnaise, two-thirds of the sliced scallions, the lemon zest and juice, nutritional yeast, Worcestershire sauce, seafood seasoning, hot sauce, garlic powder, and season with salt and pepper. Mix well. Fold the jackfruit into the cream cheeze mixture and transfer to a 1-quart baking dish. Sprinkle the bread crumbs on top.

Bake for 35 to 40 minutes, or until the dip is bubbly and the bread crumbs are golden.

Allow to cool for 5 minutes. Garnish with the remaining sliced scallions and serve with crackers.

NACHO *AVERAGE* NACHOS

I love a towering platter of nachos with an obnoxious amount of toppings. It's the perfect combination of spice and textures, no utensils needed! My easy "all in a blender" homemade queso turns cashews into an explosively flavorful cheesy sauce that gets depth from mild jalapeño, smoky chipotle chiles, and good-quality salt (like pink Himalayan salt) to counteract the cashews' sweetness. Finish it off with the zest and juice of a lime. If you are here for this kind of fierce flavor, run—don't walk!—to your pantry.

FOR THE QUESO

2 carrots, scrubbed and trimmed (no need to peel), coarsely chopped

1 chipotle chile in adobo sauce

1 jalapeño, stemmed and seeded, or 8 slices pickled jalapeño

2 garlic cloves

2 cups unsweetened, unflavored plant-based milk

2 cups raw cashews, soaked and drained (see page 35)

¼ cup nutritional yeast

1 tablespoon onion powder

1 teaspoon smoked paprika

2 teaspoons fine pink Himalayan salt, or to taste

½ teaspoon ground cumin

1 teaspoon garlic powder

1 teaspoon chili powder

½ teaspoon ground turmeric

¼ teaspoon ground black pepper

Zest and juice of 1 lime

SERVES 8

FOR THE NACHOS

1 (16-ounce) bag tortilla chips

2 cups cooked beans (black, pinto, red, or chili beans, rinsed and drained, if canned), or refried beans, warmed

2 cups Walnut Chorizo (page 105), warmed

3 cups chopped romaine lettuce

2 tomatoes, seeded and diced

Optional garnishes: Pickled jalapeños, pickled or fresh sliced red onion, chopped fresh cilantro, diced avocado and/or guacamole, Brazil Nut Sour Cream (page 57), grilled and diced pineapple (yes, so good!), sliced scallions (green and white parts)

TIP:

I usually add 1 chipotle and 1 seeded jalapeño to the queso and it's mild enough for even my kids. If you're a heat monster, feel free to add more. For a deeper, more fermented taste, add 1 heaping teaspoon white miso paste.

MAKE THE QUESO: In a high-speed blender, combine the carrots, chipotle chile, jalapeño, garlic, milk, cashews, nutritional yeast, onion powder, paprika, salt, cumin, garlic powder, chili powder, turmeric, and black pepper. Blend on high until completely smooth and the exterior of the blender is warm, 2 to 3 minutes. Add the lime zest and juice and blend for 10 seconds. Taste for consistency and flavor. Adjust the seasoning, if necessary.

Use immediately or store in an airtight container in the refrigerator for up to 1 week, or in the freezer for up to 6 months.

MAKE THE NACHOS: Arrange half of the tortilla chips on a large sheet pan or platter. Top with half of the queso, beans, and Walnut Chorizo. Add the remaining tortilla chips, beans, Walnut Chorizo, and queso.

Top with the lettuce, tomato, and any garnishes (if using). Serve immediately.

GET CREATIVE!

Swap out tortilla chips for roasted potatoes to make "potachos" just like the ones you saw in *The Game Changers*. Mix queso with cooked pasta and cooked plant-based ground "meat" for an excellent stove-top taco mac flavored with Taco Seasoning (page 86). Queso is also great drizzled over roasted vegetables or loaded baked potatoes.

BUFFALO
CHIK'N TACOS
with Kale & Avocado-Lime Ranch Slaw

8 ounces soy curls
(see page 37)

3 tablespoons plant-based
butter

1 cup hot sauce (I like
Frank's RedHot Sauce)

1 bunch kale (any variety),
stems discarded, leaves
thinly sliced crosswise

½ small head red cabbage,
cored and shredded

3 scallions (green and
white parts), thinly sliced

1¼ cups Avocado-Lime
Ranch Dressing (page 67)

2 tablespoons neutral
oil, such as avocado or
grapeseed

12 (6-inch) corn tortillas,
warmed

Chopped fresh cilantro, for
garnish

MAKES 12 TACOS

My son, King-Elias, always reminds me, "Mom, it's Tuesday." That's his way of asking for tacos. Since he was three years old, he has also loved spicy Buffalo sauce (just like his mama!), so eventually I had the idea to combine his favorite dishes into one. It was a true moment of satisfaction for him, me—and even Derrick! For those who can't handle *caliente,* the slaw adds freshness, and the avocado and ranch dressing counteract the heat. Do yourself a favor and make the soy curls up to 2 days in advance. The heroic Buffalo sauce gets soaked into the curls, leaving them tasting heavenly.

In a small bowl, cover the soy curls with hot water and soak for about 15 minutes, until rehydrated. Drain and gently squeeze out any excess water.

To make the Buffalo sauce, combine the butter and hot sauce in a small saucepan. Heat over medium until the butter melts, whisking to combine. Remove from the heat and set aside to cool.

In a large bowl, combine the kale, cabbage, and scallions. Add the Avocado-Lime Ranch Dressing and toss to coat. Refrigerate until serving, or for up to 24 hours.

Heat the oil in a large nonstick skillet over medium-high heat. When the oil is hot and shimmering, add the soy curls and sauté, tossing occasionally, for 4 to 5 minutes, until lightly browned. Pour the Buffalo sauce over the soy curls, stirring to coat.

Divide the soy curls among the tortillas. Top with the slaw, garnish with cilantro, and serve.

GET CREATIVE!
You can also use the marinated soy curls as a filling for quesadillas loaded with plant-based cheese, burritos, a Buffalo chik'n sandwich, or some fun Buffalo-filled no-egg rolls dunked into Classic Herby Ranch Dressing (page 66).

LEMON-PEPPER *WINGZ*

FOR THE WINGZ

1 cup all-purpose gluten-free flour blend (see Note) or all-purpose flour

1 tablespoon cornstarch

1 tablespoon nutritional yeast

1 tablespoon lemon-pepper seasoning

2 teaspoons garlic powder

2 teaspoons onion powder

½ teaspoon fine pink Himalayan salt, or to taste

1½ cups unsweetened, unflavored plant-based milk

1 head cauliflower, cored and separated into florets (4 to 4½ cups)

Nonstick cooking spray for baking or neutral oil for frying (I prefer rice bran oil)

SERVES 4

FOR THE SAUCE

½ cup plant-based butter

2 lemons

¼ cup nutritional yeast

4 garlic cloves, minced

1 teaspoon ground black pepper

½ teaspoon fine pink Himalayan salt, or to taste

NOTE:

If using a gluten-free flour blend, be sure your flour blend contains rice flour, which gives the wingz a nice crispy coating.

Derrick and I have always loved entertaining, whether that means family members from out of town, friends, neighbors, or teammates trying to score a home-cooked meal—all are welcome. These extra-saucy lemon-pepper wings made with cauliflower instead of poultry have always been a fan favorite. Derrick calls them a "palate destroyer," because they're so packed with flavor that anything else you eat after tastes less desirable—sorry! I make mine with so much zesty, buttery sauce they're known as "wet wingz" in our house.

MAKE THE WINGZ: In a large bowl, whisk together the flour, cornstarch, nutritional yeast, lemon-pepper seasoning, garlic powder, onion powder, and salt. Whisk in the milk until the batter is smooth. If using gluten-free flour, let the batter sit for 5 minutes to thicken. Make sure the cauliflower is dry after washing to ensure the coating sticks, then add it to the batter and toss well to coat.

TO BAKE THE CAULIFLOWER: Preheat the oven to 425°F. Line a large sheet pan with parchment paper and lightly coat with nonstick cooking spray. Transfer the florets to the prepared pan, leaving lots of space between the pieces (to allow cauliflower to crisp). Bake for 20 to 25 minutes, or until golden and crispy.

TO FRY THE CAULIFLOWER: In a large pot or Dutch oven, heat 2 inches of oil to 350°F. Preheat the oven to 200°F or the warming setting. Line a sheet pan with paper towels. Working with a few pieces at a time,

recipe continues >>

add the cauliflower to the hot oil. (Don't fry too much cauliflower at once, which will lower the temperature of the oil and result in soggy, oil-soaked cauliflower.) Fry until golden and crispy, 2 to 3 minutes per side. Transfer the fried cauliflower to the prepared pan and keep warm in the oven. Let the temperature of the oil return to 350°F before frying each batch, adding more oil if necessary.

MAKE THE SAUCE: Warm the butter in a small saucepan set over the lowest heat setting. Let it soften slightly, but do not melt to a liquefied state. Once the butter is just starting to melt, remove the pan from the heat. Zest the lemons into the pan, then halve the lemons and squeeze the juice into the pan. Add the nutritional yeast, garlic, pepper, and salt. Whisk to a creamy consistency.

In a large bowl, gently toss the cauliflower with sauce. Transfer to a serving platter and serve immediately.

GET CREATIVE!

Use the lemon-pepper sauce on roasted potatoes or chickpeas, pasta, grilled tofu, or just about any steamed or roasted vegetable. Or, make one of my favorite dinners, grilled cauliflower steaks: cut a head of cauliflower vertically into ½-inch-thick "steaks," brush with oil, grill on both sides, then drizzle the lemon-pepper sauce over them before serving. Make sure to serve with Creamy Mashed Potatoes (page 226) or steamed rice to soak up the yummy sauce.

PASTELILLOS

with Saffron Aïoli

¾ cup plus 1 tablespoon water

¼ cup uncooked red quinoa

¼ cup uncooked black or green lentils

1 tablespoon neutral oil, such as avocado or grapeseed

½ small green bell pepper, stemmed, seeded, and finely diced

½ small Spanish or yellow onion, finely diced

1 garlic clove, minced

2 tablespoons Puerto Rican Sofrito (page 74), or about 1 frozen cube of sofrito from an ice tray

¼ cup pitted Spanish Manzanilla olives, chopped

3 tablespoons tomato paste

½ teaspoon sazón seasoning (use a brand that doesn't contain MSG) (see page 38)

¼ teaspoon adobo seasoning (see page 38)

⅛ teaspoon fine pink Himalayan salt, or to taste

1 recipe Flaky Pie Dough (page 253), chilled

All-purpose flour, for rolling

Nonstick cooking spray for baking or neutral oil for frying (I prefer rice bran oil)

FOR THE SAFFRON AÏOLI

1½ cups Mayonnaise (page 53) or any plant-based mayonnaise

Juice of ½ lime

½ teaspoon fine pink Himalayan salt, or to taste

¼ teaspoon ground white pepper

¼ teaspoon ground saffron or a pinch of saffron threads

¼ teaspoon sweet or smoked paprika

⅛ teaspoon ground turmeric

1 garlic clove, peeled

Eating these Puerto Rican hand pies—usually stuffed with meat—takes me right back to my childhood. I got so excited when my mother made them and I'd often "help" her roll tiny scraps of dough (she was really just getting me out of her hair!). I truly thought I was doing big things. Now when I make them, I do the same thing with my daughter, Love Lee. I give her a tiny piece of dough and let her do her thing, whether that's rolling it one hundred times or stretching it into different shapes (her piece is strictly for fun—after all that handling, the dough would yield a seriously tough pastry shell). This recipe is very close to what my Puerto Rican mother makes, minus the beef: I replace it with a quinoa and lentil filling for a meaty texture and keep the classic pastelillo ingredients like salty Manzanilla olives, sazón, and adobo seasonings, all charged by the flavors of sofrito. Frying pastelillos is a Puerto Rican tradition; however, I've included a baking option as well.

MAKE THE PASTELILLOS: In a small saucepan, combine ¾ cup of water with the quinoa and lentils and bring to a boil. Cover and cook on low for 15 to 18 minutes, until the lentils are slightly tender but not mushy. Drain off any excess water.

Meanwhile, heat a large skillet over medium-high heat. Add the oil. Once the oil is hot and shimmering, add the bell pepper and onion. Sauté for 3 to 4 minutes, until the onion is slightly translucent. Add the garlic and sofrito and sauté for an additional 2 minutes. Stir in the lentil-quinoa mixture, olives, tomato paste, sazón seasoning, adobo seasoning,

MAKES 12 HAND PIES

recipe continues >>

salt, and the remaining 1 tablespoon water. Cook for a few minutes to allow all these flavors to come together. Turn off the heat. Transfer to a medium bowl and set aside to cool completely before filling the pastry, at least 30 minutes. (The filling can be refrigerated, covered, for up to 3 days. Take it out of the refrigerator 10 minutes before using.)

Lightly flour your work surface and rolling pin and fill a small bowl with water. Line a sheet pan with parchment paper and if baking, lightly coat with nonstick cooking spray.

Roll the dough to a thickness of ⅛ inch. Using a 4-inch lid or ring mold, cut the dough into rounds as close together as possible (to minimize scraps). Gather the scraps and reroll them to make 12 rounds total. Discard any remaining scraps.

Working with one dough round at a time (cover the remaining with a damp towel), dampen the top outer edge with a little water. Place 1 packed tablespoon of filling in the center of the dough circle. Fold the dough in half. Press around the edges with the tines of a fork to seal the dough. Transfer the pastelillo to the prepared sheet pan. Repeat with the remaining pastry rounds and filling. (Save any remaining filling for tacos or to add to a Pro-Bowl, page 152.) Refrigerate the pastelillos for 20 minutes to firm up the dough and filling.

MAKE THE SAFFRON AÏOLI: In a small bowl, combine the mayonnaise, lime juice, salt, pepper, ground saffron, paprika, and turmeric. Using a Microplane, grate the garlic into the bowl (make sure to give the Microplane a good whack to release all of the garlic). Whisk until completely combined. Cover and refrigerate until serving.

TO BAKE THE PASTELILLOS: Preheat the oven to 400°F. Bake on the parchment-lined sheet pan until crispy and golden, 30 to 35 minutes.

TO FRY THE PASTELILLOS: Fill a deep skillet or Dutch oven with 1½ inches of oil and heat to 375°F. Line a sheet pan with paper towels. Fry a few pastelillos at a time until golden brown and crispy, 1½ to 2½ minutes per side. Use tongs or a slotted spoon to transfer them to the paper towel–lined pan to drain. Repeat with the remaining pastelillos. Let the temperature of the oil return to 375°F before frying each batch, adding more oil if necessary.

Serve the pastelillos with the aïoli.

IT'S FRY-YAY!

SOUTHERN POUTINE WITH WHISKEY
CARAMELIZED ONIONS, PAGE 178

BUFFALO CHEEZY SWEET POTATO FRIES,
PAGE 179

SOUTHERN *POUTINE*

with Whiskey Caramelized Onions

Fries are always a crowd-pleaser, but fries topped with a rich brown gravy and cheese? Well, that is a party on a plate. You can thank Canada's province of Quebec for this saucy French fry sensation, and you can thank *me* for inventing a Nashville-inspired, plant-based version layered with spices, sweet caramelized onions, and a splash of Tennessee whiskey for good measure.

1 recipe (2 tablespoons) Smoke Signal (page 87)

3 tablespoons nutritional yeast

1 cup water

7 ounces extra-firm tofu (about ½ block), pressed (see page 101)

1 tablespoon neutral oil, such as avocado or grapeseed

1 small yellow onion, halved and sliced

¼ cup Tennessee whiskey

1 recipe Chips (page 195), or 2 pounds frozen French fries

1 tablespoon BBQ Seasoning (page 83)

1 recipe Savory Brown Gravy (page 91), warmed

¼ cup chopped fresh flat-leaf parsley, for garnish

¼ cup Shiitake Bae'con (page 88), or any cooked plant-based bacon (optional), coarsely chopped

SERVES 6

In a medium bowl, whisk together the Smoke Signal, nutritional yeast, and water.

Crumble the tofu into the marinade and toss to coat. Cover and marinate at room temperature for at least 1 hour, or up to overnight in the refrigerator. Make sure to bring to room temperature for serving.

Heat a medium skillet over medium-high heat. Add the oil. Once the oil is hot and shimmering, add the onion and cook, stirring occasionally, for 8 to 10 minutes, until the onions start to caramelize and are light brown. Add the whiskey and stir, scraping up any browned bits from the bottom of the pan. Cook until the whiskey evaporates, 1 to 2 minutes. Remove from the heat and set aside.

Make the Chips or prepare frozen French fries according to package directions. While hot, sprinkle the fries with the BBQ Seasoning.

To assemble, drain the tofu. Transfer the chips or fries to a serving platter and top with a generous amount of gravy, the caramelized whiskey onions, and smoky tofu curds. Garnish with parsley and bae'con (if using) and serve immediately.

BUFFALO CHEEZY *SWEET POTATO* FRIES

3 tablespoons neutral oil, such as avocado or grapeseed

4 large sweet potatoes, peeled and cut into ¼- to ½-inch-thick fries or wedges

Fine pink Himalayan salt and ground black pepper

3 tablespoons plant-based butter

½ cup hot sauce (I like Frank's RedHot Sauce)

½ recipe Buffalo cheeze sauce (from Buffalo Mac & Cheezy, page 194), warmed

½ recipe Classic Herby Ranch Dressing (page 66)

3 celery stalks, thinly sliced

2 carrots, shredded

¼ cup minced fresh flat-leaf parsley

SERVES 6

TIP:
Sweet potatoes don't get crisp the same way russet potatoes do when roasted or fried because of their higher sugar content. The method of placing them on a very hot sheet pan helps to crisp up the exterior quickly without making them mushy. The oil also helps build crispiness. The fries can be made in an air fryer, too.

GET CREATIVE!
Try topping with Buffalo soy curls (page 168) for added protein and meaty texture. Feel free to swap Tater Tots for sweet potato fries or roasted potatoes, which will hold up longer without getting soggy if you are transporting this dish.

One thing my NFL clients did not let me waiver on was Burger Day, which was every Friday. I needed something to accompany those huge, juicy burgers. These sweet potato fries created the perfect complement with their contrast of sweet and heat. Sweet potatoes are also a good source of potassium and magnesium and are rich in vitamins C and B_6—so you're getting a good dose of nutrition with your indulgence.

Preheat the oven to 425°F. Place a large sheet pan in the oven while it preheats.

In a large bowl, drizzle the oil over the sweet potatoes and season with salt and pepper. Toss to coat. Carefully remove the hot pan from the oven and arrange the potatoes on the sheet pan in a single layer. Bake for 45 to 50 minutes, stirring halfway through, or until crisp on the outside and tender on the inside.

To make the Buffalo sauce, combine the butter and hot sauce in a small saucepan. Heat over medium until the butter melts, whisking to combine. Remove from heat and set aside.

To assemble, ladle about ½ cup Buffalo cheeze sauce onto a serving platter. Place the fries on top of the sauce. Spoon some of the Buffalo sauce over the fries, then drizzle with more cheeze sauce and ranch dressing. Garnish with celery, carrots, and parsley and serve.

PLAYMAKING MAINS

GOCHUJANG JACKFRUIT NOODLE BOWL, PAGE 215

VEGETABLE PHO

FOR THE BROTH

6 quarts (24 cups) water

1 head garlic, halved horizontally

3 carrots, scrubbed, trimmed, and cut into large chunks

2- to 3-inch piece ginger, scrubbed, skin left on

1 large yellow onion, halved, first layer of skin removed

1 tablespoon fine pink Himalayan salt, or to taste

2 tablespoons rock sugar or turbinado sugar

1 cup Fyshy Sauce (page 65), or ¼ cup soy sauce or tamari (if you're gluten-free)

½ bunch cilantro stems, leaves reserved for garnish

5 whole star anise

2 whole cloves

2 bay leaves

1 black cardamom pod, lightly crushed

1 cinnamon stick

1 teaspoon fennel seeds

1 teaspoon coriander seeds

1 teaspoon whole black peppercorns

SERVES 10

FOR SERVING
(USE ANY OR ALL)

Noodles: 2 ounces dried pho rice noodles (thin rice noodles) per person, cooked according to package directions

Tofu: marinated or Roasted Tofu (page 98)

Lime wedges

Vegetables: Lightly steamed broccoli florets, sautéed mushrooms, shredded carrots, thinly sliced serrano rings, thinly sliced white onion, mung bean sprouts, sliced scallions (green and white parts)

Herbs: Thai basil, cilantro leaves

Condiments: Sriracha, chile paste (I like sambal oelek), hoisin sauce

Little Saigon in Orange County is the largest and oldest Vietnamese community in the country. I used to make weekend visits there to explore, eat, and shop with my friend Suzie Vuong. It was there that I experienced my first bowl of pho, a soup consisting of a rich, intensely flavorful broth made with toasted spices (think star anise, fennel seeds, coriander seeds, cardamom, cinnamon stick, and cloves), served with rice noodles and fresh aromatics like Thai basil, mint, and/or cilantro. I was struck by how flavorful a broth could be and quickly became obsessed. When I couldn't go to all my favorite spots any more since they used only beef or chicken stock (always be sure to ask!), I created a vegan version that is absolutely worth obsessing over.

MAKE THE BROTH: Pour the water into a very large pot and bring to a boil over high heat. Meanwhile, set an oven rack in the middle position and preheat the broiler. Arrange the garlic, carrots, ginger, and onion in a single layer on a large sheet pan and broil for 10 minutes, turning the vegetables halfway through the cooking time. Brown, but do not burn, the vegetables.

Once the vegetables are browned, remove them from the oven. Transfer the ginger to a cutting board and smash it with the flat side of a knife. Add the smashed ginger and broiled vegetables to the boiling water along with the salt, sugar, Fyshy Sauce, and cilantro stems. Reduce the heat so the broth simmers while you toast the spices.

recipe continues >>

In a large dry skillet, combine the star anise, cloves, bay leaves, cardamom, cinnamon stick, fennel seeds, coriander seeds, and peppercorns. Toast over medium-high heat, stirring occasionally, until the spices become fragrant, 2 to 3 minutes. Transfer the toasted spices to the broth. Simmer, uncovered, until the broth is rich in color and the flavors have released from the aromatics, about 1 hour.

Remove the soup from the heat. Cool, then strain and discard the vegetables and spices. Add more salt, if desired. Store in a tightly sealed container in the refrigerator for up to 1 week, or portion it into pint-size deli containers and freeze for up to 3 months. Thaw and reheat as needed.

TO SERVE: Reheat 2 cups of broth per serving and pour into each bowl. Serve with the cooked rice noodles and desired garnishes.

TIP:

Traditional pho broth calls for both fish sauce (which is salty) and salt. This helps give it a deep flavor. I use 1 tablespoon of salt to start. This is one of those recipes where you shouldn't be reluctant to use salt.

GET CREATIVE!

Add roasted vegetables and/or marinated plant-based proteins like tofu or mushrooms in place of the traditional meat. Use *The* Marinade (page 73) or Quick Stir-Fry Sauce (page 64) as the base of the marinade, then add lemongrass and tamari or soy sauce. Roast according to the directions on page 44.

CHICKPEA *TIKKA* MASALA

FOR THE SPICE BLEND

2 teaspoons fine pink Himalayan salt, or to taste

1 teaspoon garam masala

1 teaspoon ground coriander

1 teaspoon ground cumin

½ teaspoon ground turmeric

½ teaspoon sweet paprika

¼ teaspoon ground Indian red chile powder, such as Kashmiri or deggi mirch, or substitute ¼ teaspoon ground cayenne pepper and another ¼ teaspoon sweet paprika

SERVES 6 TO 8

FOR THE TIKKA MASALA

3 tablespoons butter-flavored coconut oil, such as Nutiva, or a neutral oil, such as avocado or grapeseed

1 large yellow onion, finely diced

1½-inch piece ginger, peeled and minced or grated

3 garlic cloves, minced

1 (28-ounce) can tomato purée

1½ cups vegetable broth or water

2 teaspoons coconut sugar

3 carrots, diced

2 cups cooked chickpeas (rinsed and drained, if canned)

2 cups cauliflower florets

1 cup fresh or frozen okra, diced (no need to thaw)

1 cup cut fresh or frozen green beans (2-inch pieces; no need to thaw if frozen)

½ cup fresh or frozen peas (no need to thaw)

1 cup Cashew Heavy Cream (page 55)

½ bunch cilantro, chopped, plus more for garnish

Hot cooked brown or white basmati rice

Before I cut out meat, I would frequent Indian restaurants where I could be found chowing down on bowls of chicken tikka masala, sopping up every last bit of its creamy, spiced tomato gravy with a basket or two of freshly made naan. Luckily, one of the many great things about Indian food is that it can be easily adapted to become vegan. My Cashew Heavy Cream achieves the richness of the dairy and ghee that are classically used, and chickpeas soak up all the spices beautifully. I love serving this with steamed white or brown basmati rice and vegan naan or roti (some ready-made frozen options are vegan; be sure to check the label).

MAKE THE SPICE BLEND: In a small bowl, combine the salt, garam masala, coriander, cumin, turmeric, paprika, and chile powder. Set aside.

MAKE THE TIKKA MASALA: Heat a large pot or Dutch oven over medium-high heat and add the oil. Once the oil is hot and shimmering, add the onion and sauté for 2 minutes. Add the ginger and garlic and sauté, stirring often, until fragrant, about 30 seconds. Reduce the heat to medium and add the spice blend. Toast the spices until fragrant, 1 to 2 minutes, stirring every few seconds to prevent burning. Add the tomato purée and cook, stirring, until fragrant and lightly caramelized, about 1 minute. Add the broth and sugar. Stir until smooth and all of the ingredients are well combined.

recipe continues >>

Add the carrots, chickpeas, cauliflower, okra, and green beans. Increase the heat to medium-high and bring to a simmer. Cover, reduce the heat to medium-low, and cook until the vegetables are tender, 20 to 30 minutes, stirring occasionally to prevent the vegetables from sticking and to help them cook evenly. Stir in the peas.

Slowly whisk the Cashew Heavy Cream into the tomato gravy. Simmer, uncovered, for an additional 5 minutes to allow the flavors and cream to marry, stirring frequently. Add the chopped cilantro and adjust the seasoning, if necessary.

Serve over basmati rice. Garnish with additional cilantro.

TIP:
You never know how long the spices you buy at the store have been sitting on the shelves. Wake up their flavor! Toast them to unlock their essential oils and make them extra potent and fragrant. Keep the heat low and move the spices around with a wooden spoon or spatula to prevent burning. Toast until they smell fragrant—time depends on your pan and stove—then remove from the heat to prevent them from burning.

GET CREATIVE!
Try using other vegetables, such as Yukon gold potatoes, sweet potatoes, broccoli, asparagus, or zucchini. Or add roasted (see page 98) and cubed firm tofu or plant-based chik'n for added protein.

VEGGIES & DUMPLINGS

When my client Miley Cyrus told me she hadn't eaten chicken and dumplings—her favorite dish—for more than four years since she'd gone vegan, I thought, "Easy fix!" I swapped in my Butta Biscuit dough to make the rich dumplings she craved, then I simmered them until plump and tender in a comforting, herbaceous vegetable stew. It quickly became her new favorite. She loved my version so much that she requested it to be on her Southern classics–studded wedding menu. All of her carnivorous guests could not believe it was vegan—her grandma thought we were pulling a fast one on her!

1 tablespoon neutral oil, such as avocado or grapeseed

1 large yellow onion, diced

4 celery stalks, diced

3 carrots, diced

2 garlic cloves, minced

1 teaspoon poultry seasoning

2 teaspoons fine pink Himalayan salt, or to taste

½ teaspoon ground black pepper, or to taste

5 cups Chik'n Broth (page 50) or any vegetable broth

SERVES 6

2 cups chopped plant-based chik'n, soy curls (see page 37), or cooked chickpeas (optional)

1 cup cut fresh or frozen green beans (1-inch pieces)

1 cup fresh or frozen green peas (no need to thaw)

2 sprigs fresh thyme

1 sprig fresh rosemary

1 bay leaf

All-purpose flour, for shaping

1 recipe Butta Biscuit dough (page 94), unrolled

½ cup coarsely chopped fresh flat-leaf parsley, for garnish

Heat a large pot or Dutch oven over medium heat. Add the oil. Once the oil is hot and shimmering, add the onion and cook, stirring, until slightly translucent, 3 to 4 minutes. Add the celery and carrots and sauté to slightly soften, about 2 minutes. Then add the garlic, stirring occasionally, until fragrant, about 30 seconds. Season with poultry seasoning, salt, and pepper. Add the broth, plant-based chik'n (if using), green beans, peas, thyme, rosemary, and bay leaf. Stir well and bring the broth to a simmer over medium-low heat.

Meanwhile, lightly flour your work surface. Roll out the biscuit dough to a thickness of ½ inch. Use a knife or dough cutter to cut the dough into 1- by 3-inch pieces. Arrange the dough on the surface of the simmering broth, trying to keep the dumplings as separate as possible.

Reduce the heat to low. Cover the pot and gently simmer, undisturbed, for 45 minutes, or until the dumplings are firm and cooked through and the broth is thickened into an opaque gravy. Give everything a gentle stir to submerge all of the dumplings. Remove from the heat. Cover and let stand for 10 minutes. Remove and discard the thyme, rosemary, and bay leaf before serving. Divide among bowls and garnish with parsley.

TIP:
Don't brush off too much of the flour from the biscuit dough—just put the dough as is into the pot. The excess flour on the dumplings will help the broth thicken into a gravy-like stew—and that's just what you want.

GET CREATIVE!
Add fresh chopped herbs, such as rosemary, oregano, chives, thyme, basil, or flat-leaf parsley, to the biscuit dough for an extra savory herb dumpling.

CAULIFLOWER MARBELLA

This is my vegan version of the famous recipe that appeared in *The Silver Palate Cookbook* by Julee Rosso and the late Sheila Lukins. The savory-sweet marinade made of vinegar, brown sugar, garlic, sweet prunes, briny capers, and meaty green olives turns into a rich sauce as it bakes with versatile cauliflower and a splash of white wine. This makes a beautiful family-style meal that can be served straight from the gratin dish it's baked in, with creamy whipped mashed potatoes on the side.

1½ cups pitted prunes

1 cup pitted green olives

½ cup extra-virgin olive oil

½ cup red wine vinegar

¼ cup capers, drained

6 bay leaves

10 garlic cloves, crushed

2 tablespoons fresh oregano, coarsely chopped, or 2 teaspoons dried

1 teaspoon fine pink Himalayan salt, or to taste

½ teaspoon ground black pepper

½ teaspoon crushed red pepper flakes

6 cups cauliflower florets (about 1 large head)

¼ cup (packed) light or dark brown sugar

¼ cup dry white wine

Creamy Mashed Potatoes (page 226), for serving

3 tablespoons chopped fresh flat-leaf parsley, for garnish (optional)

SERVES 6

In a large bowl, combine the prunes, olives, olive oil, vinegar, capers, bay leaves, garlic, oregano, ½ teaspoon of the salt, ¼ teaspoon of the black pepper, and the red pepper flakes. Whisk until well combined. Add the cauliflower and toss until coated. Cover and marinate in the refrigerator for 1 to 6 hours, stirring halfway through the marinating time.

Preheat the oven to 400°F.

Transfer the cauliflower and marinade to a roasting pan or glass casserole dish. Sprinkle the brown sugar, the remaining ½ teaspoon salt, and remaining ¼ teaspoon black pepper over the cauliflower (no need to stir). Pour the wine around the cauliflower. Bake for 35 to 45 minutes, until the cauliflower is tender with browned edges and the sauce has thickened and caramelized.

Remove from oven and let cool for 10 minutes. Discard the bay leaves. Serve over the Creamy Mashed Potatoes and topped with the pan sauce and parsley (if using).

MAC & CHEEZY THREE WAYS

After I debuted my mac and cheeze, it immediately became a favorite for every single one of my clients. I'd make a pan for the Titans' Brett Kern and his wife Tiffany, and I'd be sure Miley Cyrus had enough to get her through a weekend. Then I would cook up a double batch for my family so they wouldn't get jealous! There's the original, fan-favorite recipe for Truffle Mac & Cheezy. After getting so many requests, I was inspired to make new variations: smoky Bae'con and spicy Buffalo. No matter which one I'm whipping up, I start with a cashew cheeze sauce made in the blender so there's no need for a roux—or another pot. Then I bake the mac and cheeze until golden brown and bubbly and finish with something crunchy like toasty bread crumbs or Shiitake Bae'con pieces. Try all three versions!

TIP:
Do not overbake Mac & Cheezy. Just bake it in the oven long enough to thicken the sauce, create golden edges, and bring the flavors of the dish together. If you overbake it, chances are the dish will be dry.

GET CREATIVE!
There are so many fancy pasta shapes available. Try a beautiful pasta, such as conchiglie (shells), pipe rigate ("smoking pipes"), or fusilli (also called rotini or corkscrew pasta)—not only for presentation, but also because those shapes can hold pockets of sauce!

Truffle Mac & Cheezy

FOR THE TOPPING

1 cup panko bread crumbs or homemade bread crumbs (page 46)

2 tablespoons nutritional yeast

2 tablespoons plant-based butter, melted

½ teaspoon fine pink Himalayan salt, or to taste

2 tablespoons truffle oil

FOR THE MAC

1 pound elbow macaroni or shell pasta

Avocado oil or extra-virgin olive oil

FOR THE CHEEZE SAUCE

4 cups raw cashews, soaked and drained (see page 35)

3½ cups unsweetened, unflavored plant-based milk

¼ cup nutritional yeast

2 garlic cloves

1 tablespoon onion powder

1 tablespoon truffle salt, or to taste

1 teaspoon garlic powder

½ teaspoon ground black pepper

SERVES 6 TO 8

MAKE THE TOPPING: In a medium bowl, combine the bread crumbs, nutritional yeast, melted butter, and salt; set aside.

Preheat the oven to 375°F. Lightly oil a 3-quart baking dish.

MAKE THE MAC: Cook the pasta in salted water according to the package directions, minus 2 minutes of cooking time (leaving a slightly undercooked pasta allows it to continue cooking in the oven without getting mushy); drain. Toss with a little bit of oil to prevent sticking. Transfer the cooked pasta to the prepared baking dish.

MAKE THE CHEEZE SAUCE: In a high-speed blender, combine the drained cashews, milk, nutritional yeast, garlic, onion powder, truffle salt, garlic powder, and pepper. Blend on high until completely smooth and the exterior of the blender is warm, 2 to 3 minutes.

Pour the cheeze sauce over the pasta and stir to make sure the sauce is evenly distributed. Sprinkle with the topping. Bake for 15 to 20 minutes, until the mac and cheeze is hot throughout and the bread crumbs are golden brown. Remove from the oven and allow to cool for 5 to 8 minutes. Drizzle the truffle oil on top, right before serving hot. (Never add truffle oil before baking, as it will lose its delicate flavor.)

Bae'con Mac & Cheezy

Prepare the Mac & Cheezy as directed for the truffle version, but omit the bread crumb topping and truffle oil. Substitute 1 tablespoon fine pink Himalayan salt, or to taste, for the truffle salt in the cheeze sauce. Add 1 recipe (2 tablespoons) Smoke Signal (page 87) to the blender with the other cheeze sauce ingredients. Bake as directed. Top with 1 cup coarsely chopped Shiitake Bae'con (page 88) or any crispy cooked plant-based bacon pieces before serving.

Buffalo Mac & Cheezy

Prepare the Mac & Cheezy as directed for the truffle version, but omit the bread crumb topping and truffle oil. Substitute 1 tablespoon fine pink Himalayan salt, or to taste, for the truffle salt in the cheeze sauce. Add ¼ cup hot sauce (I like Frank's RedHot Sauce), 2 teaspoons sweet paprika, ½ teaspoon ground celery seed, and 1 teaspoon dry mustard to the blender with the other cheeze sauce ingredients. Bake as directed. Combine ½ cup hot sauce with 2 tablespoons melted plant-based butter. Before serving, drizzle the Buffalo sauce and ½ cup Classic Herby Ranch Dressing (page 66) over the baked Mac & Cheezy. Garnish with ½ cup shredded carrot and ½ cup thinly sliced celery.

BEER-BATTERED FYSH & CHIPS

with Tartar Sauce

FOR THE TARTAR SAUCE

1 cup Mayonnaise (page 53) or any plant-based mayonnaise

2 tablespoons sweet relish

1 tablespoon capers, drained and minced

1 teaspoon Dijon mustard

1 teaspoon vegan Worcestershire sauce

1 teaspoon fresh lemon juice

½ teaspoon hot sauce (I like Tabasco)

¼ teaspoon fine pink Himalayan salt, or to taste

¼ teaspoon ground black pepper, or to taste

FOR THE CHIPS

2 pounds Yukon gold or russet potatoes, unpeeled and cut into ¼- to ½-inch-thick sticks

Fine pink Himalayan salt and ground black pepper

SERVES 6

FOR THE FYSH

1 (12-ounce) bottle cold dark ale

1 cup rice flour

1 cup all-purpose flour or all-purpose gluten-free flour blend

1 tablespoon baking powder

2 teaspoons seafood seasoning (such as Old Bay)

2 teaspoons Nori Dust (page 38) or kelp powder

1 teaspoon fine pink Himalayan salt, or to taste

¼ teaspoon ground white pepper

½ cup water

Neutral oil for frying (I prefer rice bran oil)

2 (18-ounce) cans banana blossoms, drained and patted dry (6 whole blossoms)

Chopped fresh flat-leaf parsley, lemon wedges, and malt vinegar, for serving

Fysh fry at the Morgans'! I remember falling in love with fish and chips on my first visit to London, eons ago. Being a (former) seafood lover, it was only right I created a plant-based version. I wanted a crispy batter with snap and a malty beer flavor—just like the UK classic. Take note of the rice flour in the batter as this helps create a nice crisp crust when fried. But what is the fish? Banana blossoms! Also known as banana hearts, they have a flaky, meaty texture that truly mimics fish (see page 36). They're a gift from nature; I cannot take credit for the bountiful gifts from God. This is Derrick's favorite cheat meal, and it definitely scratches his seafood itch. Serve with splashes of malt vinegar (or hot sauce) and plenty of tartar sauce.

MAKE THE TARTAR SAUCE: In a small bowl, combine the mayonnaise, relish, capers, mustard, Worcestershire, lemon juice, hot sauce, salt, and pepper. Stir until well combined. Cover and refrigerate until serving.

PREP THE CHIPS: Place the cut potatoes in a large bowl and cover with ice and water. Chill in the refrigerator for 30 minutes.

PREP THE FYSH: In a large bowl, combine the ale, rice flour, all-purpose flour, baking powder, seafood seasoning, Nori Dust, salt, pepper, and water. Whisk until well combined.

Preheat the oven to 200°F or the warming setting. Line two large sheet pans with paper towels. In a large Dutch oven, heat 3 to 4 inches of oil to 375°F.

recipe continues >>

COOK THE FYSH: Banana blossoms are very delicate, so you need to be careful when handling them. Hold the blossom with both hands, dip it in the batter to generously coat all sides (do not let excess batter drip off; keep a thick coating), and then gently place it in the hot oil. Repeat with 2 or 3 blossoms at a time. (Don't fry too many at once, which would lower the temperature of the oil and result in soggy, oil-soaked fysh.) Fry on both sides until golden brown, 3 to 4 minutes total. Using tongs, transfer the fried blossoms to one of the paper towel-lined pans and keep warm in the oven. Let the temperature of the oil return to 375°F before frying each batch of fysh, adding more oil if necessary.

FRY THE CHIPS: Drain the potatoes in a strainer and thoroughly pat them dry. Add more oil to the pot used to fry the banana blossoms, if necessary, to return the oil to a depth of 3 to 4 inches. Heat to 375°F.

Working in small batches, fry the potatoes in the hot oil until golden and crispy, 3 to 4 minutes total, stirring and turning frequently. Using tongs, transfer the potatoes to the other paper towel-lined pan and season with salt and pepper immediately after removing them from the oil. Transfer the pan to the warm oven. Let the temperature of the oil return to 375°F before frying each batch, adding more oil, if necessary.

Serve the fysh and chips hot, garnished with parsley and with the tartar sauce, lemon wedges, and malt vinegar.

GET CREATIVE!

Try the fysh on a toasted bun with the tartar sauce or remoulade (page 201), crisp lettuce, and tomato slices for a delicious fysh sandwich.

LOBZTER PENNE ALLA VODKA

1 ounce dried lobster mushrooms (about 1 cup)

1 pound penne pasta or other tube pasta, such as rigatoni

5 tablespoons extra-virgin olive oil, avocado oil, or grapeseed oil

1 white or yellow onion, finely diced

2 garlic cloves, minced

¼ teaspoon crushed red pepper flakes

1 (6-ounce) can tomato paste

½ cup vodka

2 teaspoons fine pink Himalayan salt, or to taste

¼ teaspoon ground black pepper, or to taste

¼ cup dry white wine

1 cup Cashew Heavy Cream (page 55)

2 tablespoons nutritional yeast

½ cup homemade bread crumbs (see page 46) or panko bread crumbs (optional)

¼ cup thinly sliced fresh basil, for garnish

SERVES 6

If you're a pink vodka sauce fan, then you'll love this version, which is just as rich, creamy, and rosy as the one from your neighborhood trattoria. I use lobster mushrooms (see page 38), which have deep red and orange hues, a chewy texture, and a seafood-like essence. These beauties can be found at specialty stores and many online vendors—yes, including *that* one! The vodka works to balance the sweetness of the tomatoes and intensifies the aroma and flavor. Serve with Lemon Parm-y Kale Salad (page 139) or The Classic Caesar (page 140) and a loaf of warm crusty bread.

In a medium pot, pour boiling water over the mushrooms to cover completely. Cover and soak for 30 minutes to rehydrate the mushrooms. Drain and coarsely chop them into ½-inch pieces, if necessary. Set aside.

Salt a large pot of water and bring to a boil. Cook the pasta al dente according to the package directions. Reserve 2 cups of the pasta water, then drain the pasta and toss with 1 tablespoon of the oil to prevent sticking.

Meanwhile, heat a large pot or Dutch oven over medium heat. Add 3 tablespoons of the oil. Once the oil is hot and shimmering, add the onion and cook for 8 to 10 minutes, until softened and the edges are slightly browned. Add the garlic and sauté until fragrant, about 30 seconds.

recipe continues >>

Add the red pepper flakes and tomato paste. Cook, stirring constantly, until the tomato paste turns a dark red-brick color, about 2 minutes. Add the vodka and stir, scraping the bottom of the pan to deglaze and loosen any browned bits. Season with the salt and black pepper. Stir in 1 cup of the reserved pasta water. Reduce the heat to low and simmer until reduced by half, 3 to 5 minutes.

Meanwhile, heat a small skillet over medium-high heat. Add the remaining 1 tablespoon of oil. Once the oil is hot and shimmering, add the mushrooms and season lightly with salt and black pepper. Sauté for about 2 minutes to warm and slightly brown them. Add the wine and cook, stirring frequently, until the wine is reduced by half, 1 to 2 minutes. Remove from the heat. Set aside.

Add the Cashew Heavy Cream, nutritional yeast, and remaining 1 cup reserved pasta water to the tomato sauce and stir until well-combined. Add the pasta. Mix well and add the mushrooms. Cook for 1 to 2 minutes, just to bring everything together, then remove from the heat.

Divide among serving bowls. Garnish with bread crumbs (if using) and fresh basil.

TIP:
The Cashew Heavy Cream will thicken the sauce as it simmers. Add water a tablespoon at a time to thin the sauce, if needed.

GET CREATIVE!
Add 1 cup diced fresh or sun-dried tomatoes. Use the sauce on pizza, in lasagna, or as a sauce for meatballs (made from the Unbelievably Vegan Protein Burger mixture, page 217). You can also get creative with a different variety of pasta, or add some dried or chopped fresh herbs, such as oregano, thyme, parsley, or basil.

CREOLE
KRAB CAKES

with Tarragon Remoulade

FOR THE PATTIES

1 tablespoon neutral oil, such as avocado or grapeseed, plus more for searing

2 celery stalks, finely diced

½ yellow onion, finely diced

½ large red bell pepper, stemmed, seeded, and finely diced

3 garlic cloves, minced

1 teaspoon Creole-Cajun Seasoning (page 85)

2 teaspoons seafood seasoning (such as Old Bay)

1 (18-ounce) can banana blossoms (see page 36), drained

1 (14-ounce) can hearts of palm, drained

1½ cups cooked chickpeas (rinsed and drained, if canned)

2 scallions (green and white parts), finely chopped

¼ cup minced fresh flat-leaf parsley

1 heaping tablespoon Mayonnaise (page 53) or any plant-based mayonnaise

2 teaspoons fresh lemon juice

2 teaspoons Nori Dust (page 38) or kelp powder

2 teaspoons Creole mustard or Dijon mustard

1 to 2 teaspoons hot sauce (depending on how spicy you want it; I like Frank's RedHot)

½ teaspoon fine pink Himalayan salt, or to taste

¼ cup all-purpose flour or all-purpose gluten-free flour blend

FOR THE REMOULADE

1½ cups Mayonnaise (page 53) or any plant-based mayonnaise

1 scallion (green part only), minced

2 teaspoons chopped fresh tarragon, or 1 teaspoon dried

1 teaspoon hot sauce (I like Tabasco)

1 teaspoon Creole mustard or Dijon mustard

1 teaspoon fresh lemon juice

½ teaspoon lemon zest

½ teaspoon Creole-Cajun Seasoning (page 85)

¼ teaspoon smoked paprika

1 large garlic clove

The combination of flaky banana blossoms and hearts of palm create a great crab-free cake that is crispy on the outside and moist on the inside. Crab cakes are traditionally associated with the area surrounding the Chesapeake Bay, but I prefer the version from a little farther south, flavored with the holy trinity (onion, bell pepper, and celery) along with a good dose of Creole seasoning. I serve them with remoulade, which is similar to tartar sauce but has more of a kick, thanks to my favorite condiment—hot sauce—plus Creole seasoning and mustard.

MAKE THE PATTIES: Heat a large nonstick pan or cast-iron skillet over medium-high heat. Add the oil. Once the oil is hot and shimmering, add the celery, onion, and bell pepper. Sauté until the onion is translucent, 5 to 7 minutes. Add the garlic and sauté for another 30 seconds, or just until fragrant. Stir in the Creole-Cajun Seasoning and 1 teaspoon of the seafood seasoning, remove from the heat, and transfer to a bowl to cool. Wipe out the skillet and set aside.

Combine the banana blossoms, hearts of palm, and chickpeas in a food processor and pulse a few times so the mixture is coarse and has a lot of texture. (To mix by hand, smash the chickpeas in a bowl using a fork—keeping them slightly coarse—and coarsely chop the banana blossoms and hearts of palm by hand. Mix together.) Transfer the mixture to a large bowl.

MAKES 12 KRAB CAKES

recipe continues >>

Add the cooked and cooled vegetables, the scallions, parsley, mayonnaise, lemon juice, Nori Dust, mustard, hot sauce, remaining 1 teaspoon seafood seasoning, and salt. Using clean hands, gently mix until the ingredients are well combined. Add the flour and mix. Cover and chill in the refrigerator for 20 minutes to allow the mixture to cool and firm up before shaping.

Line a sheet pan with parchment paper. Using a ½-cup measure, scoop up the "krab" mixture and shape each portion into a 3-inch-wide and 1-inch-thick patty. Set on the prepared sheet pan. Repeat until all the mixture has been formed into patties. Chill the patties in the refrigerator for 30 to 40 minutes to allow the mixture to firm up and the flavors to meld, or freeze to cook at later time (see Note).

MAKE THE REMOULADE: In a medium bowl, combine the mayonnaise, scallion, tarragon, hot sauce, mustard, lemon juice and zest, Creole-Cajun Seasoning, and smoked paprika. Using a Microplane, grate the garlic into the bowl (make sure to give the Microplane a good whack to release all of the garlic). Whisk until smooth, cover, and chill in the refrigerator until you are ready to use it, or store in an airtight container in the refrigerator for up to 1 week.

When you are ready to cook, preheat the oven to 200°F or the warming setting. Line a large sheet pan with paper towels.

Heat a cast-iron skillet or nonstick pan over medium-high heat. Add a thin layer of oil. Once the oil is hot and shimmering, add the krab cakes in batches and cook until golden brown, 2 to 4 minutes per side, then drain on the prepared sheet pan. Transfer the sheet pan to the warm oven. Repeat with the remaining krab cakes, adding more oil as needed. Serve hot with the remoulade.

NOTE:
You can freeze the krab cakes on a parchment-lined pan. Once the patties are completely firm, transfer them to an airtight container or reusable plastic bag with parchment or waxed paper between each patty. These will keep for up to 6 months. To cook, slightly thaw in refrigerator for a few hours or at room temperature for 30 minutes, then cook as directed.

GET CREATIVE!
The krab mix can be used in various ways: try these cooked cakes in a sandwich (or on a hero-style bun for a po'boy), in place of the tofu for an upgraded Benedict (page 98), on top of Kick'n Cajun Caesar Salad (page 143), or use the uncooked filling to stuff wonton or spring roll wrappers.

EXTRA CRISPY KRAB CAKES

Make the patties as directed but do not cook. Put 1½ cups all-purpose flour in a shallow bowl, ½ recipe eggz batter (used to make the fried chik'n on page 206) in another, and 2 cups panko bread crumbs seasoned with 2 teaspoons Creole-Cajun Seasoning (page 85) in a third. Dredge each krab cake in flour, then eggz batter, then bread crumbs. Repeat with the remaining krab cakes. Heat a large pan with ½ inch of neutral oil. Once the oil is hot and shimmering, gently slide the cakes into the oil (do not overcrowd the pan) and cook on each side for 2 to 3 minutes, until golden and crispy. Drain on a paper towel and serve hot.

PAY AZTECA

(Enchilada Casserole)

This Mexican lasagna–like dish is similar to enchiladas but has a bit more personality with layers of creamy, cheesy, and spicy flavors. It's an adaptation of a family recipe from my close friend Marcela Valdez, who lives in Guadalajara, Mexico. I layer corn tortillas with roasted poblano chiles, homemade Rojo Sauce, and Cream Cheeze and bake it until golden brown and bubbly. Then I finish with avocado, cilantro, and scallions. This makes a fantastic vegan entrée for holiday celebrations, family get-togethers, and potluck dinners. It also reheats beautifully and tastes so good the next day. Thank you, Marcela, for blessing me with this idea.

Nonstick cooking spray

4 cups store-bought plant-based chik'n, rehydrated soy curls (see page 37), or vegan refried beans, warmed

Fine pink Himalayan salt and ground black pepper

2 cups Cream Cheeze (page 56) or any plant-based cream cheese

2 cups plant-based cheese shreds

1 recipe Rojo Sauce (page 61)

12 (6-inch) yellow corn tortillas

4 large poblano chiles, roasted, skinned, seeded (see page 43), and cut into thin strips

Optional toppings: Sliced avocado, Brazil Nut Sour Cream (page 57), chopped fresh cilantro, sliced black olives, and/or sliced scallions (green and white parts)

SERVES 8

Preheat the oven to 375°F. Lightly spray a 9 × 13-inch baking dish with nonstick cooking spray.

Season the chik'n with salt and pepper to taste. In a medium bowl, combine the Cream Cheeze and shredded cheese.

Spread about 1 cup of the Rojo Sauce in the bottom of the baking dish. Line the bottom with half of the tortillas, overlapping them to fit in the dish. Cover the tortillas with half of the chik'n, then half of the poblano strips, followed by half of the cheese mixture. Repeat with 1 cup of the Rojo Sauce and the remaining tortillas, chik'n, poblano strips, and cheese mixture. Keep the remaining sauce warm.

Bake until the cheese is melted and casserole has golden edges, 30 to 35 minutes. Remove from the oven and let stand for 10 minutes.

To serve, divide the remaining Rojo Sauce among 8 plates with a serving of the casserole on top. Garnish with any toppings (if using).

FRIED *CHIK'N*

with Spicy Maple Syrup

FOR THE SPICY MAPLE SYRUP

1 cup pure maple syrup

½ cup hot sauce (I like Frank's RedHot Sauce)

FOR THE EGGZ BATTER

2 cups unsweetened, unflavored plant-based milk

1 cup chickpea flour

¼ cup hot sauce (I like Frank's RedHot Sauce)

1 teaspoon Creole-Cajun Seasoning (page 85)

1 teaspoon nutritional yeast

1 teaspoon fine pink Himalayan salt, or to taste

¼ teaspoon ground black pepper

¼ teaspoon sweet or smoked paprika

½ cup water

SERVES 6

FOR THE SEASONED FLOUR

3 cups all-purpose flour or all-purpose gluten-free flour blend

2 tablespoons cornstarch

2 tablespoons nutritional yeast

1 tablespoon Creole-Cajun Seasoning (page 85)

2 teaspoons dried thyme

2 teaspoons garlic powder

2 teaspoons onion powder

2 teaspoons fine pink Himalayan salt, or to taste

1 teaspoon smoked paprika

½ teaspoon ground black pepper

FOR THE CHIK'N

1 pound fresh oyster mushrooms, broken into large pieces

Neutral oil for frying (I prefer rice bran oil)

I remember the first time I made this recipe for Derrick. I piled the fried chik'n on top of a Fluffy Vanilla Waffle (page 119) and drizzled spicy maple syrup over everything. He was in fried "chicken" bliss and said, "I have no idea what I am eating. It tastes like chicken, but I know it's not. *What is this?*"

Oyster mushrooms are the mystery guest—they are super meaty and juicy and shred just like pieces of dark meat chicken! (Thank you, Mother Nature.) It also doesn't hurt that mushrooms are a good source of zinc, folic acid, and niacin. Now, I should add that Derrick *hates* mushrooms. So I had to prove to him that he really didn't hate mushrooms—he just disliked how they were previously prepared for him. I use chickpea flour mixed with plant-based milk, and hot sauce for added flavor, to create an "egg" wash that coats the mushrooms and allows the seasoned flour to stick. My Creole-Cajun Seasoning blend kicks up the dredge, giving the mushrooms an award-winning fried chicken taste. Leftovers? If I'm lucky, I toss mine right into an air fryer to reheat and snap them back to that extra crispy chik'n.

MAKE THE SYRUP: Whisk together the maple syrup and hot sauce and set aside.

MAKE THE EGGZ BATTER: In a medium bowl, whisk together the milk, chickpea flour, hot sauce, Creole-Cajun Seasoning, nutritional yeast, salt, pepper, paprika, and water. Set aside for 10 minutes to thicken.

recipe continues >>

MAKE THE SEASONED FLOUR: In a shallow dish, whisk together the flour, cornstarch, nutritional yeast, Creole-Cajun Seasoning, thyme, garlic powder, onion powder, salt, paprika, and pepper.

Preheat the oven to 200°F or the warming setting. Line a large sheet pan with paper towels.

MAKE THE CHIK'N: Working with one piece at a time, dip a mushroom in the batter, then toss it in the seasoned flour, making sure it's evenly coated. Shake off any excess flour. Place on a sheet pan and repeat until all the mushrooms are battered.

In a large pot or Dutch oven, heat 2 inches of oil to 350°F. Add the battered mushrooms to the pot a few pieces at a time. (Don't fry too many mushrooms at once—this lowers the temperature of the oil and results in soggy, oil-soaked chik'n). Fry until golden and crispy, 2 to 3 minutes per side. Transfer the fried mushrooms to the prepared sheet pan and keep warm in the oven while frying the remaining mushrooms. Let the temperature of the oil return to 350°F before frying each batch, adding more oil if necessary.

Serve warm, drizzled with the Spicy Maple Syrup.

TIP:
When coating the mushrooms, use one hand for battering and one hand for dredging in the flour. This way your mushrooms are beautifully coated without all the mess.

GET CREATIVE!
There are so many ways you can give your fried chik'n a spiced twist. Instead of the Creole-Cajun Seasoning, try curry powder or Jerk Seasoning (page 233). Or combine ground cumin and chili powder for a fiery south-of-the-border feel. Use this recipe to make crispy po'boy chik'n sandwiches served on a toasted roll, slathered with Tarragon Remoulade (page 201).

GRANDMA *DUPLECHAN'S* CREOLE GUMBO

1 cup vegetable oil
(plus 1 tablespoon if using
plant-based shrimp)

¾ cup all-purpose flour

1 large yellow onion, diced

1 large green bell pepper,
stemmed, seeded, and diced

4 large celery stalks, diced

6 garlic cloves, minced

8 cups Chik'n Broth
(page 50) or any vegetable
broth

3 bay leaves

1 tablespoon Creole-Cajun
Seasoning (page 85), or to
taste

2 teaspoons dried thyme

2 teaspoons fine pink
Himalayan salt, or to taste

¼ teaspoon ground
cayenne pepper

¼ teaspoon ground white
pepper

3 pounds fresh or frozen
okra, trimmed and cut into
¼- to ½-inch pieces

1 (14-ounce) package plant-
based andouille or plant-
based smoked sausage,
sliced

1 (9- or 10-ounce) package
plant-based shrimp
(optional)

Ground black pepper
(optional)

1 tablespoon gumbo filé, or
to taste

¼ cup chopped scallions
(green and white parts),
plus more (optional) for
garnish

Hot cooked long-grain
white rice, for serving

Chopped fresh flat-leaf
parsley, for garnish

SERVES 8

No dish warms my heart more than the gumbo made by my grandmother Leola Duplechan. It's a Creole classic that brings together African, Spanish, Native American, and French flavors and techniques. I can still see all five feet two inches of her standing in front of the stove, stirring a pot that seemed to be twice her size, brimming with spicy andouille sausage, Gulf shrimp, crab legs, silky okra, chicken legs, and a few closely guarded secret ingredients. The thought of never having it again devastated me when I stopped eating meat, so it became my mission to create a version every bit as delicious and comforting as Grandma's.

I start with a dark roux made with vegetable oil and flour and add filé, which is made from dried and ground sassafras leaves, to thicken the magic. Some people claim that only okra, roux, *or* filé can be used to thicken a gumbo (maybe you can use two of the three, depending on who you ask). But I am here to clear the air: like my Creole grandma, I use all three! I'm sure Leola is turning over in her grave at the mere mention of plant-based gumbo . . . but I also know that she would be thrilled to find out I am carrying on her traditions with my family, in her memory.

Heat a large pot or Dutch oven over high heat. When hot, add ¾ cup of the oil. Whisk in the flour. When the mixture begins to simmer, turn the heat to its lowest setting. Cook low and slow, stirring at least every 60 seconds (I alternate between a whisk and a silicone spatula), until the roux turns blond, then light brown, and finally becomes a deep, rich chocolate color and smells nutty and buttery. (This

recipe continues >>

can take up to 1 hour; be patient—your gumbo is only as good as your roux.) It should be thick enough to coat the back of a spoon but silky textured, too.

When the roux is chocolate-colored, increase the heat to medium-high and immediately add the onion, bell pepper, and celery. Cook, stirring constantly, until slightly softened, 6 to 8 minutes. Add the garlic and sauté until fragrant, 30 to 60 seconds. Slowly pour in half of the broth while whisking vigorously, then add the remaining broth, continuing to whisk until smooth. Add the bay leaves, Creole-Cajun Seasoning, thyme, salt, cayenne, and white pepper. Bring to a simmer, lower the heat to medium-low, and simmer, uncovered, for 30 minutes.

Meanwhile, heat a very large cast-iron skillet over high heat. Add 3 tablespoons of the oil. Once the oil is hot and shimmering, add the okra. Sear the okra for 10 to 12 minutes, stirring every 2 minutes or so, until the edges are golden and most of the liquid has been released and evaporated. (This helps prevent it from getting slimy.) Transfer the okra to a sheet pan and set aside.

Add the remaining 1 tablespoon oil to the pan. Add the sausage and cook until lightly browned, 3 to 4 minutes. Add the sausage to the gumbo. Stir from the bottom to prevent sticking. If using shrimp, add 1 tablespoon oil to the hot skillet and cook the shrimp until seared, about 3 minutes. Remove from the heat. Set aside.

After the gumbo has been simmering for 30 minutes and has been thickened by the roux, add the cooked okra and simmer an additional 10 to 15 minutes, stirring frequently to make sure nothing sticks to the bottom of the pan and burns. During the last 5 minutes of simmering, add the shrimp (if using). Continue to cook just to heat through. Taste, add black pepper (if using), and adjust the seasoning, if needed.

Turn off the heat and stir in the gumbo filé and scallions. Discard the bay leaves before serving. Ladle over rice and garnish with parsley and/or scallions (if using).

Gumbo keeps in the refrigerator for up to 5 days or can be frozen in an airtight container for up to 3 months.

TIP:
Roux should never be rushed, so be sure to cook low and slow and stir often—if you scorch it, toss it out and start over.

SMOKY JAMBALAYA

6 cups Chik'n Broth
(page 50) or any
vegetable broth

2 teaspoons hot sauce
(I like Louisiana-style)

1 recipe (2 tablespoons)
Smoke Signal (page 87)

3 tablespoons neutral
oil, such as avocado or
grapeseed

1 (14-ounce) package plant-
based andouille sausage or
any plant-based sausage, or
smoked tofu, sliced

3 celery stalks, chopped

1 yellow onion, chopped

1 green bell pepper,
stemmed, seeded, and
chopped

3 cups long-grain white rice

3 garlic cloves, minced

1 tablespoon Creole-Cajun
Seasoning (page 85)

1 (14-ounce) can diced
tomatoes and their liquid,
or 2 cups chopped fresh
tomatoes

2 bay leaves

3 scallions (green and white
parts), sliced

½ teaspoon fine pink
Himalayan salt, or to taste

¼ teaspoon ground black
pepper

Chopped fresh flat-leaf
parsley or more sliced
scallions, for garnish

SERVES 10

This one-pot meal is another adaptation from my Creole grandmother. When veganizing recipes it's really important to find ways to add tons of seasoning (and love) to your plant-based dish. For this recipe, I do include plant-based sausage, which brings a lot of that Creole nostalgia, but I also create a smoky, spicy broth so that every grain of rice is penetrated with an explosion of flavor. Toasting the rice in the pot with the vegetables first, instead of just adding it to the simmering liquid, infuses the rice with flavor and also results in fluffy, separate grains.

In a medium bowl, combine the broth, hot sauce, and Smoke Signal; set aside.

Heat a large pot or Dutch oven over medium-high heat. When very hot, add 2 tablespoons of the oil. Once the oil is hot and shimmering, add the sausage. Cook, stirring occasionally, until the edges are crisp, 3 to 5 minutes. Transfer to a plate.

To the same pot, add the remaining 1 tablespoon oil along with the celery, onion, and bell pepper. Cook, stirring frequently, until the vegetables start to soften, about 3 minutes. Add the rice and cook, stirring frequently, until toasted, 3 to 5 minutes.

Add the garlic and Creole-Cajun Seasoning and sauté until fragrant, 30 to 60 seconds. Add the broth mixture, tomatoes, bay leaves, sausage, scallions, salt, and pepper. Stir, then cover and bring to a simmer. Reduce the heat to medium-low and cook until the rice is tender, 30 to 35 minutes. Remove from the heat and let stand, covered, for 10 minutes.

Discard the bay leaves. Garnish with parsley or scallions and serve.

GET CREATIVE!

For a creamy jambalaya pasta, omit the rice and broth and add 1 recipe (2 tablespoons) Smoke Signal (page 87) to the sauce. Cook the sauce for 15 minutes. Meanwhile, cook 1 pound of pasta, such as penne or bowties, in salted water according to the package directions, minus 2 minutes of cooking time. Drain and add to the sauce along with 1 recipe Cashew Heavy Cream (page 55). Simmer for 5 minutes, then serve hot, topped with blackened vegetables (see page 42), if desired.

GOCHUJANG *JACKFRUIT* NOODLE BOWL

FOR THE NOODLES

½ cup soy sauce or tamari (if you're gluten-free)

1 tablespoon gochujang

1 tablespoon (packed) light or dark brown sugar

1 tablespoon toasted sesame oil

8 ounces Korean glass noodles (sweet potato noodles) or mung bean cellophane noodles

FOR THE JACKFRUIT AND VEGETABLES

¼ cup soy sauce or tamari (if you're gluten-free)

3 tablespoons (packed) light or dark brown sugar

1 tablespoon gochujang

½ cup water

2 tablespoons neutral oil, such as avocado or grapeseed

1 tablespoon toasted sesame oil

4 ounces fresh shiitake mushrooms, cleaned, stemmed, and caps thinly sliced

SERVES 4

1½ pounds frozen and thawed, or canned and drained, young (green) jackfruit, cut into large chunks

1-inch piece ginger, peeled and grated

3 garlic cloves, minced

½ white onion, thinly sliced

1 red bell pepper, stemmed, seeded, and sliced

2 carrots, julienned

4 cups baby spinach or chopped bok choy leaves and tender stalks

Fine pink Himalayan salt and ground black pepper

FOR SERVING

1 cup shelled edamame, cooked and cooled

Kimchi (page 80) or any vegan kimchi

1 small cucumber, thinly sliced or julienned

2 scallions (green and white parts), thinly sliced diagonally

1 (0.35-ounce) package roasted seaweed snack, cut into thin strips

2 tablespoons toasted white sesame seeds

My beautiful friend Alice Kim introduced me to Korean cooking years ago. I immediately fell in love with the intense flavors of this bold cuisine: deep, rich notes of ginger, garlic, sesame, chiles, and lots of fresh vegetables. Gochujang, a spicy, sweet, brick-colored paste made from red chile flakes (gochugaru specifically, used in kimchi, page 80), is one of my favorite ingredients from the Korean pantry. Its strong umami character bumps up the impact of just about any dish. It's especially well suited to young jackfruit (see page 36) and chewy glass noodles (dangmeyun), which both readily soak up whatever sauce you match them with. When finished, the jackfruit should have the texture similar to pulled pork (a few chunks are okay—don't overthink it). If you can't find glass noodles, serve the jackfruit on a bowl of steamed rice, quinoa, or your rice noodles.

MAKE THE NOODLES: In a large bowl, mix the soy sauce, gochujang, brown sugar, and sesame oil. Set aside. Cook the noodles according to the package directions. Drain and rinse thoroughly with cold water for 1 minute; drain again. Snip with a pair of clean kitchen scissors (these noodles are very long). Add to the large bowl of sauce and toss well. Set aside and allow the noodles to marinate.

MAKE THE JACKFRUIT AND VEGETABLES: In a small bowl, combine the soy sauce, brown sugar, gochujang, and water. Stir until well combined.

recipe continues >>

Heat a large pan over medium-high heat. Add 1 tablespoon of the neutral oil and the sesame oil. Once the oils are hot and shimmering, add the mushrooms and sauté until slightly browned, 3 to 5 minutes. Add the jackfruit, reduce the heat to medium, cover, and cook, stirring occasionally, until the jackfruit becomes tender, 5 to 8 minutes. Add the ginger and garlic and sauté for a few seconds, or just until fragrant. Pour the gochujang mixture over the jackfruit. Reduce the heat to low and simmer, uncovered, for 10 minutes, stirring occasionally, until the sauce thickens into a syrup and the jackfruit is very tender. Remove from the heat and set aside while you cook the remaining vegetables.

Heat another large pan or wok over medium-high heat. Add the remaining 1 tablespoon of neutral oil. Once the oil is shimmering and hot, add the onion, bell pepper, and carrots to the pan. Cook, stirring frequently, for 3 to 5 minutes, until the vegetables are just crisp-tender. Add the spinach and let wilt for 30 seconds. Season to taste with salt and pepper.

Add the cooked noodles with their marinade to the pan with vegetables and cook, stirring often, for 1 minute, until the noodles are heated through. (Keep the noodles moving rapidly so they don't stick.) Remove from the heat.

To serve, divide the noodle-vegetable mixture among four bowls. Top with the jackfruit. Garnish with edamame, kimchi, cucumber, scallions, seaweed, and sesame seeds and serve.

GET CREATIVE!
Use the spiced jackfruit to stuff crispy spring rolls, bao buns, or sushi hand rolls.

UNBELIEVABLY VEGAN *PROTEIN* BURGER

FOR THE BURGERS

3 cups textured pea protein (TPP) or textured vegetable protein (TVP) (see page 37)

4 cups Chik'n Broth (page 50) or any vegetable broth, warmed

2 tablespoons neutral oil, such as avocado or grapeseed

1 cup finely chopped shallot or red onion

10 ounces fresh mushrooms (any variety), stems removed and caps coarsely chopped

2 teaspoons fine pink Himalayan salt, or to taste

3 garlic cloves, minced

2 tablespoons Vegemite or Marmite (see page 38)

2 tablespoons liquid aminos (see page 38)

1 teaspoon ground black pepper

1 small raw red beet (about 7 ounces), trimmed, peeled, and quartered

1 cup rolled oats

MAKES 14 BURGERS

1 cup cooked green, brown, or black lentils (rinsed and drained, if canned)

1 cup cooked chickpeas (rinsed and drained, if canned)

¼ cup nutritional yeast

2 teaspoons garlic powder

1 teaspoon onion powder

1 teaspoon smoked paprika

1 cup tapioca starch

Nonstick cooking spray

FOR SERVING

Neutral oil, such as avocado or grapeseed

Vegan buns

Toppings: Plant-based cheese slices, lettuce, tomato, pickles, thinly sliced raw or caramelized onions (see page 42), coleslaw (try the slaw that tops the tacos on page 168), and/or Shiitake Bae'con (page 88) or any cooked plant-based bacon

Condiments: Mayonnaise (page 53) or any plant-based mayonnaise, ketchup, mustard, and/or Drip Burger Sauce (recipe follows)

Burgers are the gateway to plant-based fulfillment! Many of my clients signed up for my plant-based meals once they tried a satisfying, cow-free burger, stacked with all the toppings you can imagine. My burger is a hearty, soy-free, gluten-free, and wheat-free patty that is also free of preservatives and highly processed additives—but not free of flavor, thanks to fresh and honest ingredients like vegetables, tons of spices, oats, and pea protein. This recipe makes fourteen patties, so freeze the extras (if you have any), and future-you can have a burger in only the time it takes to sear. Don't forget to give your burger some drip action with the tangy burger sauce on page 219.

MAKE THE BURGERS: In a large bowl, combine the textured pea protein and warm broth. Stir until well combined. Let stand for 10 minutes to rehydrate, then completely drain the remaining broth. Set aside.

Heat a large skillet over medium-high heat. Add the oil. Once the oil is hot and shimmering, add the shallot, mushrooms, and 1 teaspoon of the salt. Sauté until the shallots are soft and slightly translucent with lightly browned edges, 7 to 10 minutes. Add the garlic and sauté for 30 seconds, or just until fragrant. Remove from the heat. Stir in the Vegemite, liquid aminos, and pepper. Set aside to cool, about 10 minutes.

recipe continues >>

In the bowl of a large food processor, pulse the beet a few times to break it up into coarse pieces. Add the oats and shallot-mushroom mixture and pulse until there are no large chunks. Add the lentils, chickpeas, nutritional yeast, garlic power, onion powder, smoked paprika, and remaining 1 teaspoon salt. Pulse a few times to break up the lentils and chickpeas (keep the mixture slightly coarse). Transfer to the bowl with the pea protein. Add the tapioca starch and stir well to combine all the ingredients.

Preheat the oven to 400°F. Spray a sheet pan with nonstick cooking spray or line with parchment paper.

Using a ½-cup measure, form the mixture into a 4-ounce patty (however thick you like), pressing firmly to shape it with your hands or in a ring mold, and place on the prepared sheet pan. Repeat until all fourteen patties are formed.

Bake for 20 to 25 minutes, flipping halfway through. Patties should be fully cooked and firm. If you're serving any burgers right away, proceed to the next step. Allow any extras to cool, then place the patties between layers of parchment paper. Transfer to an airtight container and freeze for up to 6 months. Thaw, then sear as directed.

TO SERVE: Heat a griddle or large pan over medium-high heat. Add some oil. Once the oil is hot and shimmering, sear the patties in batches for 3 to 4 minutes on each side, or until browned and crisp, adding more oil as needed. When you flip the patties, top each with a slice of cheese, if desired, then add a teaspoon of water to the pan and place a lid over the patties to melt the cheese. Repeat with however many patties you're serving right away.

Serve on buns with the desired toppings and condiments.

GET CREATIVE!
Turn your burger into a patty melt by topping it with caramelized onions (page 42) and Chipotle BBQ Sauce (page 60) and sliding it onto a piece of grilled sourdough or rye bread. To make a hickory-smoked burger, add 1 recipe (2 tablespoons) Smoke Signal (page 87) to the patty blend and cut the salt to 1 teaspoon.

DRIP BURGER SAUCE
In a small bowl, stir together 1 cup Mayonnaise (page 53) or any plant-based mayonnaise, ¼ cup organic ketchup (see page 40), 1 tablespoon yellow mustard, 2 tablespoons sweet or dill relish, 2 teaspoons onion powder, 1 teaspoon garlic powder, ½ teaspoon fine pink Himalayan salt, or to taste, and ¼ teaspoon ground white pepper. Cover and refrigerate until serving, or store in an airtight container and refrigerate for up to 1 week.

BIG OL' BBQ MEATBALLS
Preheat the oven to 400°F. Lightly coat a large sheet pan with nonstick cooking spray; set aside. With clean hands firmly shape the burger mixture into twenty-four meatballs each about 2½ inches in diameter. Place on the prepared sheet pan. Bake for 25 to 30 minutes, rotating the meatballs halfway through, until they're firm and fully cooked. Serve with Chipotle BBQ Sauce (page 60) and garnish with 2 tablespoons chopped flat-leaf parsley.

GARLIC RAMEN NOODLES, PAGE 238

SIDELINE SIDES

SMOKY *HOLD-THE-HAM* COLLARDS

3 pounds collard greens

2 tablespoons neutral oil, such as avocado or grapeseed

1 large yellow or white onion, diced

3 garlic cloves, minced

2 or 3 teaspoons Creole-Cajun Seasoning (page 85) or any Creole seasoning (depending on your preferred spice level)

7 cups Chik'n Broth (page 50) or any vegetable broth

¼ cup distilled white vinegar

1 bay leaf

1 recipe (2 tablespoons) Smoke Signal (page 87)

1 tablespoon hot sauce, (I like Louisiana-style)

1 teaspoon pure maple syrup

1 teaspoon fine pink Himalayan salt, or to taste

½ teaspoon ground black pepper

Shiitake Bae'con (page 88) or any cooked plant-based bacon, for garnish (optional)

SERVES 8

GET CREATIVE!

Swap out the collards for mustard greens, kale, or cabbage sliced ½ inch thick. Simmer for 30 to 35 minutes instead of 1½ hours.

Nothing brings my family together faster than a huge spread of food, and to be legit, there better be a big piping-hot pot of collards. My sisters loved it when I made collards for the holidays. I still do, and now the flavor that a ham hock would normally add comes from Smoke Signal with a combination of three different smoky components: liquid smoke, smoked salt, and smoked paprika. To soak up every precious last drop of the pot licker broth, I add crumbled-up Skillet Cornbread (page 241) right to the bowl—just like my grandma taught me.

Trim the greens and discard the tougher stems. Stack a few of the leaves on top of each other (smaller leaves in the center). From the width of the leaves, tightly roll them into a large cylinder. Cut the greens crosswise into ¼- to ½-inch-thick strips. Place in a large bowl and repeat until all the greens are cut.

Heat a large pot or Dutch oven over medium-high heat. Add the oil. Once the oil is hot and shimmering, add the onion. Sauté for 3 to 5 minutes, until the onion starts to soften. Add the garlic and Creole-Cajun Seasoning and sauté for 30 seconds, or just until fragrant. Add the broth, vinegar, and bay leaf and bring to a boil. Add the greens. (If the pot is overcrowded, add the greens in batches, allowing them to cook down a bit before adding more.) Cover and simmer, stirring occasionally, for about 1½ hours, or until tender.

Season with the Smoke Signal, hot sauce, maple syrup, salt, and pepper. Remove the bay leaf before serving. Top with Shiitake Bae'con (if using).

TRUFFLE *CREAM'D* CORN

1 cup Béchamel (page 54)

4 cups fresh or frozen corn kernels (thawed if frozen)

3 tablespoons nutritional yeast

3 tablespoons Cream Cheeze (page 56) or any plant-based cream cheese

2 teaspoons organic sugar

1 teaspoon truffle salt

1 tablespoon plant-based butter

1 tablespoon truffle oil

1 tablespoon minced fresh flat-leaf parsley, for garnish

Freshly shaved truffle, for garnish (optional)

SERVES 8

Many chefs rely on heavy cream, cheese, and butter to achieve extra richness, but when you go plant-based, you need to let go of those habits and adopt *better* ones. For this sweet and creamy corn, I use a plant-based béchamel sauce and cashew cream cheese for a velvety sauce, nutritional yeast for punchy, cheesy flavor, and a double dose of truffle from infused salt and oil. Not convinced this will be as decadent as the dairy version? Just ask the entire defensive line of the Tennessee Titans, who polished off a whole chafing dish (before I even got some!) without even knowing it was vegan during Friendsgiving at my house.

In a large saucepan, combine the béchamel and corn over medium-low heat and cook, stirring frequently, for 5 to 8 minutes, until the corn is tender and heated through.

Stir in the nutritional yeast, Cream Cheeze, sugar, and truffle salt. Mix well. Stir in the butter.

Transfer to a serving dish. Drizzle with the truffle oil, garnish with parsley, and truffle (if using), and serve.

CREAMY *MASHED* POTATOES

Decadent and creamy traditional mashed potatoes are possible with a few swaps—like plant-based milk (I like oat milk here), sour cream, and butter—for that memorable and comforting taste. It really is that simple. I like mine *extra* savory, so I stir in some nutritional yeast and garlic, and sometimes truffle oil, to turn this traditional side dish into an over-the-top experience. Top with Savory Brown Gravy (page 91) or Chipotle BBQ Sauce (page 60)—which might be weird to some, but I love it!

6 large russet potatoes, peeled and cut into 3-inch chunks

3 garlic cloves, crushed

2 cups unsweetened, unflavored plant-based milk

¼ cup nutritional yeast

2 tablespoons plant-based butter

2 teaspoons fine pink Himalayan salt, or to taste

¼ teaspoon ground white pepper

½ cup Cashew Heavy Cream (page 55) or Brazil Nut Sour Cream (page 57)

1 tablespoon truffle oil, for drizzling (optional)

Chopped fresh herbs, such as chives, flat-leaf parsley, or dill (optional)

SERVES 6 TO 8

Combine the potatoes and garlic in a large pot. Cover with water. Generously salt the water. Bring to a boil over medium-high heat. Cook the potatoes until they are fork-tender, 15 to 20 minutes.

Meanwhile, combine the milk, nutritional yeast, butter, salt, and pepper in a medium saucepan. Bring to a simmer over medium heat, whisking occasionally. Turn off the heat, cover, and keep warm until the potatoes are ready.

Drain the potatoes and garlic and set aside in the colander for 5 minutes to allow the potatoes to completely drain and release most of their steam. (This ensures your mashed potatoes will be light and fluffy, not soupy.)

Return the potatoes and garlic to the same pot. Using a potato masher or handheld mixer, mash or whip the potatoes until most of the large chunks are broken up. Add half of the warm milk mixture and the Cashew Heavy Cream and continue to mash or beat until the potatoes are smooth and everything is well incorporated, then add the remaining milk mixture. Mash or beat to combine. Taste and adjust the seasoning, if necessary.

Transfer the mashed potatoes to a serving dish, drizzle with truffle oil (if using), and sprinkle with fresh herbs (if using). Serve immediately.

GET CREATIVE!
Pump up basic mashed potatoes with plant-based cheese shreds or crisp plant-based bacon pieces, diced pickled jalapeños, or roasted garlic and chives.

CHEEZY *SWEET POTATO* GRITS

1 teaspoon fine pink Himalayan salt, or to taste

1 bay leaf

1 cup stone-ground organic grits (quick grits are okay, too)

1 sweet potato, peeled and diced small

3 tablespoons Cream Cheeze (page 56) or any plant-based cream cheese

2 tablespoons nutritional yeast

1 teaspoon Creole-Cajun Seasoning (page 85), or to taste

1 teaspoon garlic powder

¼ teaspoon ground white pepper

SERVES 4

TIP:
To make basic "cheese" grits, omit the sweet potato—and boom: cheezy grits!

There are two kinds of grits eaters: those who prefer them stone-ground with a bit of texture and a touch of sugar, and those who love them smooth and loaded with lots (and lots) of cheese and savory spices. I'm on team creamy and savory all the way. I can polish off a huge bowl, especially when topped with red beans (page 234), blackened vegetables (page 42), or as part of my Cheezy Grits Bowls with Kale, Chickpea Scramble & Grilled Avocado (page 111). Since I also love the richness of cheesy grits and sweetness of sweet potatoes, I combined the two in a moment of inspiration. These grits are the best of both worlds—everybody's happy! Plant-based cream cheese makes them extra creamy and velvety smooth, and the sweet potato adds a glorious pop of orange color and nutritional value.

In a medium saucepan, bring 4 cups of water to a boil and add the salt and bay leaf. Slowly add the grits, whisking constantly to prevent clumps. Lower the heat to medium-low and simmer for 10 minutes (5 to 7 minutes if using quick grits), stirring occasionally.

Add the sweet potato and simmer, uncovered and stirring occasionally, for an additional 10 minutes, or until the sweet potato is cooked and the grits are smooth. The sweet potato should start to break up and give the grits an orange hue. Add the Cream Cheeze, nutritional yeast, Creole-Cajun Seasoning, garlic powder, and white pepper. Mix well to make sure the cheeze is melted and spices are thoroughly blended. The grits will thicken a bit upon standing and should be served immediately, while hot. Discard the bay leaf before serving.

CHIPOTLE-LIME POTATO SALAD

8 to 10 medium russet potatoes, or 12 small Yukon gold, peeled and cubed (3 pounds)

1½ cups Mayonnaise (page 53) or any plant-based mayonnaise

2 red bell peppers, roasted, peeled, and seeded (see page 43), and diced

1 to 3 chipotle chiles in adobo sauce (depending on how spicy you want the salad), minced, plus 2 teaspoons adobo sauce

Zest and juice of 1 lime

2 teaspoons ground cumin

2 teaspoons smoked paprika, plus more for garnish

1 teaspoon garlic powder

3 scallions (green and white parts), thinly sliced, plus more for garnish

Leaves from ½ bunch cilantro, coarsely chopped (about ½ cup), plus more for garnish

2 teaspoons fine pink Himalayan salt, or to taste

Ground black pepper

SERVES 10 TO 12

People who aren't even vegan show up to our backyard barbecues rubbing their hands together, wondering what will those herbivores be serving up—because they *know* it's gonna be good. Whether I'm having a cookout or feeding a 300-pound athlete, no gathering is complete in my world until the potato salad has arrived! My version screams sassy side dish, with its creamy, spicy, zesty, smoky Mexi-Cali-inspired dressing with fresh hits of cilantro and scallion. Remember to dress your potatoes while slightly warm (but not hot) for the best flavor absorption.

Bring a large pot of salted water to a boil. Add the potatoes and cook until fork-tender, 12 to 15 minutes. Drain and set aside to cool slightly.

In a very large bowl, whisk together the mayonnaise, roasted bell peppers, chiles and adobo sauce, lime zest and juice, cumin, smoked paprika, garlic powder, scallions, cilantro, salt, and black pepper. Gently fold in the potatoes, being careful not to break them up too much. Transfer to a serving bowl. Garnish with a pinch of smoked paprika and additional cilantro and scallions.

Serve warm or cover and chill in the refrigerator for at least 2 hours, and up to 2 days before serving.

SWEET POTATO CASSEROLE

Upholding food memories and traditions is very important to me, and this casserole was one recipe that I was determined to reinvent for all of us plant-loving people. It's impossibly creamy, with a crunchy pecan praline topping—it's essentially a side dish and dessert all in one. I hope it will become a tradition for your family, too. If you are feeling extra decadent, have it for dessert with a scoop of nondairy vanilla bean ice cream and a drizzle of Salted Caramel Sauce (page 245)—that's how Derrick loves it!

FOR THE SWEET POTATOES

3 medium to large sweet potatoes (about 2½ pounds)

Nonstick cooking spray

2 flax eggs (see page 36)

1 cup organic sugar

½ cup plant-based butter, melted

½ cup Cashew Heavy Cream (page 55)

1 tablespoon vanilla powder, or 2 teaspoons vanilla extract

1 teaspoon ground cinnamon

¼ teaspoon fine pink Himalayan salt, or to taste

FOR THE TOPPING

1 cup coarsely chopped pecans or walnuts

1 cup (packed) light or dark brown sugar

½ cup all-purpose flour or all-purpose gluten-free flour blend

⅓ cup plant-based butter, melted

SERVES 6 TO 8

Preheat the oven to 425°F.

PREPARE THE SWEET POTATOES: Wrap each sweet potato in foil and bake until fork-tender, 40 to 45 minutes. Remove from the oven and let cool. Once cool, remove the foil and peel away the skins.

Reduce the oven temperature to 350°F. Spray a shallow 3-quart baking dish with nonstick cooking spray.

Put the sweet potato flesh in a large mixing bowl (if using a handheld mixer) or the bowl of a stand mixer fitted with the paddle attachment. Beat on medium to high speed until fluffy. Add the flax eggs, sugar, melted butter, Cashew Heavy Cream, vanilla, cinnamon, and salt. Beat on medium to high speed until well combined. Transfer the mixture to the prepared baking dish and bake until firm, about 35 minutes.

MEANWHILE, MAKE THE TOPPING: In a small bowl, combine the nuts, brown sugar, flour, and melted butter. Mix well, then set aside.

Remove the casserole from the oven and increase the oven temperature to 375°F. Sprinkle the topping evenly over the sweet potatoes and bake for an additional 10 to 15 minutes, until the topping is crisp and has golden edges. Allow to cool for 10 minutes before serving.

JERK-SPICED LENTILS

with Coconut Rice & Mango Salsa

I used to constantly crave jerk chicken and have many fond memories of eating the aromatic, spicy meal at local Jamaican restaurants close to home or in the Caribbean while on vacation. But eventually I realized what I wanted was the spice and seasonings—not the meat! Now I find as many ways as possible to use my homemade jerk seasoning—like in these hearty lentils with coconut rice and a zesty mango salsa for just enough sweetness to help cool your taste buds.

FOR THE LENTILS

1 tablespoon neutral oil, such as avocado or grapeseed

1 yellow or white onion, diced

2 celery stalks, diced

1 teaspoon fine pink Himalayan salt, or to taste

2 garlic cloves, minced

1½-inch piece ginger, peeled and grated

1 recipe Jerk Seasoning (see opposite page)

4 cups Chik'n Broth (page 50) or any vegetable broth

2 cups dried black lentils

2 tablespoons soy sauce or tamari (if you're gluten-free)

2 tablespoons fresh orange juice

1 tablespoon fresh lime juice

2 scallions (green and white parts), sliced

1 whole Scotch bonnet chile (optional)

SERVES 6 TO 8

FOR THE SALSA

2 cups diced fresh ripe mango (about 2 large mangoes; see page 157)

1 small red onion, finely diced

½ red bell pepper, stemmed, seeded, and finely diced

1 jalapeño, stemmed, seeded, and minced

2 garlic cloves, minced

1-inch piece ginger, peeled and minced

¼ cup fresh lime juice (from 2 to 3 limes)

¼ cup chopped fresh cilantro

¼ teaspoon fine pink Himalayan salt, or to taste

⅛ teaspoon ground black pepper, or to taste

FOR THE RICE

1 tablespoon coconut oil

2 garlic cloves, minced

½ teaspoon dried thyme

2 cups Chik'n Broth (page 50) or any vegetable broth

1 cup full-fat coconut milk

2 cups long-grain white rice

1 teaspoon fine pink Himalayan salt, or to taste

2 scallions, trimmed and left whole

MAKE THE LENTILS: Heat a large pot or Dutch oven over medium-high heat. Add the oil. Once the oil is hot and shimmering, add the onion, celery, and salt. Sauté until the onions are slightly translucent, 3 to 4 minutes. Add the garlic and ginger and sauté until fragrant, about 30 seconds. Add the Jerk Seasoning and stir, toasting the spices for 30 to 60 seconds. Add the broth and bring to a simmer. Add the lentils, soy sauce, orange juice, lime juice, scallions, and Scotch bonnet chile (if using). Simmer, covered, for 45 to 50 minutes, until the lentils are tender.

MAKE THE SALSA: In a medium bowl, stir together the mango, red onion, bell pepper, jalapeño, garlic, ginger, lime juice, cilantro, salt, and black pepper. Cover and chill up to 2 days before serving.

MAKE THE RICE: Heat a medium pot over medium heat. Add the coconut oil. Once the oil is hot and shimmering, add the garlic and thyme and sauté until fragrant, about 1 minute. Add the broth and coconut milk. Bring to a simmer and stir in the rice, salt, and whole scallions. Reduce the heat to low, cover, and cook until the rice is tender and the liquid has been absorbed, 15 to 20 minutes. Remove from the heat and place a clean, dry paper towel between the lid and the pot. Let stand for 10 minutes.

To serve, discard the scallions and fluff the rice with a fork. Divide the rice among serving bowls and top with lentils and salsa.

JERK SEASONING

Use this spice blend to season plant-based chik'n, cubed tofu, roasted chickpeas, or another favorite of mine—jerk cauliflower steaks. Rub the seasoning on the cauliflower steaks, place on an oiled pan or grill, sear until browned, tender, and cooked through.

In a small bowl, stir together 3 (packed) tablespoons dark brown sugar, 2 teaspoons ground allspice, 1 teaspoon garlic powder, 1 teaspoon onion powder, 1 teaspoon dried thyme, ½ teaspoon ground black pepper, ¼ teaspoon fine pink Himalayan salt, ⅛ teaspoon ground cinnamon, ⅛ teaspoon freshly grated nutmeg, and ⅛ teaspoon ground cloves. (Makes enough for one batch of lentils.)

GET CREATIVE!

Turn the lentils into a delicious jerk lentil soup: Add an additional 2 cups of broth and one (13.5-ounce) can unsweetened coconut cream or coconut milk to the lentils. Cook the lentils as directed. Once they're tender, use an immersion blender and blend in two or three spots for 5 to 10 seconds at a time for added creaminess.

RED BEANS & RICE

Rice and beans are one of the simplest, cheapest, and most nutritious vegan dishes in existence. But make no mistake: this is no ordinary rice and beans recipe, this is a *Louisiana-style* red beans and rice, and it is my favorite. As the daughter of a Creole father, red beans and rice is a quintessential meal in our home. The original recipe gets its distinctive smoky flavor from a ham hock or andouille sausages cooked slowly with the beans. I use my trusty Smoke Signal seasoning blend and vegan smoked sausages to pull in a classic Bayou flavor. I include a traditional slow-and-low stovetop method for cooking the beans, and a quick multicooker version for all the Instant Pot lovers.

1 pound dark kidney beans, picked over for any rocks, soaked in water overnight (see page 46)

2 tablespoons neutral oil, such as avocado or grapeseed

4 smoked plant-based sausage links (about 13 ounces), diced (optional)

1 large white or yellow onion, diced

1 large green or red bell pepper, stemmed, seeded, and diced

3 celery stalks, diced

5 garlic cloves, minced

2 teaspoons Creole-Cajun Seasoning (page 85), or to taste

1 teaspoon hot sauce (I like Louisiana-style), plus more for serving

Ground black pepper

6 cups Chik'n Broth (page 50) or any vegetable broth

1 bay leaf

1 recipe (2 tablespoons) Smoke Signal (page 87)

½ bunch flat-leaf parsley, coarsely chopped, reserving some for garnish

3 scallions (green and white parts), sliced, reserving some for garnish

1 teaspoon fine pink Himalayan salt, or to taste

Hot cooked long-grain white rice, for serving

SERVES 8

Drain the beans. Rinse and drain again; set aside.

Heat a large pot or Dutch oven over medium-high heat. Add the oil. Once the oil is hot and shimmering, add the sausage (if using), onion, bell pepper, and celery. Sauté until the onion is translucent and the sausages are browned, 5 to 7 minutes. Add the garlic and sauté for about 30 seconds, or just until fragrant. Season with the Creole-Cajun Seasoning, hot sauce, and black pepper.

Add the broth, bay leaf, and beans. Bring to a boil, then reduce the heat to low. Cover and simmer for 2 hours, or until the beans are tender.

Remove and discard the bay leaf. Add the Smoke Signal, parsley, scallions, and salt. Using the back of a spoon, smash a few spoonfuls of beans against the side of the pot to slightly thicken the mixture. Stir well to combine. Taste and add more Creole-Cajun Seasoning or salt, if necessary.

Serve with hot cooked rice and more hot sauce. Garnish with the remaining scallions and parsley.

TIP:
Check the beans and stir frequently to ensure they don't stick to the bottom of the pot.

GET CREATIVE!
Leftover red beans are good for a quick burrito filling. Roll up warm beans and rice with plant-based cheese shreds in a warm tortilla. Add Tofu Scramble (page 108) or Scrambled Chickpea Eggz (page 106) for a breakfast burrito.

MULTICOOKER METHOD

The timing can be cut in half if you use a multicooker. Add the soaked beans, broth, and bay leaf to the cooker. Pressure cook for 20 minutes or your manufacturer's recommended time, then allow the pressure to release naturally. While the beans are cooking, sauté the sausage, onion, bell pepper, and celery in the oil in a large pan or cast-iron skillet, 5 to 7 minutes. Add the garlic and Creole-Cajun Seasoning to the vegetables and sauté for 30 seconds. Add the hot sauce, salt, and black pepper. When the beans are cooked through, add the vegetable mixture to the beans. Lightly smash some of the beans against the side of the pot to thicken the mixture. Stir in the Smoke Signal and the parsley and scallions. Use the simmer function to simmer for 20 minutes, so the beans thicken slightly and the flavors meld. Remove and discard the bay leaf and serve as directed.

ARROZ *CON* GANDULES

(Puerto Rican Rice & Peas)

It's been debated for decades who makes the best arroz con gandules ("party rice") in our family: my mother, Migdalia; her sister, Hortencia Valentin; or uncle Luis Valentin? I have a clear winner—and my recipe is based on theirs—but to keep the peace, I shall refrain from sharing who inspired it! For mine, I cook the rice and protein-rich gandules verdes (also known as green pigeon peas) with garlicky, herbaceous homemade Puerto Rican Sofrito. The rice gets its beautiful orange color and nutty-sweet aroma from annatto seeds (also called achiote). The smell alone brings me right back to my mother's kitchen! This is so good served alongside Pastelillos (page 173).

¼ cup neutral oil, such as avocado or grapeseed

2 tablespoons annatto seeds (see page 38)

2½ cups medium- or long-grain rice

¼ cup Puerto Rican Sofrito (page 74), or 2 frozen sofrito cubes from an ice tray

1½ teaspoons MSG-free sazón seasoning (about 1 packet) (see page 38)

1 teaspoon adobo seasoning (see page 38)

1 teaspoon fine pink Himalayan salt, or to taste

½ teaspoon ground cumin

½ teaspoon dried oregano

¼ teaspoon ground black pepper, or to taste

3 cups Chik'n Broth (page 50) or any vegetable broth

½ cup pitted Spanish Manzanilla olives, sliced

1 (15-ounce) can green pigeon peas (gandules verdes), rinsed and drained, or 1½ cups frozen pigeon peas, thawed

1 teaspoon liquid smoke or Smoke Signal (page 87)

1 bay leaf

SERVES 8

Heat a heavy cast-iron pot or Dutch oven over medium heat. Add the oil. Once the oil is hot and shimmering, add the annatto seeds. Cook, stirring occasionally, for 2 to 3 minutes, until the oil is a deep red color. Turn off the heat, allow to cool slightly (5 to 10 minutes), then strain through a fine-mesh strainer set over a heatproof bowl. Return the annatto oil to the pot; discard the seeds.

Heat the annatto oil over medium-high heat and add the rice. Toast the rice, stirring frequently, until the edges are slightly golden and it has a nutty aroma, 3 to 5 minutes. Add the sofrito, sazón, adobo seasoning, salt, cumin, oregano, and pepper. Sauté until fragrant, 1 to 2 minutes. Add the broth, olives, pigeon peas, liquid smoke, and bay leaf. Bring to a simmer, cover, and cook over low heat for 18 to 20 minutes, until all of the liquid has been absorbed and the rice is tender.

Remove and discard the bay leaf and fluff with a fork before serving.

GARLIC *RAMEN* NOODLES

I used to frequent a famous Vietnamese restaurant known for its signature dish of garlic noodles served with a choice of roasted crab, lobster, or prawns. Legend has it that the secret recipe for the noodles has been handed down for three generations, so my chances of getting it were slim to none. My "almost famous" version is citrusy, buttery, and big on umami flavor with a hint of sweetness from hoisin. I use dried ramen to make it fun, but this recipe can use any egg-free noodle. The garlic flavor is pretty intense—this is probably not a date-night meal!

1 pound dried ramen noodles (make sure they are egg-free)

6 garlic cloves (8 cloves if they're small)

2 tablespoons plant-based butter

1 tablespoon toasted sesame oil

½ cup Chik'n Broth (page 50) or any vegetable broth

¼ cup hoisin sauce

3 tablespoons nutritional yeast

2 tablespoons soy sauce or tamari (if you're gluten-free)

Juice of 1 lime

2 teaspoons Fyshy Sauce (page 65) (optional)

Coarsely chopped fresh cilantro, for garnish (optional)

Thinly sliced scallions (green and white parts), for garnish (optional)

SERVES 8

Bring a large pot of water to a boil. Add the noodles and cook just until the ramen has loosened from its bricks, 1½ to 2 minutes. (It's okay if some of the noodles are slightly undercooked—they'll finish cooking in the sauce.) Drain and rinse with cool water; set aside.

Using a Microplane, grate the garlic into a large, cold sauté pan (make sure to give the Microplane a good whack to release all of the garlic). Add the butter and sesame oil and set the pan over medium-high heat. Once the butter melts, sauté the garlic for 30 seconds, or just until fragrant. Add half of the broth, the hoisin sauce, nutritional yeast, soy sauce, lime juice, and Fyshy Sauce (if using); stir to combine. Cook until the sauce begins to form tiny bubbles and starts to thicken slightly, 1 to 2 minutes.

Add the ramen and the remaining broth and toss until all of the noodles are evenly coated with the sauce. Remove from the heat and transfer to a serving bowl or platter. Top with cilantro and scallions (if using) and serve.

GET CREATIVE!

Turn this into a main dish by adding some grilled or stir-fried veggies and/or plant-based proteins, such as Roasted Tofu (page 98) or plant-based chik'n or shrimp.

SKILLET CORNBREAD

1¼ cups fine- to medium-grind cornmeal

1 cup gluten-free 1-to-1 baking flour blend or all-purpose flour

¼ cup organic sugar

2 teaspoons baking powder

1½ teaspoons fine pink Himalayan salt

1 teaspoon baking soda

1½ cups unsweetened, unflavored plant-based milk

½ cup unsweetened applesauce

½ cup neutral oil, such as avocado or grapeseed plus more for the pan

1 tablespoon apple cider vinegar

MAKES ONE 9- OR 10-INCH CORNBREAD

This is *the* bread of the South: golden, crumbly, sweet, and a perfect side to soups, barbecue, collard greens (page 222), and of course, chili (page 136). Start by preheating a well-seasoned cast-iron pan in a hot oven while you assemble the ingredients, then pour in the batter. That sizzle you hear results in the golden crust that truly sets Southern cornbread apart. My recipe was created with individuals who struggle with digesting gluten in mind, so I use a gluten-free flour blend that can be swapped easily for all-purpose flour. Applesauce handles the functions of an egg by adding structure, moisture, and emulsifying the batter, plus it helps with browning, thanks to its natural sugars.

Preheat the oven to 400°F. Generously oil the bottom and sides of a 9- or 10-inch cast-iron skillet. Place in the oven to get hot while you make the batter.

In a large bowl, whisk together the cornmeal, flour, sugar, baking powder, salt, and baking soda. Add the milk, applesauce, oil, and apple cider vinegar. Whisk until smooth. Carefully pour the batter into the hot pan. Bake for 5 minutes, then lower the oven temperature to 375°F and bake for an additional 30 to 35 minutes, or until the top is golden brown and a wooden toothpick or cake tester inserted in the center comes out clean. Cool for 10 minutes before serving.

GET CREATIVE!

Try adding diced green chiles, plant-based cheese shreds, and/or corn kernels to the batter. Don't have a cast-iron pan? Use a muffin tin with paper muffin liners and bake for 20 to 25 minutes.

NO-BAKE PEANUT BUTTER CHEEZECAKE, PAGE 268

SWEET
VICTORIES

VANILLA
COCO WHIP

1 (14-ounce) can coconut cream or full-fat coconut milk

3 tablespoons confectioners' sugar

1 tablespoon vanilla powder, or 2 teaspoons vanilla extract

MAKES ABOUT 1½ CUPS

Here's a simple plant-based whipped cream that you can use to complement any dessert in this chapter and create an amazing grand finale—or to simply dress up a bowl of fresh fruit. The technique is easy, just note that the coconut cream needs to be chilled for a few hours before whipping. (You can be prepared by always have a can or two in the fridge.) Try giving it your own twist by adding different flavors. One of my favorites is a splash of orange liqueur to make Orange Coco Whip for Strawberry-Orange Shortcakes (page 261).

Chill the can of coconut cream upside-down in the refrigerator overnight or in the freezer for 4 hours. Chill a stand mixer bowl or large bowl for 10 minutes in the freezer to keep the whip chilled and stable. When you are ready, turn the can right side up and open it. Scoop out all the fat/solids that have solidified into the chilled bowl; save the liquid for another use. Using a stand mixer or handheld mixer with a whisk attachment, beat until fluffy and the mixture forms stiff peaks, 1 to 2 minutes. Fold in the confectioners' sugar and vanilla. Use immediately or store in an airtight container in the refrigerator for up to 1 week.

ORANGE COCO WHIP
Follow the recipe above, adding 1 teaspoon orange liqueur or orange juice to the mixer with the sugar and vanilla.

SALTED *CARAMEL* SAUCE

I absolutely adore caramel. Given the choice between chocolate sauce or caramel sauce, I am going for caramel every single time. In its simplest form, caramel is sugar cooked until it turns a deep amber brown. It can be used as is for crème caramel and flan, or to make caramel corn. However, add in some butter and heavy cream—plant-based, of course!—and now you now have a delicious, creamy, slightly sweet, slightly bitter, salty sauce that is exceptional with . . . everything. Try it in my Salted Caramel Apple Crisp (page 248) or drizzled over Sweet Potato Cheezecake (page 278). I love adding a spoonful to my coffee for a delicious salted caramel latte. See the photo on page 279.

1 cup organic sugar

¼ cup water

1 recipe Cashew Heavy Cream (page 55), at room temperature

2 tablespoons plant-based butter

1 teaspoon vanilla extract

½ teaspoon fine pink Himalayan salt

MAKES 1¼ CUPS

Combine the sugar and water in a medium saucepan. Make sure all of the sugar is moistened by the water. Place the pan on the stove over medium-high heat. Allow the sugar to melt. Have a cup with warm water and a pastry brush nearby. Use the wet pastry brush to clean the sides of the pan if any sugar starts to stick to or crystalize on the sides. The sugar will melt, then bubble (do not stir). Cook for 6 to 8 minutes, until the mixture turns a golden color, reduce the heat to medium-low, and continue to cook to a deep amber color, another 3 to 5 minutes. Remove from the heat. (If the mixture starts to smell nutty, *quickly* remove it from the heat. Caramel can go from perfect to burnt in seconds.)

Vigorously whisk in the Cashew Heavy Cream until the sauce is smooth. Whisk in the butter, vanilla, and salt. Allow to cool slightly before using. (The sauce will thicken as it cools.)

Store in an airtight container in the refrigerator for up to 1 week.

NOTE:
Be sure your saucepan is clean and completely dry, as moisture can cause the caramel to crystallize. It's easier to monitor the caramel color if you use a saucepan with a light interior.

CHOCOLATE *GANACHE*

1 cup semisweet vegan chocolate chips or chopped chocolate bar

½ cup Cashew Heavy Cream (page 55)

¼ cup unsweetened, unflavored plant-based milk

MAKES 1½ CUPS

Chocolate is still on the table and ganache can be poured all over desserts in this book. Find a high-quality dairy-free chocolate with a cacao content of at least 50 percent, then combine it with rich Cashew Heavy Cream and a splash of your favorite nondairy milk to create the smoothest, silkiest, chocolatiest vegan ganache. Serve it warm, drizzled over cakes, cookies, ice cream, or just about any dessert in this book. Or make it the dessert! I whipped some leftover chocolate ganache with Coco Whip for a last-minute dessert one day and, low and behold, not only was it a *phenomenal* mousse (see box), it was easy and versatile.

Heat 2 to 3 inches of water in a large saucepan over medium-low heat. Place a metal bowl on the pan, making sure the water doesn't touch the bottom of the bowl. Add the chocolate chips to the bowl. When the chips begin to melt, turn off the heat.

Slowly whisk in the Cashew Heavy Cream and milk. Continue whisking until the mixture becomes smooth and pourable.

Use immediately or store in an airtight container in the refrigerator for up to 1 week.

WHIPPED GANACHE (CHOCOLATE MOUSSE)

Chill the ganache in the refrigerator until cold and firm but not solid, 30 minutes to 1 hour. If the ganache has set in the refrigerator overnight, place it on the counter for 30 minutes to 1 hour to slightly soften. While the ganache is chilling, make the Vanilla Coco Whip (page 244; you can also use 1½ cups of any plant-based whipped topping). Using a stand mixer fitted with a whisk attachment, a handheld mixer, or a whisk, beat the ganache for 1 minute, until slightly fluffy. Using a spatula, fold ¾ cup of the Vanilla Coco Whip into the ganache until well incorporated, then repeat with the remaining ¾ cup whip. Refrigerate for 30 minutes to 1 hour to chill and allow the flavors to meld. Serve immediately or store in an airtight container in the refrigerator for up to 2 weeks. Makes 3 cups.

SALTED CARAMEL APPLE CRISP

Every Friday I let my NFL clients choose what dessert they want and make whatever their sugary imaginations dream up, whether it's a brand-new dessert or a repeat. Well, let's just say I made *a lot* of apple crisp thanks to Jurrell Casey, because it was his all-time favorite. This warm, comforting, and casual dessert isn't labor intensive, so I didn't mind. It can be ready to eat in no time *and* keeps well, making it a light lift for barbecues and shindigs. Mildly sweet graham cracker crumbs add a nutty richness to the crumble topping (well guys, there's my secret).

Serve family-style, baked in a large casserole dish, or in ramekins for adorable individual portions (cut the baking time to 35 to 40 minutes) or even in mini cast-iron pans. And every time you show up with this crispy-topped dessert with syrupy fruit and caramel collecting around the rim, just know you, too, will be asked to make this often.

FOR THE CRUMBLE

1¼ cups all-purpose flour or all-purpose gluten-free flour blend

1 cup rolled oats

¾ cup graham cracker crumbs (see Note)

½ cup (packed) dark or light brown sugar

1 cup plant-based butter, cut into cubes and chilled

SERVES 8

FOR THE FILLING

8 cooking apples (see Tip), peeled, cored, and sliced ¼ to ⅜ inch thick

Juice of 1 lemon

1 cup (packed) dark brown sugar

3 tablespoons cornstarch

2 teaspoons vanilla extract

2 teaspoons ground cinnamon

1 recipe Salted Caramel Sauce (page 245)

Nondairy vanilla ice cream or Vanilla Coco Whip (page 244), for serving

TIP:
Good cooking varieties hold their shape well and include Granny Smith, Golden Delicious (great for combining with another apple), Jonagold, Honeycrisp, Braeburn, Crispin, Pink Lady, and Winesap. Never cook with Red Delicious apples because they will fall apart, and you will be serving applesauce.

NOTE:
You can buy graham cracker crumbs or crush whole crackers in a plastic bag with a rolling pin. If you're using whole crackers, it will take 5 or 6 to get ¾ cup of crumbs.

GET CREATIVE!
While apples are probably the most classic fruit for a crisp, almost any fruit that works in a pie will do here, too. Some of my favorites are pears, plums, peaches, and fresh berries—or a combination of any and all.

Preheat the oven to 375°F.

MAKE THE CRUMBLE: In a medium bowl, stir together the flour, oats, graham cracker crumbs, and brown sugar until well combined. Add the butter and, using a pastry blender or two forks, cut the butter into the flour mixture until it is the texture of small peas; set aside. (If using your hands instead of the pastry blender, work quickly so the butter doesn't melt.)

MAKE THE FILLING: In a large bowl, combine the apples and lemon juice. Add the brown sugar, cornstarch, vanilla, and cinnamon. Mix and toss until all of the apples are evenly coated with the mixture.

Transfer the apples to a large ovenproof baking dish. Sprinkle the crumble over the top. Bake for 55 to 60 minutes, until the fruit is tender, the filling is bubbling, and the crumble is golden brown and crisp.

Let cool slightly and drizzle with as much Salted Caramel Sauce as desired. Serve warm with ice cream or Vanilla Coco Whip.

CHILDHOOD *CHOCOLATE* CHIP COOKIES

½ cup unsweetened, unflavored plant-based milk

3 tablespoons ground flaxseeds

3 tablespoons unsweetened applesauce

2½ cups all-purpose flour or gluten-free 1-to-1 baking flour

2 teaspoons baking soda

1 teaspoon fine pink Himalayan salt

1 cup plant-based butter, set out for 15 minutes to soften slightly

¾ cup organic sugar

¾ cup (packed) dark or light brown sugar

2 teaspoons vanilla extract

1½ cups vegan chocolate chips

1 cup chopped nuts (optional)

MAKES 2½ DOZEN COOKIES

GET CREATIVE!

Make blondies: Spread the dough in a greased 10- or 12-inch square baking pan. Bake for 30 to 35 minutes. Cool and cut into bars. Drizzle with Chocolate Ganache (page 247) or top individual bars with a scoop of plant-based ice cream.

There are a lot of delicious vegan chocolate chip cookie recipes out there, but I was in serious need of one that didn't taste like coconut. I wanted a version that tasted like the cookies of my childhood: full of buttery, toffee-like flavor and bursting with semisweet chocolate morsels. It also needed the perfect texture, with a balance of crispy edges and chewy center. Well . . . here ya go! This is your new favorite chocolate chip cookie recipe that can be used in various ways: iced, frosted, crumbled, or baked in a cast-iron pan for a gooey skillet-size cookie. Whatever way your little creative heart desires, just enjoy—it's plant-based!

Preheat the oven to 350°F. Line a large sheet pan or cookie sheet with parchment paper; set aside.

In a small bowl, whisk together the milk, flaxseeds and applesauce; let thicken for 3 to 5 minutes.

In a medium bowl, whisk together the flour, baking soda, and salt; set aside.

In a large mixing bowl (if using a handheld mixer) or in the bowl of a stand mixer fitted with the paddle attachment, cream the butter for 1 minute on medium-high until fluffy. Add the organic sugar and brown sugar. Beat on medium to high speed just until well combined, about 30 seconds. (Do not overmix or the mixture may break.)

Add the flaxseed mixture and vanilla to the butter mixture. Beat on medium speed for 10 to 20 seconds, then turn to low and add half of the flour mixture.

Beat until incorporated. Add the remaining flour mixture and beat until the dough is smooth, 30 to 60 seconds. Stir in the chocolate chips and nuts (if using).

Scoop out the dough in heaping tablespoonfuls, shape into balls, and place them 2 inches apart on the prepared pan. Bake in two batches or wrap the remaining dough in plastic and keep in the refrigerator for up to 2 weeks.

For soft cookies, bake for 10 to 12 minutes, until golden. For crispy cookies, bake for 12 to 15 minutes, or until the edges are golden brown. Cool the cookies on the pan for 5 minutes, then transfer to a wire rack to cool completely.

FROZEN MOUSSE ICE CREAM SANDWICHES

Make sure the cookies have cooled completely. Spoon a thick layer of Whipped Ganache (page 247) onto one flat side of a cookie, then top with another cookie and gently press down. Wrap in plastic. Place in the freezer for at least 2 hours, or for up to 2 months.

FLAKY PIE DOUGH

3 cups all-purpose flour

2 teaspoons baking powder

1 teaspoon fine pink Himalayan salt

¾ cup cold nonhydrogenated vegetable shortening or plant-based butter, cut into small chunks

½ cup ice water

MAKES ENOUGH FOR 12 HAND PIES OR 1 DOUBLE-CRUST PIE

I use my tried-and-true pie dough for everything from my sweet Hand Pies (page 255) to savory Puerto Rican Pastelillos (page 173) in this book, as well as for old-fashioned double- and single-crust pies. You can use all nonhydrogenated vegetable shortening for a super flaky crust or all plant-based butter for the richest flavor—or a combination of both. The addition of baking powder lightens the pastry, enhancing its layers for an *extra*-flaky crust. Pie dough freezes beautifully for up to 3 months, so make extra and store disks well wrapped in plastic—just in case a pie craving creeps up.

In a large bowl, whisk together the flour, baking powder, and salt. Using a pastry blender or two forks, cut the shortening into the flour mixture until it is the texture of small peas. Add the ice water, a couple of tablespoons at a time, mixing the water into the flour mixture after each addition. When all of the water has been added, form the dough into a smooth ball. Press lightly into a disk (two if you're making a double-crust pie) and wrap in plastic wrap. Chill in the refrigerator for at least 1 hour, or up to 5 days. (Wrapped dough can also be stored in an airtight resealable plastic bag in the freezer for up to 3 months.)

HAND PIES

My clients loved it when I delivered lunches with a little surprise: pastry bags filled with homemade hand pies that make great on-the-go desserts. Mixed berry and peach are two of my classic fillings, but you can get creative: try new shapes, icings, and your favorite pie fillings like strawberry-rhubarb, cherry, and apple-cinnamon. Hand pies can be assembled, placed in an even layer on a sheet pan to freeze, and stored in the freezer for up to 3 months, ready to be baked or fried whenever you want to show off your pastry skills.

All-purpose flour, for shaping

1 recipe Flaky Pie Dough (page 253)

Mixed Berry Filling or Peach Cobbler Filling (recipes follow)

FOR THE GLAZE

1 cup sifted confectioners' sugar

2 tablespoons unsweetened, unflavored plant-based milk

1 teaspoon fresh lemon juice

MAKES 12 HAND PIES

Preheat the oven to 375°F. Line a large sheet pan with parchment; set aside.

Lightly dust your work surface with flour. Roll the disk of pie dough to a thickness of ⅛ inch, flouring the dough as needed to prevent sticking. Using a 5-inch round cookie cutter, cut the dough into circles. Gather the scraps, press them together, re-roll, and cut until you have 12 rounds.

Place a small bowl of water next to your work surface. Working with one dough circle at a time, dip your finger into the water and moisten the outside edge of the circle. Place 1 heaping tablespoon of fruit filling in the center of each dough circle. Fold the circle in half and seal the edges with the tines of a fork. Use the fork to pierce the top of the pie in a few places to allow steam to escape. Transfer to the prepared pan. Repeat with the remaining dough circles.

Bake for 25 to 30 minutes, until golden brown. Carefully transfer to a cooling rack with parchment paper underneath. Let cool completely.

WHILE THE HAND PIES COOL, MAKE THE GLAZE: In a medium bowl, whisk together the confectioners' sugar, milk, and lemon juice until smooth.

Drizzle about 1 teaspoon of glaze over each cooled pie. Let set for 5 to 10 minutes before serving.

TIP:

Hand pies make cute and creative desserts for kids' parties *and* you can involve the kids in making them. Use flavoring extracts and natural food coloring to make the dough or glaze an assortment of vibrant colors, and let the kids have fun decorating. Love and King have a ball decorating (and licking the frosting off) these.

recipe continues >>

MIXED BERRY FILLING

MAKES 2 CUPS

2 tablespoons cornstarch

¼ cup water

3 cups mixed fresh berries (sliced strawberries, blueberries, blackberries, and/or raspberries)

½ cup (packed) dark or light brown sugar

1 tablespoon fresh lemon juice

2 teaspoons vanilla extract

In a small bowl, stir together the cornstarch and water to make a slurry.

In a medium saucepan, combine the berries, brown sugar, lemon juice, and vanilla. Cook over medium-high heat until tiny bubbles start to form, 2 to 3 minutes. Stir in the slurry and continue cooking just until the berries burst and the mixture is thickened, 2 to 3 minutes more. Cool completely before using, about 20 minutes.

TIP:
There may be a little pie filling leftover (never a bad thing). Use it to top Fluffy Vanilla Pancakes (page 119), Eggless French Toast (page 117), or shortcakes (page 261).

PEACH COBBLER FILLING

MAKES 2 CUPS

2 tablespoons cornstarch

¼ cup water

3 cups peeled and diced fresh or frozen and thawed peaches (see Note)

½ cup (packed) dark or light brown sugar

2 teaspoons ground cinnamon

¼ teaspoon freshly grated nutmeg

1 tablespoon fresh lemon juice

2 teaspoons vanilla extract

In a small bowl, stir together the cornstarch and water to make a slurry.

In a medium saucepan, combine the peaches, brown sugar, cinnamon, nutmeg, lemon juice, and vanilla. Cook over medium-high heat until tiny bubbles start to form, 2 to 3 minutes. Stir in the slurry and continue cooking until the peaches are just tender and the mixture is thickened, 2 to 3 minutes more. Cool completely before using, about 20 minutes.

NOTE:
Before dicing ripe peaches, remove their skins. Prepare an ice bath in a large bowl. Bring a pot of water to a boil. Make an X on the bottom of each peach with a sharp knife. Gently drop the peaches into the water and allow each to be submerged no longer than 30 seconds. Use a slotted spoon to remove the peaches and immediately place them in the ice bath. Peel the skins off by pulling away from the X and discard.

PECAN *STICKY* BUNS

FOR THE DOUGH

2 cups unsweetened, unflavored plant-based milk, such as oat milk, warmed (105°F to 110°F)

¼ cup plant-based butter, melted

3 tablespoons organic sugar

1 (0.25-ounce) packet active dry yeast (2¼ teaspoons)

4½ cups all-purpose flour, plus extra if needed

2 teaspoons fine pink Himalayan salt

MAKES 12 BUNS

FOR THE FILLING

½ cup (packed) light or dark brown sugar

2 teaspoons ground cinnamon

¼ cup plant-based butter, set out for 15 minutes to soften slightly

FOR THE TOPPING

Nonstick cooking spray

1 cup (packed) light or dark brown sugar

¼ cup plant-based butter, melted

6 tablespoons brown rice syrup

1 cup chopped pecans

These are a real treat for "cheat day," usually Fridays, for my NFL clients. Once I sent a batch of still-warm sticky buns to the team for lunch and then texted the group to ask if everyone grabbed some dessert. Jurrell Casey and DaQuan Jones immediately replied, "What dessert?" Uh oh! I quickly texted Derrick. "Hey, can you check the lunch room to make sure everybody grabbed their dessert?" He replied, "Yep, and I'm eating mine right now. It's bangin'!" After some investigation, the guilty individual confessed: Wesley Woodyard. It wasn't the first time, and it wouldn't be the last, that he swiped the good stuff as a joke on his teammates. (I don't think Jurrell and DaQuan thought it was too funny.) These light, buttery rolls are packed with sweet cinnamon filling and cooked in brown sugar, rice syrup, and pecans, creating a gooey, sticky caramel topping. Now you see why they are worth snagging! Here ya go, Wesley!

MAKE THE DOUGH: In a large bowl, combine the milk, melted butter, and organic sugar. Whisk to combine. Sprinkle the yeast over the top and set aside for 3 to 5 minutes, until the yeast blooms on the surface of the liquid. Add 4 cups of the flour and sprinkle the salt on top. Using a wooden spoon, stir until the ingredients are well combined and a sticky ball of dough forms. Cover the bowl and let the dough rise in a warm place until doubled in size, 1 to 1½ hours.

Sprinkle the remaining ½ cup flour on your work surface. Turn the dough out onto the surface and lightly knead for about 3 minutes to make it less sticky, adding a little more flour as needed. Lightly

recipe continues >>

cover the dough with plastic wrap and let it rest for 10 minutes.

Roll the dough into an 18 × 15-inch rectangle (the dough will be soft). If the dough begins to stick, sprinkle the dough with more flour, as needed.

MAKE THE FILLING: In a small bowl, stir together the brown sugar and cinnamon. Brush the softened butter over the dough, then sprinkle the brown sugar mixture evenly over the dough, leaving a ¼-inch border all around. Tightly roll the dough, beginning at the long side closest to you and ending seam side down. Using a serrated knife, cut the log into twelve even slices.

Spray a 9 × 13-inch baking dish with nonstick cooking spray.

MAKE THE TOPPING: In a small bowl, combine the brown sugar, melted butter, and brown rice syrup. Stir in the pecans. Spread in the prepared baking dish. Arrange the rolls in the baking dish, spacing them evenly into four rows of three each. Cover the dish loosely with plastic wrap and set aside to rise in a warm place until doubled in size, 45 to 60 minutes. (Or you can refrigerate the buns for up to 14 hours, then remove them from the refrigerator and let rise in a warm place for 1 to 2 hours, or until doubled in size.)

Preheat the oven to 375°F.

Put the baking dish on a sheet pan (to prevent any bubbling caramel from spilling over). Bake until the edges of the rolls are golden brown and the center of the dough is baked through, 30 to 35 minutes, rotating the dish once and tenting loosely with foil if the buns begin to brown too quickly.

Immediately invert the buns onto a serving dish. Spread any pecans and sauce remaining in the dish over the rolls. Cool for at least 5 minutes before serving.

TIP:
Convert these into classic cinnamon rolls by skipping the topping and icing them with Cream Cheeze Frosting (page 273) instead.

STRAWBERRY-ORANGE *SHORTCAKES*

1 recipe Butta Biscuit dough (page 94), cut into biscuits, but not baked

2 tablespoons plant-based butter, melted

½ cup plus 3 tablespoons organic sugar

5 cups fresh strawberries, hulled and thinly sliced

2 teaspoons grated orange zest

Orange Coco Whip (page 244)

SERVES 8

GET CREATIVE!
Add spices like cinnamon, cardamom, or unsweetened cacao powder to the biscuit dough. Substitute chopped fresh peaches or nectarines, blackberries, raspberries, or blueberries for the strawberries. Drizzle Chocolate Ganache (page 247) or Salted Caramel Sauce (page 245) on the biscuit tops for a beautifully plated dessert.

Here's the deal: shortcakes are just biscuits cut a little bigger and a little thicker *and* they are fabulous piled high with just about any fresh, seasonal fruit. They're also one of the easiest desserts to whip up when you need something quick. I make strawberry shortcakes when my garden is bursting with red, plump, juicy, sweet strawberries, and I add orange zest for a bit of brightness. Since no strawberry shortcake is complete without whipped cream, my homemade Orange Coco Whip completes this classic.

Preheat the oven to 425°F. Line a sheet pan with parchment paper and evenly space out the biscuits.

Brush the tops of the biscuits with the melted butter and sprinkle with 3 tablespoons of the sugar. Bake for 15 to 20 minutes, until fluffy and golden. Transfer to a wire rack to cool completely.

In a large bowl, combine the strawberries and orange zest. Toss gently to combine. Sprinkle the remaining ½ cup of sugar over the top and gently stir to evenly coat the strawberries. Cover and let stand for 30 minutes at room temperature, or overnight in the refrigerator.

To assemble the shortcakes, split the biscuits in half horizontally. Place a spoonful of strawberries and their juices on the bottom half of each biscuit. Pipe or spoon a dollop of Orange Coco Whip over the strawberries. Cover with the other biscuit half and serve immediately.

HOMEMADE *VANILLA* WAFERS

Golden, crispy, and packed with vanilla flavor, I created these vanilla wafers to satisfy a hardcore craving for banana pudding (find that recipe on page 266). Most commercial wafers contain milk derivatives and other non-vegan ingredients, so homemade is the way to go. Plus, these are just so good! I use vanilla paste to get an intensely vanilla cookie—extract just doesn't cut it here. Use the dough to make press-in piecrust for a sweet filled pie, crumble the cookies between layers of Whipped Ganache (page 247) for parfaits, or simply serve alongside coffee or tea.

2½ cups all-purpose flour

2 teaspoons baking powder

¼ teaspoon pink Himalayan salt

1 cup plant-based butter, set out for 15 minutes to soften slightly

½ cup organic sugar

½ cup unsweetened applesauce

1 tablespoon vanilla paste

MAKES 3½ DOZEN WAFERS

In a medium bowl, whisk together the flour, baking powder, and salt and set aside.

In a large bowl (if using a handheld mixer) or in the bowl of a stand mixer fitted with the paddle attachment, beat the butter on medium-high speed for 30 seconds, until fluffy. Add the sugar and beat until well combined, then add the applesauce and vanilla paste. Beat for 30 seconds, or until well combined. Add half the flour mixture and beat on low until incorporated. Add the remaining flour mixture and beat until the dough forms a ball (do not overbeat).

Remove the dough from the bowl and form it into two 10-inch logs or one 20-inch log. Tightly wrap in plastic and place in the refrigerator for at least 2 hours, or up to 5 days (or in the freezer for up to 3 months).

When you are ready to bake, preheat the oven to 350°F. Line a large sheet pan with parchment paper.

Cut the dough log into ¼-inch-thick slices, rolling the log after each cut to keep a nice round cylinder. Arrange the slices 1 inch apart on the prepared pan.

Bake for 15 to 16 minutes, until crisp. Cool on the pan for 5 minutes, then transfer the cookies to a wire rack to cool completely.

GET CREATIVE!

Instead of shaping it into logs, roll the dough to a thickness of ⅜ inch and use cookie cutters to cut out shapes. Bake, cool, and drizzle or ice the cookies with a glaze (try the one on page 255); mix the glaze with natural food coloring for even more stunning cookies.

CHOCOLATE CHIP *BANANA BREAD*

FOR THE BREAD

Nonstick cooking spray

2 cups gluten-free 1-to-1 baking flour or all-purpose flour

1 teaspoon baking powder

1 teaspoon baking soda

½ teaspoon fine pink Himalayan salt

3 (or 4 if small) very ripe bananas, peeled

½ cup expeller-pressed safflower oil or other neutral oil such as expeller-pressed canola oil

1 teaspoon vanilla extract

¼ cup (packed) light brown sugar

¼ cup organic sugar

1 flax egg (page 36)

½ cup vegan chocolate chips (⅓ cup if using vegan mini chocolate chips)

½ cup chopped walnuts or pecans (optional)

MAKES ONE 9 × 5-INCH LOAF

FOR THE CHOCOLATE GLAZE

1 cup confectioners' sugar, sifted

1 tablespoon unsweetened cacao powder

1 teaspoon vanilla extract

2 tablespoons unflavored sweetened or unsweetened plant-based milk

---

Overripe bananas are very useful for an egg-free baking lifestyle. I use them to create a luscious custard for Eggless French Toast (page 117) and, of course, for baking lots and lots of banana bread. This chocolate-studded version is made doubly rich with a drizzle (or heavy pour) of chocolate glaze, because too much chocolate is not a thing. However, if you are a banana bread purist and prefer yours unadorned, feel free to omit the chocolate. Either way, it's full of rich banana flavor. I always use a gluten-free flour blend so the treat accommodates anyone regardless of their dietary restrictions, but you can use all-purpose flour, if you prefer.

Preheat the oven to 350°F. Spray a 9 × 5-inch loaf pan with nonstick spray and set aside.

MAKE THE BREAD: In a medium bowl, whisk together the flour, baking powder, baking soda, and salt and set aside.

In a large bowl (if using a handheld mixer) or in the bowl of a stand mixer fitted with the paddle attachment, mash the bananas. Add the oil and vanilla and mix on medium speed until incorporated, about 1 minute. Add the brown sugar and organic sugar and beat on medium-low speed until well combined, 1 minute. Add the flax egg and beat on medium-low until well blended, about 1 minute. Add the flour mixture and mix on low speed until fully combined, then increase the speed to medium and mix for about another minute (do not overmix

recipe continues >>

the batter). Fold in the chocolate chips and nuts (if using).

Transfer the batter to the prepared pan and spread it into an even layer. Bake for 50 to 55 minutes, until a wooden toothpick or cake tester inserted near the center comes out clean. (If necessary, cover loosely with foil during the last 15 minutes of baking to prevent overbrowning.)

Cool in the pan on a wire rack for 10 minutes. Remove the bread from the pan and cool completely on the wire rack.

MAKE THE GLAZE: While the bread cools, whisk together the confectioners' sugar, cacao powder, vanilla, and milk in a small bowl until smooth.

Once the bread is cool, drizzle the glaze over the top. Let the glaze set for 10 to 15 minutes before slicing.

NOTE:
To make muffins, spray a 12-cup muffin pan with nonstick spray or line with muffin liners. Divide the batter evenly among the cups (they should each be two-thirds full). Bake for 25 to 30 minutes, until a wooden toothpick or cake tester inserted into a center comes out clean. Cool in the pan for 10 minutes, then transfer to a wire rack and cool completely. Once cool, drizzle with the glaze and let stand to set.

GET CREATIVE!
Try adding fresh berries and citrus for a change up and make a Banana Blueberry Lemon Loaf! Substitute 2 teaspoons lemon extract for the vanilla extract, omit the chocolate chips and nuts, and add 1 cup fresh blueberries and 1 teaspoon lemon zest. Bake as directed. Cool completely, then top with the lemon glaze on page 271.

BANANA PUDDING

with Homemade Vanilla Wafers

I always wondered why my mother made her pudding from scratch when she could have just used the box version from the grocery store. Later in life, it all began to make sense. Sure, pudding mix is convenient, but it's also full of artificial ingredients (and you know how I feel about those). Making it from scratch is simple and tastes so rich and creamy, too. When the pudding is layered with ripe (but not too ripe) bananas, homemade vanilla wafers, and whipped coconut cream, it creates the ultimate vintage dessert.

FOR THE PUDDING

¾ cup organic sugar

½ cup cornstarch

1 tablespoon vanilla powder or 2 teaspoons vanilla extract

Fine pink Himalayan salt

3 cups unsweetened, unflavored plant-based milk

1 cup Cashew Heavy Cream (page 55)

SERVES 8

FOR ASSEMBLY

Homemade Vanilla Wafers (page 262), or 42 store-bought vegan vanilla wafers

4 ripe bananas with just a few brown spots, peeled and thinly sliced

1½ cups Vanilla Coco Whip (page 244) or any plant-based whipped topping

Ground cinnamon for garnish (optional)

MAKE THE PUDDING: In a saucepan, whisk together the sugar, cornstarch, vanilla powder, and a pinch of salt. Pour ½ cup of the milk into the pan and whisk to create a paste. Whisk in the remaining 2½ cups milk.

Bring the mixture to a boil over medium-high heat, whisking constantly, until the pudding thickens, 5 to 10 minutes. Remove from the heat. Whisk in the Cashew Heavy Cream. Leave to cool for 30 minutes, whisking every few minutes to allow more steam to release. Transfer the pudding to a nonreactive bowl and cover with plastic wrap, making sure the plastic wrap touches the surface of the pudding (this prevents a skin from forming). Chill in the refrigerator for at least 2 hours, or until completely cool.

TO ASSEMBLE: Whisk the chilled pudding until light and fluffy. Layer one-third of the cookies in the bottom and up the sides of an 8 × 8-inch baking dish, trifle dish, or punch bowl. Arrange half of the sliced bananas over the cookies. Spoon half of the pudding over the bananas. Repeat with another layer of one-third of the cookies and the remaining bananas. Top with the remaining half of the pudding. Finish with the Vanilla Coco Whip, then crumble the remaining cookies on top.

Chill for at least 2 hours and up to 24 so the cookies can soften. Garnish with a sprinkle of cinnamon (if using) before serving.

NO-BAKE
PEANUT BUTTER
CHEEZECAKE

My husband is obsessed with peanut butter, so I'm always looking for ways to create more (and more) peanutty desserts for this peanut butter–crazed man. As soon as he tried this decadent cheezecake with a chocolate cookie crust, it became his favorite. If you are a peanut butter lover like my husband—and *especially* if you love it with chocolate—then this will become a new favorite of yours, too. For a grand finale, drizzle with Chocolate Ganache (page 247) or Salted Caramel Sauce (page 245) and top with fresh banana slices.

FOR THE CRUST

24 vegan chocolate sandwich cookies

5 tablespoons plant-based butter, melted

MAKES ONE 9-INCH CHEEZECAKE

FOR THE FILLING

2 cups Cream Cheeze (page 56), or any plant-based cream cheese

1 cup creamy peanut butter

1 cup confectioners' sugar, sifted

1½ cups Vanilla Coco Whip (page 244), or 1 (9-ounce) container plant-based whipped topping, plus extra for serving (optional)

Salted Caramel Sauce (page 245), for serving (optional)

MAKE THE CRUST: Put the cookies in a food processor or high-speed blender and process to fine crumbs. Transfer to a bowl and slowly drizzle in the melted butter along the sides of the bowl, using a fork to mix until the crumbs are all moistened.

Transfer the crumbs to a 9-inch pie dish and spread them in an even layer in the bottom and up the sides of the dish. Use the bottom of a drinking glass to compress the crumbs, then freeze for 20 minutes to firm up.

MAKE THE FILLING: In a mixing bowl (if using a handheld mixer) or the bowl of a stand mixer fitted with the paddle attachment, beat the Cream Cheeze and peanut butter on high speed for 30 seconds, until smooth and well combined. Add the confectioners' sugar and beat on low speed until all the sugar is incorporated, about 30 seconds. Increase the speed to medium-high and beat for another 30 to 60 seconds, until smooth.

Use a rubber spatula to fold half of the Vanilla Coco Whip into the peanut butter mixture until well combined. Then fold in the remaining half, just until the mixture is fluffy and well incorporated.

Pour the filling into the crust and spread into an even layer. Cover with plastic wrap and refrigerate until firm, at least 5 hours, or up to overnight.

When serving, wipe your knife between slices to make clean cuts. Top with dollops of Vanilla Coco Whip and drizzle with Salted Caramel Sauce, if desired.

POUND CAKE

with Lemon Glaze

FOR THE CAKE

1 cup plant-based butter,
set out for 15 minutes to
soften slightly, plus more
for greasing

3 cups all-purpose or cake
flour, plus more for the pan

1 tablespoon baking powder

½ teaspoon fine pink
Himalayan salt

1 cup organic sugar

1 cup unsweetened
applesauce

½ cup unflavored,
sweetened or unsweetened
plant-based milk

2 teaspoons vanilla extract

2 teaspoons lemon extract,
or 1 tablespoon fresh lemon
juice

MAKES ONE 9 × 5-INCH
LOAF

FOR THE GLAZE

1 cup confectioners' sugar,
sifted

Zest of 1 lemon plus
2 tablespoons lemon juice

I have to be honest: one of the things that I was certain I would never be able to eat again when I went plant-based was pound cake. I mean, when two of the four ingredients used to make this iconic cake are off-limits (eggs and butter) and both play a vital role in the texture and flavor of the cake, you kind of have to accept the facts and move on, right? Or do you? Determined not to give up on anything I loved, I started experimenting with ingredients. After many attempts, I landed on a recipe that created a pound cake that reminded me of the ones my mom and my big sister always made growing up.

Preheat the oven to 350°F. Grease a 9 × 5-inch loaf pan with butter. Sprinkle a little flour into the pan, rotating the pan until the entire bottom and sides are evenly coated. Tap out any excess flour and set the pan aside.

MAKE THE CAKE: Sift the 3 cups of flour and the baking powder into a medium bowl. Whisk in the salt and set aside.

In a large mixing bowl (if using a handheld mixer) or in the bowl of a stand mixer fitted with the paddle attachment, beat the butter on medium speed for 1 minute, or until fluffy. Add the organic sugar and beat for 30 seconds. Add the applesauce, milk, and vanilla and beat on medium speed until just blended, stopping to scrape down the sides of the bowl as necessary.

GET CREATIVE!

Add 1 tablespoon unsweetened cacao powder and omit the lemon extract for a chocolate pound cake and use the glaze from Chocolate Chip Banana Bread (page 263). Substitute orange juice and zest for the lemon to make an orange pound cake, or stir chopped dried fruit or fresh berries into the batter before baking. The options are limitless!

recipe continues >>

Add half of the flour mixture and beat on low until the flour is incorporated, about 30 seconds. Add the remaining flour mixture and lemon extract and beat on low until well combined, 30 to 60 seconds, stopping to scrape down the sides and bottom of the bowl.

Transfer the batter to the prepared pan. Bake for 45 minutes, then loosely cover with foil (this helps prevent overbrowning). Bake for an additional 20 to 25 minutes, until the cake is golden brown and a wooden toothpick or cake tester inserted into the center of the cake comes out clean. If the cake is still a little wet in the center, bake for another 5 minutes, then turn off the oven and allow the residual heat to bake the cake completely for up to another 10 minutes. *Do not* open the oven during this process; the carryover heat continues to bake the cake, and opening the oven will release the heat.

Cool the cake in the pan on a wire rack for 10 minutes. Remove from the pan and cool completely.

MAKE THE GLAZE: In a small bowl, combine the confectioners' sugar, lemon zest, and lemon juice. Whisk until completely smooth.

Drizzle the glaze over the cooled cake. Let stand for 30 minutes to allow the glaze to set before slicing. Store tightly covered at room temperature for up to 3 days.

CARROT CAKE

with Cream Cheeze Frosting

FOR THE CAKE

Nonstick cooking spray

4 cups all-purpose flour, plus more for the pan

1 cup organic sugar

1 cup (packed) light or brown sugar

1 tablespoon ground cinnamon

2 teaspoons baking soda

2 teaspoons baking powder

1 teaspoon pumpkin pie spice

½ teaspoon fine pink Himalayan salt

1 (20-ounce) can crushed pineapple in juice, drained

1½ cups expeller-pressed safflower or other neutral oil, such as expeller-pressed canola oil

½ cup unsweetened applesauce

1 tablespoon vanilla extract

3 cups lightly packed grated carrots (about 6 carrots)

1 cup golden raisins (optional)

1 cup coarsely chopped walnuts or pecans (optional)

SERVES 12

FOR THE CREAM CHEEZE FROSTING

1 cup Cream Cheeze (page 56), or 8 ounces any plant-based cream cheese

3 cups confectioners' sugar, sifted

¼ cup tapioca starch

¼ cup plant-based butter, set out for 15 minutes to soften slightly

1 tablespoon vanilla powder, or 2 teaspoons vanilla extract

¼ teaspoon fine pink Himalayan salt

Whenever I make this jaw-dropping carrot cake, my sister Danielle eats it for breakfast, lunch, and dinner (seriously). My mother's version was loaded with raisins, walnuts, and her secret ingredient: crushed pineapple, which gives the cake an extra tender crumb, moistness, and natural sweetness. (Why are moms so smart?) I keep pretty true to my mother's recipe, only switching out the eggs for applesauce and reducing the amount of raisins (and sometimes just leaving them out completely). In addition to the cinnamon, I also include a generous pinch of pumpkin pie spice because it makes my home smell heavenly. Take note of the frosting: most vegan cream cheeses are not as firm as a dairy cream cheese, so the tapioca starch is added to stabilize the frosting.

Preheat the oven to 350°F. Spray two 8-inch round baking pans with nonstick cooking spray. Sprinkle a little flour into each pan, rotating the pan until the entire bottom and sides are evenly coated with flour. Tap out any excess flour; set the pans aside.

MAKE THE CAKE: In a large mixing bowl (if using a handheld mixer) or the bowl of a stand mixer fitted with the paddle attachment, combine the flour, organic sugar, brown sugar, cinnamon, baking soda, baking powder, pumpkin pie spice, and salt. Mix on low for 30 seconds until well combined.

Add the pineapple, oil, applesauce, and vanilla. Beat on medium-high speed until well blended, 2 to 3 minutes. Add the carrots, 1 cup at a time, beating on low speed after each addition, until just combined.

recipe continues >>

Stir in the raisins and/or nuts (if using). Divide the batter evenly between the prepared pans, leaving ½ inch at the top to allow the cake to rise.

Bake for 45 to 50 minutes, until a wooden toothpick or cake tester inserted into the center of the cake comes out clean. Cool the cakes in the pans on a wire rack for 10 minutes, then invert them onto the rack to cool completely. Use a cake leveler or serrated knife to slice off the rounded tops of the layers, if necessary.

MAKE THE FROSTING: In a large mixing bowl (if using a handheld mixer) or the bowl of a stand mixer fitted with the whisk attachment, combine the Cream Cheeze, confectioners' sugar, tapioca starch, butter, vanilla, and salt. Beat on low speed for 1 minute to combine, then on medium-high speed for 2 to 3 minutes, until light and fluffy. Cover and refrigerate until firm, at least 1 hour. (The frosting can be made in a day in advance and kept refrigerated.)

To assemble the cake, place one layer on a serving platter. Using an offset spatula, spread ½ to 1 cup of frosting on top of the cake. Top with the second layer, trimmed side down. For a crumb coat, spread a thin layer of frosting on the top and sides of the cake, then chill for 30 minutes to allow the frosting to set. Once set, remove the cake from the refrigerator and frost the entire cake evenly with the remaining frosting. Refrigerate until you are ready to serve, or up to 48 hours.

BAKED
CHEEZECAKES

Cookies N' Cream Cheezecake

FOR THE CRUST

24 vegan chocolate sandwich cookies

5 tablespoons plant-based butter, melted

MAKES ONE 8- OR 9-INCH CHEEZECAKE

FOR THE FILLING

1 cup Cream Cheeze (page 56), or 8 ounces any plant-based cream cheese

2 cups raw cashews, soaked and drained (see page 35)

2 cups unsweetened, unflavored plant-based milk

1 cup pure maple syrup

2 tablespoons arrowroot powder

2 teaspoons vanilla extract

12 vegan chocolate sandwich cookies, coarsely chopped

FOR SERVING

Vanilla Coco Whip (page 244), Chocolate Ganache (page 247), and/or cookie halves or crumbles

This recipe takes advantage of cashews' natural sweetness and turns them into a sublime dessert. I opt for maple syrup to sweeten the filling, and it pairs perfectly with rich dark chocolate cookies for a classic cookies 'n' cream taste. Be prepared to make it again—it gets requested quite often around these parts.

Preheat the oven to 350°F.

MAKE THE CRUST: In a food processor or blender, process the cookies to fine crumbs. Transfer to a bowl and drizzle the melted butter around the sides of the bowl, using a fork to stir until the crumbs are all moistened.

Transfer the crumbs to an 8- or 9-inch springform pan and evenly spread across the bottom and up the pan's sides. Use the bottom of a glass or measuring cup to compress the crumbs. Wrap the outside of the pan in aluminum foil to prevent leaks. Bake for 10 minutes to allow the cookie crust to firm up. Remove from the oven and cool completely. Do not remove the foil wrap.

MAKE THE FILLING: In a high-speed blender or food processor, combine the Cream Cheeze, drained cashews, milk, maple syrup, arrowroot powder, and vanilla and process until smooth. Pour the batter into a medium bowl. Fold in the chopped cookies.

Pour the batter into the crust. Place the springform pan in a roasting pan and pour enough hot water into the pan to reach halfway up the sides of the springform (this helps prevent cracking). Bake until the cheezecake is firm and set, 50 to 60 minutes.

Remove from the water bath and cool completely on a wire rack, then chill in the refrigerator for at least 5 hours, or up to overnight. Serve chilled with the toppings of your choice.

Sweet Potato Cheezecake

FOR THE FILLING

2 sweet potatoes, scrubbed, unpeeled, and wrapped in foil

1 cup Cream Cheeze (page 56), or 8 ounces any plant-based cream cheese

2 cups raw cashews, soaked and drained (see page 35)

2 cups unsweetened, unflavored plant-based milk

1 cup pure maple syrup

2 tablespoons arrowroot powder

1 tablespoon vanilla extract

2 teaspoons pumpkin pie spice

2 teaspoons ground cinnamon

MAKES ONE 8- OR 9-INCH CHEEZECAKE

FOR THE CRUST

2 cups graham cracker crumbs (see page 248)

¼ cup confectioners' sugar

2 teaspoons ground cinnamon

6 tablespoons plant-based butter, melted

FOR SERVING

Salted Caramel Sauce (page 245) or Vanilla Coco Whip (page 244)

GET CREATIVE!

Top this cheezecake with the praline from my Sweet Potato Casserole (page 231). Mix the topping and sprinkle it evenly over the cheezecake during the last 15 minutes of baking.

For fifteen years, my contribution to holiday meals was a delicious sweet potato cheesecake. With a few plant-based swaps of soaked cashews and plant-based cream cheese, no one can tell the difference between the original and this no-cheese version. Firm and creamy, this cheezecake will soon be one of your family's fall favorites as well.

Preheat the oven to 425°F.

MAKE THE FILLING: Bake the sweet potatoes until fork-tender, 40 to 45 minutes. Unwrap and set aside to cool completely. Reduce the oven temperature to 350°F.

MAKE THE CRUST: In a medium bowl, combine the graham cracker crumbs, confectioners' sugar, and cinnamon. Whisk to combine, then slowly drizzle the melted butter along the sides of the bowl, using a fork to moisten the crumbs.

Transfer the crumbs to an 8- or 9-inch springform pan and evenly spread across the bottom and up the pan's sides. Use the bottom of a glass or measuring cup to compress the crumbs. Wrap the outside of the pan in aluminum foil. Bake until firm, about 10 minutes. Remove from the oven and allow the crust to cool completely. Do not remove the foil wrap.

Peel and discard the cooled sweet potato's skin and add to a high-speed blender or food processor with the Cream Cheeze, drained cashews, milk, maple syrup, arrowroot powder, vanilla, pumpkin pie spice, and cinnamon. Blend until smooth, 2 to 3 minutes.

Pour the batter into the crust. Place the springform pan in a roasting pan and pour enough hot water into the pan to reach halfway up the sides of the springform (this helps prevent cracking). Bake until the cheezecake is firm and set, 45 to 50 minutes.

Remove from the water bath and cool completely on a wire rack, then chill in the refrigerator for at least 5 hours, or up to overnight. Serve chilled with Salted Caramel Sauce or Vanilla Coco Whip.

KEY PLAYERS

First and foremost, this book could not have happened without my beautiful, supportive, and ever enthusiastic taste-testing family allowing me days of isolation for writing. My husband, **Derrick,** who I forced to find words to describe every bite, LMAO. I know I annoyed you so much during the process of this book. My babies, **Love Lee** and **King-Elias,** you are the reason WHY I do anything. Always remember you can achieve anything you put your minds to and never care what others have to say! Your love for food, spice, and cruelty-free ingredients have constantly pushed me for greatness. You are the future, and the future is looking bright based on your compassion and knowledge of integrity, food, and our planet.

Thank you to my father, **Wayne Duplechan,** for instilling in me the gifts of creativity, discipline, and self-love. Our spirits are always connected, and your wisdom is so rare to find. Thank you Mom, **Migdalia Tirado,** for giving me the passion for cooking.

My siblings that have been so encouraging: **Seranequia** (my official pound cake tester); **Enoch,** the best big brother; **Naomi,** my ride-or-die little sis; and **Israel, aka Izzy-Iz,** thanks for always cleaning out my refrigerator LOL.

Thank you to all my family members from my Tirado and Duplechan sides, who have always thought of me as being greater than I am. You make me live up to the hype. (LOL) Thank you for your input on Duplechan family history, recipes, and your loving support: **Uncle Danny** and **Auntie Tonya, Kelly Dixon, Auntie Hester, Desiree Duplechan, DJ Duplechan**, and **Sir Daniel, Sir Doyle, Davina,** and the entire Duplechan tribe. You helped me out so much when I was overthinking every tiny detail. Your support is always appreciated.

Danielle Frost, thank you for being the wisest voice of reason. You have always been the closest family member to support me and you've help push me past my fears and anxiety. Thank you for always having my back and for being the world's greatest sister.

Pamela "Mima" Paul, Fredrick "Pop Pop" and **Louella "Gi Gi" Morgan,** thank you for always holding down your grandbabies and Derrick and I.

Marcela (Marcelita) Centeno, thank you for being the backbone of our family, for helping out in any way possible, and for organizing our lives. You supported our family during such crazy times with so many sacrifices. Your love for people, nutrition, and health is what the world needs more of.

Trinity Weathersby, thank you "lil sis" for being such a supportive friend. You are always the first to be there whenever I need anything. A true friend.

Thank you to one of the best in the industry, **Andrea "Andy" Barzvi.** You are an agent with strength, knowledge, and persistence. Thank you for teaching me about the publishing world (and sooo much more) and seeing the project the WHOLE way through and being there, even if I just needed a wise opinion. You are truly not the typical agent. I value you beyond words.

My Clarkson Potter family that has made my dreams come true: **Raquel Pelzel,** you saw something in me, reached out, and believed in me as a first-time author. I thank you so much for listening to your inner voice and sending that email to me. Your integrity in the food space and fine skill of paying attention to detail is such a value to every book you touch. **Marysarah Quinn,** you are the most amazing art director and magician! You made this book a piece of art that I will hold to my heart for eternity. Thank you for all of your hard work in making this a creative, modern cookbook. I couldn't have done this without the rest of the Potter team: editorial MVP **Bianca Cruz; Kate Tyler** and **Kristin Casemore,** for handling PR like pros; and the best marketing team in the game, **Windy Dorrestyn** and **Monica Stanton.** I am honored to have rock-star women like you on my team. There are many background players who I did not communicate much with but who helped to bring this book to life. THANK YOU.

James Wilks and Joseph Pace, you guys are the real Game-Changers in this space! You have educated millions of people on what a plant-based diet is all about. You gave me a huge platform to share my voice and demonstrate the possibilities of plants and performance. The Game Changers is truly an epic documentary and will be for years to come.

Kathryn Goldman, you have been responsible for all of the dirty work. Contracts, contracts, contracts. Thank you for not just sending me marked-up contracts but rather teaching me the best ways to protect myself and my work. Many attorneys would never take so much of their time to do that. I learned so much about law because of you. Thank you!

Emily Stephenson, Wow! What can I say chyle, you jumped in during the fourth quarter with bells ringing and a positive attitude ready to pull this book together. Thank you for guiding me to articulate my story, organizing every detail with your "hawk eyes." You are a true editor (and all of the above) in the publishing space, and every suggestion, opinion, and thought you had helped this rookie bring her passion for cooking to the publishing world. Biggest gratitude to you! You are so amazing.

Emily Dorio and team, I loved sharing such a memorable time with you and your keen eye for beauty and pushing all the boundaries. My food looks so beautiful. I am very proud of what we accomplished in a short time. Thank you for bringing on a stellar crew as well.

Tami Hardman, "more sauce, Honey, more drip!" Thank you for your hard work and gorgeous food styling that must dripeth over.

Matthew Mossart, your professionalism and natural superpower to nail recipes is a gift. Thank you for testing and making all of my recipes look amazing.

Antoinette Licalsi (owner of The Wild Muffin), best vegan baker in Nashville, thank you for testing my baked goodies and being an awesome friend to me.

Chef Anthony DeGeorge, boy did you come through when I needed a professional opinion and was overthinking my recipes. Thank you for testing my burger recipe and giving me your honest opinion of my work. I am excited to see where our love for food takes us.

Tina Ujlaki, thank you for jumping in last-minute to help me test these recipes!

Thank you to my DAY ONE Titan players, who allowed me to just create. You guys let me whip up whatever I wanted and gave me so much confidence in my passion to cook. Thank you for all the fond memories that Derrick and I hold in our hearts forever. Jurrell Casey, DaQuan Jones, Wesley Woodyard, Tye Smith, Brian Orakpo, Rishard Matthews, Brett Kern, Johnathan Cyprien, Daren Bates, Erik Walden, and the many others who signed on after these guys raved about the food. I thank you for having an open mind and trusting me.

My awesome niece Imonee Williams, thank you for always being there for me and the endless deliveries of fresh flowers. To my tía Hortensia Valentine, thank you so much for being so supportive in everything I do (and sending me fresh mangoes from your tree!).

To my friends, who I call family, who have supported and inspired so much of this: Alice Kim, Suzie Vuong, Ashley Norris, Terra Bell, Marcela Centeno (Senior). I know I'm forgetting some people. Please know it's not intentional; this list could be a book on its own.

I thank all of my friends (and social media friends) who have asked for a book for years. You truly are the reason this book came together. You asked and asked, and I had to deliver. Thank you for inspiring me to inspire you.

Thank you to so many other vegan creators who are here to take over the culinary space to say, "But that's not the only way." Whether you're vegan, plant-based, or Plegan, we are in this together.

INDEX

Published in the United States by Clarkson Potter/Publishers, an imprint
of Random House, a division of Penguin Random House LLC, New York.
clarksonpotter.com

CLARKSON POTTER is a trademark and POTTER with colophon is a
registered trademark of Penguin Random House LLC.

Plegan is a registered trademark of Plant Life Chef LLC.
Plegan is a transitional space that refers to people who *eat* grains and
animal-free diets, avoiding meat, fish, dairy, and eggs, but who may
still use animal by-products, such as leather. The term *Plegan* is an
inclusive space for people that have a non-animal-based diet. But it's
also a non-exclusionary term for people growing in their awareness and
consciousness, making an effort to discover the healthiest and most
sustainable diet available.

Library of Congress Cataloging-in-Publication Data is on file with
the publisher.

ISBN 978-0-593-23298-9
Ebook ISBN 978-0-593-23299-6

Printed in China

Editor: Raquel Pelzel
Art Director: Marysarah Quinn
Writer: Emily Stephenson
Photographer: Emily Dorio
Designer: Karina Ponce
Food Stylist: Tami Hardman
Prop Stylist: Lily Noel
Production Manager: Philip Leung
Production Editor: Terry Deal
Composition: Merri Ann Morrell
Copy Editor: Andrea Chesman
Indexer: Elizabeth Parson

10 9 8 7 6 5 4 3 2 1

First Edition